Discover the Holy Land

Discover the Holy Land

A Travel Guide to Israel and Jordan

Max Miller

CASCADE *Books* · Eugene, Oregon

DISCOVER THE HOLY LAND
A Travel Guide to Israel and Jordan

Cascade Books
An Imprint of Wipf and Stock Publishers
199 W. 8th Ave., Suite 3
Eugene, OR 97401

www.wipfandstock.com

PAPERBACK ISBN: 978-1-5326-6031-3
HARDCOVER ISBN: 978-1-5326-6032-0
EBOOK ISBN: 978-1-5326-6033-7

Cataloguing-in-Publication data:

Names: Miller, J. Maxwell (James Maxwell), 1937–, author.

Title: Discover the Holy Land : a travel guide to Israel and Jordan / Max Miller.

Description: Eugene, OR: Cascade Books, 2020.

Identifiers: ISBN 978-1-5326-6031-3 (paperback). | ISBN 978-1-5326-6032-0 (hardcover). | ISBN 978-1-5326-6033-7 (ebook).

Subjects: LCSH: Excavations (Archaeology)—Palestine—Antiquities—Guidebooks. | Palestine—Guidebooks.

Classification: DS111 M853 2020 (print). | DS111 (ebook).

All maps and site plans in this book are original, and all photographs are by the author.

Manufactured in the U.S.A.   01/14/20

Contents

Maps, Figures, Sidebars, and Photos

Maps

Figures

Sidebars

Photos

Introduction

CHRISTIAN PILGRIMS HAVE BEEN making their way to the Holy Land for almost two thousand years. Before modern times the journey was slow, difficult, and dangerous. Many reached the Holy Land on foot. Some died along the way. Even those who traveled in what would have been upscale style for their time took physical discomfort and risk for granted. Present-day Holy Land tours continue this long pilgrimage tradition, but under very different conditions. Travel is so much easier now, especially for relatively affluent Americans and Europeans. One can fly to the Holy Land, explore it from one end to the other in air-conditioned busses, eat and sleep in comfortable hotels, and return home within two weeks. Some packaged tours manage it in even less time than that.

One of the first packaged "church tours" in modern times was organized by Henry Ward Beecher's Plymouth Church in New York. This group consisted of one hundred and fifty Americans who set out in 1867, traveled through Europe, and from there to the Holy Land and Egypt. In the group was Samuel Clemens, a relatively unknown newspaper correspondent at the time who would come to be better known by his pen name, Mark Twain. His account of the trip, *The Innocents Abroad*, remains a classic.

The real pioneer of modern-era Holy Land tourism, however, was Thomas Cook from Derbyshire England. A cabinetmaker, Baptist lay preacher, and publisher of Baptist and Temperance pamphlets, Cook began his travel career by arranging excursions to Liverpool and London for temperance meetings and holidays. Soon he was arranging trips to Paris, Italy, and the Alps. In 1869 he organized and accompanied a group of ten travelers to Palestine. This first Cook's Tour to Palestine went by steamship to Sidon and by horseback from there to Jerusalem, often riding seven to eight hours a day. They slept in tents, they were robbed one night as they camped outside Jerusalem's walls, and one of their number died during the trip.

Thomas Cook & Son was firmly established as the go-to company for travel arrangements by the outbreak of World War I almost a half century later. Travel possibilities and conditions had improved somewhat, but a trip to the Holy Land was still an arduous undertaking. *Cook's Tourist's Handbook for Palestine and Syria* (1911) offered two options.

> Travel in Palestine and Syria has of late years undergone a considerable change. Owing to the construction of better roads, the introduction of railways and improved hotel accommodation, travellers are no longer under the necessity of journeying on horseback and sleeping in tents, although for the fairly robust this still remains the best method of visiting the country. Travelers in the holy Land may now, therefore, be divided into two categories, viz.:—
>
> Those who travel by rail and carriage and sleep in hotels,
>
> Those who ride on horseback and sleep in tents . . .
>
> Traveling by rail and carriage is especially suitable for ladies, or when time is limited; those who prefer the saddle and camp, enjoying the delightful sense of freedom afforded by this nomadic life, will find the specimen itineraries (pp. 282–4), based upon more than forty years of practical experience, of great assistance in determining their routes.

I arrived in Jerusalem for my first time over a half century ago (1960). Fresh out of college and exploring the world on a shoestring budget, I had hitchhiked much of the way through Turkey, Syria, and Jordan to get there. Jerusalem's walled Old City and the West Bank were Jordanian territory at the time. The new state of Israel was only twelve years old. And as it happened, I entered the Old City through the Damascus Gate on my twenty-third birthday.

Jordan's capital city, Amman, was still a relatively small place back then. Third Circle, now near the center of a sprawling city, was on the outskirts of town. After Amman, I rented a bicycle in Madaba and pedaled to Mount Nebo on a gravel road. Later I crossed the Jordan River, slept out under the stars on the shore of the Dead Sea, rented another bicycle in Jericho, and pedaled on another gravel road to Qumran where the Dead Sea Scrolls had been discovered just a few years earlier. Then I took a local bus from Jericho to Jerusalem.

For a young man who had grown up in a Bible-reading family this first visit to Jerusalem was a powerful experience. Captivated by the sights, sounds, and smells, I found an inexpensive place to stay inside the Damascus Gate and spent the next two weeks exploring Jerusalem's Old City and making excursions by local bus to archaeological sites in what is now the West Bank. Then I crossed through the Mandelbaum Gate into the new state of Israel and explored it in similar fashion.

This early adventure was to have a powerful impact on my career. Little did I realize at the time that I would return to Jordan and Israel often during the years ahead—as an archaeologist and historian of biblical times during my academic career and also as a lecturer with educational travel groups. From 1980 through 2014, I directed an annual travel seminar to Middle Eastern countries for seminarians and community leaders. Through this program alone, sponsored by Emory University's Candler School of Theology, I introduced Jordan and Israel to more than a thousand first-time visitors.

This travel guide is based on my travel notes and is intended primarily for Holy Land travelers. Accordingly, it treats places that Christian Holy Land tour groups usually visit and gives major attention to connections between the Bible and the land. It is neither comprehensive nor encyclopedic even in that regard. I have not attempted to cover every place that a Christian tour group might possibly visit, but those that typically are visited. Also, I should alert readers in advance that I do not take all of the Bible stories to be fully accurate history. The biblical narratives and poetry have come down to us from people who actually lived in the Holy Land during ancient times. They pertain to real places that can be located and visited still today. And they provide a great deal of valuable historical information. But much of this historical information is deeply embedded in folk traditions that often are difficult to square with other ancient sources and/or archaeology. I have explored this matter of Bible and history extensively in other publications. See especially J. Maxwell Miller and John H. Hayes, *A History of Ancient Israel and Judah* (2nd ed., 2006).

The Holy Land has a rich archaeological and historical heritage that goes back thousands of years. The places to be visited there were all part of this rich heritage, so in order to discuss them it will be necessary for me to rely to some degree on archaeological and historical terminology—terms like *Bronze Age, Iron Age, Hellenistic Period,* and *Byzantine Period.* Also, Holy Land travelers must try to envision historical Palestine in terms of its natural geophysical features rather than present-day political boundaries, which are relatively recent. The modern states of Israel and Jordan did not exist when Mark Twain and Thomas Cook visited Palestine, and the boundaries that separate them have shifted significantly since my first visit. I will begin the travel notes with a brief overview of archaeological and historical terminology, followed by a description of the natural lay of the land.

Most Holy Land travel groups visit only modern Israel and the Palestinian areas controlled by Israel, all west of the Jordan River. Indeed, the Holy Land and present-day Israel sometimes seem to be regarded as synonymous. But the biblical narratives and poetry involve places on both sides of the Jordan River. It is more accurate to think of the Holy Land as corresponding approximately to historic Palestine, which overlaps both present-day Israel and present-day Jordan. The biblical sites east of the Jordan River (in present-day Jordan) tend to draw one's attention more often to the Old Testament world, while the Gospel narratives and Acts of the Apostles unfold almost entirely west of the Jordan River (in present-day Israel and the Palestinian areas). I will begin with Jordan, therefore, and turn next to Israel and the Palestinian areas.

While this travel guide focuses mainly on biblical times and places, and while the Holy Land overlaps rather than corresponds to present-day political boundaries, the current political scene cannot and should not be ignored. Jordan, Israel, and the Palestinians have each their own national story, political complexities, and corresponding terminologies. I will conclude my travel guide with a brief overview of recent political developments and some of the resulting terminology that Holy Land travelers are likely to hear during the course of their trip—terms such as *Hashemite*, *Israeli Arab*, and *Palestinian areas*.

Max Miller

$$1$$

The Long Sweep of History

In view of the Holy Land's long archaeological and historical heritage, it will be useful at the outset to give some attention to the following four topics: (1) archaeological and historical terminology for dealing with the long sweep of our human past; (2) *tells*, which represent the earliest urban settlements in the Middle East; (3) how ancient Israel fits into the overall archaeological and historical story of the Holy Land; and (4) how place-names in the Holy Land have changed over time.

Archaeological and Geological Terminology

First, keep in mind that geologists differ from archaeologists in the way they divide time. Geologists deal with the long eons and epochs of the earth's past, pay special attention to changes in the physical features of the earth's surface, and attempt to trace the fossil record of all life forms. Archaeologists focus more specifically on our human past, which began late in geological time, and concentrate on developments in human material culture. As shown in the first diagram below, the latest four geological epochs (Lower Pleistocene, Middle Pleistocene, Upper Pleistocene and Holocene) overlap with the earliest six archaeological periods (Lower Paleolithic, Middle Paleolithic, Upper Paleolithic, Epipaleolithic, Neolithic, and Chalcolithic).

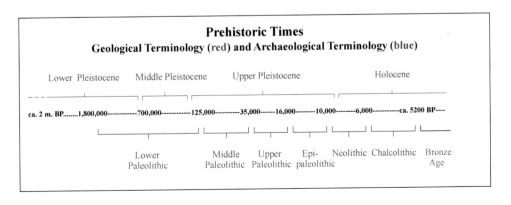

Historians, in contrast, draw mainly on written records, the first of which do not appear until late in both geological and archaeological time—approximately 5200 BP. Accordingly, historians sometimes refer to the long, mostly stone-age centuries of our human past before writing (the Lower Paleolithic through Chalcolithic periods) as "prehistoric time" and the centuries that follow, beginning with the Bronze Age, as "historic time." BP stands for "Before the Present," thus 5200 BP corresponds to 3200 BC in our Western Christian calendar, which has long served as the international standard. BCE (Before the Common Era) and CE (Common Era) are theologically neutral terminology for BC and AD. They mean the same thing.

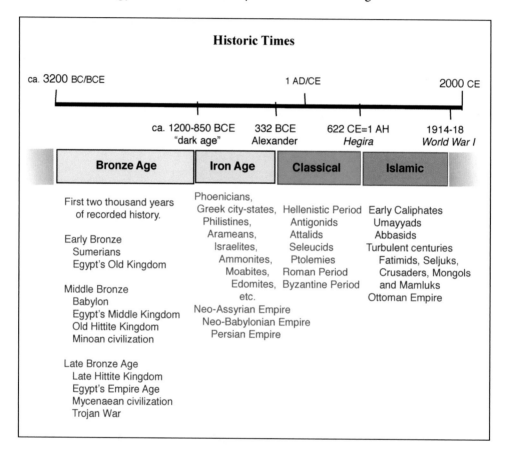

Now look at the second diagram, titled "Historic Times," and note the horizontal timeline that extends from approximately 3200 BCE, the era of the earliest writing and the beginning of the Bronze Age, to our current century (2000 CE). Marked along this timeline and labeled below it are four threshold moments in the history of the lands east of the Mediterranean Sea. (1) In approximately 1200 BCE the region underwent a widespread collapse of urban society that resulted in a "dark age" throughout much of the eastern Mediterranean world. (2) Alexander the Great of Macedonia conquered the Persian Empire in 332 BCE. (3) Mohammed's flight (hegira) from Mecca to Medina in 622 CE marked a pivotal moment in the rise of Islam and corresponds to year

1 of the Islamic calendar. (4) World War I, 1914–1918, ended the Ottoman Empire and reset the map for the Middle East as we know it today.

Look now at the four named blocks below the timeline. These represent four long historical phases that are demarcated by the four threshold moments.

- *Bronze Age*—the first two thousand years of recorded history; from the beginning of writing to the widespread collapse of urban society that occurred around 1200 BCE. Archaeologists and historians subdivide this long block of time into three subphases: *Early Bronze, Middle Bronze,* and *Late Bronze.*

- *Iron Age*—another roughly thousand-year period between the urban collapse and Alexander the Great's conquest of the East. Archaeologists working in Palestine and the Transjordan recognize two subphases: *Iron I* and *Iron II.*

- *Classical Times*—from Alexander to the rise of Islam. Greek- and Latin-speaking peoples dominated the eastern Mediterranean world. There were three subphases—*Hellenistic Period, Roman Period,* and *Byzantine Period.*

- *Islamic Times*—from the rise of Islam to World War I. Arabic- and Turkish-speaking peoples, for whom Islam was the predominant religion, ruled the Middle East. *Three Arab Caliphates* (Umayyads, Abbasids, Fatimids) dominated the region, each in turn, until a *period of turbulence* from roughly 1070 to 1260 CE (featuring Seljuk Turks, European Crusaders, and Mongols), after which Turkish-speaking rulers (Mamluks in Egypt and Ottomans in Asia Minor) controlled Syria-Palestine.

I will refer often to these archaeological and historical phases and subphases in the travel notes ahead, so please examine the two diagrams closely for a big-picture overview and refer back to them as needed.

Tells

Scattered throughout the Middle East are mounds of occupational debris that represent the stratified remains of ancient cities from the Bronze and Iron Ages. They often look like hills that stand somewhat isolated from their surrounding topography. And often they bear names that begin with *Tell* (Arabic) or *Tel* (Hebrew), which basically means "hill." Consequently, *tell* has come to be used as a standard archaeological term for this kind of ancient city ruin.

Ancient cities naturally emerged in places that were conducive to communal living—near water, agricultural land, and trade routes. When people lived in one place over a period of time, they produced occupational debris—remnants of buildings and defensive walls, broken pieces of pottery, other artifacts. When a well-situated city was destroyed or abandoned for some reason, its site often would be resettled at a later period, with the new settlers building over (and often partially reusing) remains from the previous phase of the city. This cycle often repeated itself again and again during the course of the Bronze and Iron Ages, with each new settlement phase adding to the height of the mound of debris, which is how the tells came to be.

Most of the larger tells in Palestine gained their impressive size during the Bronze Age, especially during the Middle Bronze Age, which was before the ancient Israelites appeared on the scene. Iron Age strata typically indicate less extensive settlements perched for better protection on top of tells that had already formed during the Bronze Age. This calls to mind the biblical account of the Israelite conquest of Canaan, specifically Josh 11:12–13, where the implication seems to be that the Israelites conquered and destroyed all the towns and villages of the land but not the cities situated on tells (translated "mounds" below). Hazor was the exception.

> And all the towns of those kings, and all their kings, Joshua took, and struck them with the edge of the sword, utterly destroying them, as Moses the servant of the LORD had commanded. But Israel burned none of the towns that stood on *mounds* except Hazor, which Joshua did burn.

Ancient Israel in the Land of Canaan

The Hebrew Bible/Old Testament provides two overlapping accounts of biblical Israel. Genesis through 2 Kings (excluding Ruth, which has been repositioned between Judges and 1 Samuel in Christian translations) begins with creation and concludes its account with the Babylonian destruction of Jerusalem. First and Second Chronicles, sometimes referred to as the Chronicler's History, covers essentially the same time frame with an added notice about how Cyrus the Persian called for rebuilding the Jerusalem temple. The books of Ezra and Nehemiah pick up at that point and focus on the careers of Ezra and Nehemiah. How to correlate these biblical accounts with other written sources from ancient times and with archaeology is much debated by biblical scholars, archaeologists, and historians.

The widest differences of opinion have to do with the biblical presentation of Israel's origins and early history—from creation through the exodus from Egypt and conquest of Canaan. Some authorities challenge even the historicity of the biblical account of the exodus, for example, and are reluctant to date it. Those more confident of the historical accuracy of the biblical record often connect the exodus with the reign of Ramesses II (ca. 1279–1213 BCE). Accordingly, both the exodus and the conquest would have occurred at the very end of the Late Bronze Age. One reason for identifying Ramesses II as the pharaoh of the exodus is that an inscription from the reign of his son, Merneptah (ca. 1213–1203 BCE), mentions "Israel" as a people located in Palestine. This is the first reference to Israel in any known written source outside the Bible, and it is the only such reference before the ninth century BCE.

The earliest individual mentioned in both the Bible and ancient written sources from his own time is Pharaoh Sheshonq I, founder of Egypt's Dynasty 22. Sheshonq commemorated a campaign into Palestine with an inscription on the walls of the great temple to Amun at Karnak. According to 1 Kgs 14:25, King Shishaq came up from Egypt and plundered Solomon's temple and palace during the fifth year of Solomon's son and successor Rehoboam. Sheshonq's inscription does not include Jerusalem on the list of cities that he claims to have conquered, but it seems obvious that Sheshonq and Shishak were the same individual. Egyptian chronology remains somewhat uncertain for Dynasty 22, so the approximate date generally given for Sheshonq's Palestinian Campaign (ca. 925 BCE) depends heavily on biblical chronology. Depending on biblical chronology as well, King David is thought to have lived ca. 1000 BCE, and Solomon would have ruled during the early decades of the tenth century BCE.

In short, the Bronze Age strata of the tells scattered throughout the Holy Land hark back to pre-Israelite times, while their Iron Age strata represent occupational remains from the time of the biblical Israelites. Among the tells with notable Iron Age remains and biblical connections that you are likely to see and possibly visit during your Holy Land tour are Tell Hesban (ancient Heshbon), Tell el-Mutesellim (ancient Megiddo), Tell el-Qedah (ancient Hazor), and Tell el-Qadi (ancient Dan).

Keeping Up with Place-Names

Alexander the Great's conquests gave rise to successor states ruled by Greek-speaking dynasties that would dominate the eastern Mediterranean world for more than two centuries. While their rulers spoke Greek and encouraged Greek culture, what emerged was a Macedonian version of Greek culture that both influenced and was influenced by the local traditions of the conquered lands. Historians refer to these states as Hellenistic and the period following Alexander as the Hellenistic Period, by which they mean "Greek-like" or "Greek-ish." Two of these Hellenistic states competed for control of Palestine—the Ptolemaic state centered in Egypt, and the Seleucid state centered in Syria.

The Ptolemaic and Seleucid rulers founded many new cities while rebuilding and expanding others. Their cities tended to be more spread out than their predecessors perched on tells, and often were situated at the foot of an ancient tell. Many of these Hellenistic cities would remain active and continue to grow through the Roman Period, whose emperors also founded new cities and rebuilt others. Often, the Hellenistic-Roman cities remained active through the Byzantine Period as well, and some even into Islamic times. When the Hellenistic and Roman rulers founded or rebuilt cities, they usually gave them new names (Philadelphia, Scythopolis, Caesarea, and so on). Where older names persisted, usually Semitic in origin, they often were pronounced differently under Greek or Latin influence (Heshbon became Esbus, Megiddo became Armageddon, and so on).

Tell el-Husn in the background represents the stratified remains of ancient Beth-shean. In the foreground, at the foot of the tell, are the remains of Hellenistic-Roman Scythopolis.

The arrival of Arabic-speaking rulers and administrators from the seventh century CE forward resulted in another wave of new names and pronunciations of older ones (Gerasa became Arabic Jerash, Sepphoris became Saffuriyeh, Paneas became Banias, and so on). Moreover, it appears that many of the older Semitic names that may have survived only locally through the Hellenistic, Roman, and Byzantine Periods reemerged now with Arabic variations (biblical Bethel became Arabic Beitin, nearby biblical Michmash became Mukhmas, the site of ancient Heshbon became Tell Hesban, and so on). Perhaps these older names reemerged because Arabic also is a Semitic language, and the older Semitic names seemed more natural. In any case, the fact that so many of the Arabic names in the Holy Land hark back to pre-Hellenistic times has turned out to be very useful for locating and identifying places mentioned in the Hebrew Bible/Old Testament.

Yet another name-change process is occurring in modern Israel. Along with new Hebrew names and Hebrew renditions of Arabic names, new Israeli settlements sometimes adopt the name of a biblical town or village that may have been located nearby the new settlement, but not necessarily at the same place. Road signs north of Jerusalem, for example, point to the large Israeli settlement of Bet El or Bethel. The actual site of biblical Bethel was that of the former Arab village Beitin, which is nearby but now largely obscured by modern development.

Almost every place that you will visit in the Holy Land has gone by two or three different names over the past centuries. Keeping up with all the names may seem a little daunting at first. It helps to keep in mind that the name changes follow a pattern:

- The oldest names that date back to the Bronze and Iron Ages, including those that appear in the Hebrew Bible/Old Testament, are based on Semitic languages. Hebrew, Ammonite, and Moabite were dialects of the same language that linguists designate as Canaanite.

- Many new names appeared during Classical times (in the Hellenistic, Roman, and Byzantine Periods), as did different pronunciations of older names under the influence of Greek and Latin. These are the names that appear in the New Testament and other early Christian writings.

- Another layer of Arabic names emerged during the Islamic centuries, many of which remain in use still today or were recorded by nineteenth century travelers. These Arabic names provide useful clues for locating places mentioned in the Old Testament.

- Hebrew names are rapidly replacing Arabic names in present-day Israel. But Israeli towns or settlements with biblical names do not necessarily represent the actual locations of biblical sites.

2

The Lay of the Land

TODAY THE JORDAN RIVER and Dead Sea serve as a political boundary between the modern state of Israel and the Hashemite Kingdom of Jordan. But this is a present-day boundary between two relatively young nations, not a boundary of the Holy Land. Although *Holy Land* is, admittedly, a loose designation, the biblical narratives unfold on both sides of the Jordan River during times when movement back and forth from one side to the other seems to have been much more fluid than it is today. I prefer to think of the Holy Land as corresponding roughly to Palestine, where the latter is understood in its traditional regional sense rather than as a political term. This requires some explanation.

Like many of the traditional names we use in English for various regions of the Middle East, both *Syria* and *Palestine* were coined by Greek geographers. Probably the Greeks derived the name Syria from Assyria, then applied it more broadly to the eastern Mediterranean seaboard. Herodotus, writing in the fifth century BCE and wishing to refer to the southern part of the seaboard, with its Philistine cities near the coast, called this southern part *Syria hē palaistinē* (Philistine Syria). Whether or not this designation was original with Herodotus, this southern seaboard region came to be known as Palestine. In 1865, for example, an organization called the Palestine Exploration Fund was established in London. Among its early projects were two archaeological surveys published under the titles *Survey of Western Palestine* (1883) and *Survey of Eastern Palestine* (1889). *Western Palestine* referred in this case to the region west of the Jordan River and Dead Sea. *Eastern Palestine*, the survey of which was never completed, referred to the region east of the Jordan River and Dead Sea.

From time to time, however, the name Palestine has been used as a political designation. When Hadrian crushed the Bar Kochba Revolt in 132–135 CE, for example, he attached Judea to the Roman province of Syria and renamed the province Syria Palaestina. Between World I and the establishment of Israel in 1948, Britain administered the region west of the Jordan River and Dead Sea as the Mandate of Palestine. I will say more about both of these situations below; the point here is that, unless otherwise indicated, I will be using the name Palestine in its traditional sense as a loosely defined geographical region that overlapped both present-day Jordan and present-day Israel, not as a political entity.

Palestine consists essentially of five north-south geographical zones that begin in Syria and Lebanon. These zones are, from west to east: (1) the Mediterranean Coastal Plain, (2) Galilee and the Central Hill Country, (3) the Jordan River Basin, (4) the Transjordanian Highlands, and (5) the Syria-Arabian Desert.

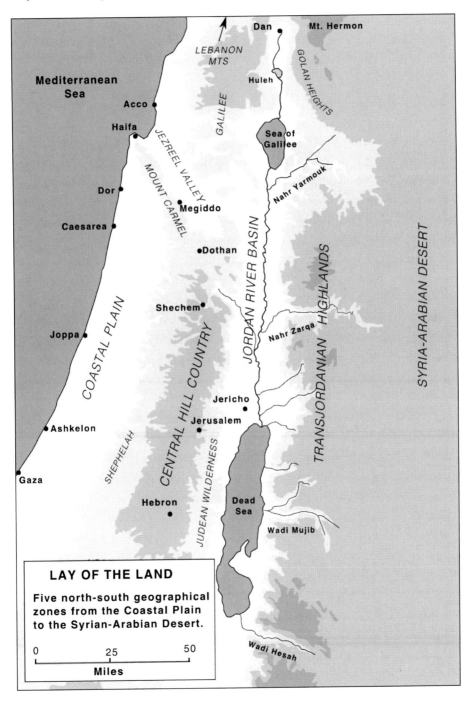

LAY OF THE LAND

Five north-south geographical zones from the Coastal Plain to the Syrian-Arabian Desert.

0   25   50
Miles

The Mediterranean Coastal Plain

The Lebanon Mountains rise immediately from the water, creating natural coves and harbors for the small and fragile ships of the ancient world, and the Phoenicians made good use of this landscape to become a seafaring people. The Palestinian coast, especially south of Mount Carmel, becomes smooth, sand dunes render much of it even less accessible from the sea, and a coastal plain appears. Between Mount Carmel and Joppa, this plain was called the Sharon (Song 2:1; Isa 65:10). South of Joppa was the Philistine Plain. Acco, Dor, Joppa, and Ashkelon offered minor ports. Herod the Great built a large artificial harbor at Caesarea Maritima.

Galilee and the Central Hill Country

Between the coastal plain and the Jordan River Basin, and continuous with the Lebanon Mountains, one finds a spine of low mountains and hill country. Both this mountain range and the coastal plain are interrupted by lowlands—valleys and plains known inclusively as the Jezreel Valley—that extend northwestward from the Jordan River Basin to the Gulf of Acco. This Jezreel Valley separates the mountainous area into two parts: Galilee to the north and the Central Hill Country to the south.

Paralleling the Jezreel Valley on its southwestern side and jutting out into the Mediterranean Sea at present-day Haifa is Mount Carmel. This is actually a mountain ridge, which has been a barrier throughout the ages to traffic between the coastal plain and the Jezreel Valley. Caravans and armies moving from Egypt through the coastal plain toward Syria or Mesopotamia (and vice versa) have been forced either to detour inward through valleys in the Mount Carmel ridge or to squeeze through the few hundred feet that separate Mount Carmel's northwest promontory from the Mediterranean Sea. The Wadi Ara passage through Mount Carmel, guarded by the ancient city of Megiddo, offered the most convenient route. The ancient city of Jokneam guarded another crossing. A third option, which avoided Mount Carmel altogether, was to veer east, past the ancient city of Dothan toward Gilead in the Transjordan. The narrow passage between Mounts Ebal and Gerizim, where the ancient city of Shechem once stood, provided another important east-west pass through the North-Central Hill Country and a juncture with routes that led in various directions.

It is useful to distinguish between the North-Central and the South-Central Hill Country, with Jerusalem almost midway between. The early Israelite tribes of Manasseh, Ephraim, and Benjamin settled in the North-Central Hill Country. The northern Israelite kingdom emerged there with Shechem and Samaria as its chief cities, and the region was still known as Samaria during New Testament times. The South-Central Hill Country was home to other early tribes, especially Judah. Its chief cities were Jerusalem and Hebron, both of which figured prominently in King David's rise to power. Foothills known as the Shephelah (lowland) marked a frontier between the kingdom of Judah and the Philistines. South of the hill country and Shephelah is the Negeb (literally "dry land"), an area of transition between Palestine proper and Sinai.

Mediterranean winds release rainfall over the land between mid-October and April, but the distribution is uneven. Generally speaking, rain falls less frequently the farther south one goes. Also, The Central Hill Country gets its best rain coverage along its western side and crest, leaving the eastern side from Jericho southward as an arid wasteland, the Judean Wilderness. A similar pattern occurs in the Transjordanian Highlands (more about that below).

The Jordan River Basin

This basin is a segment of the Great Rift Valley, a major fault line in the earth's crust that extends from Iskandarun in southern Turkey to Lake Malawi in Africa. Along the way it forms the Bekaa Valley, which lies between the Lebanon and Anti-Lebanon Mountains. South of the Bekaa Valley, it forms the Jordan River Basin, the Gulf of Aqaba, and the Red Sea. The Jordan River itself is fed by three main branches that emerge from the southern foothills of the Lebanon and Anti-Lebanon Mountains. Situated at the sources of two of these branches were cultic shrines—Dan and Paneas (also called Caesarea Philippi).

The Jordan River Basin includes the Sea of Galilee, the Dead Sea, and a continuation of the depression southward from the Dead Sea to the Gulf of Aqaba. In the Hebrew Bible/Old Testament, this basin is referred to as the Arabah. In Arabic it is called the Ghor. The Jordan River Basin is well watered and offers good farmland in the north but becomes increasingly dry and barren as one proceeds southward toward the Dead Sea. Some of Palestine's oldest cities stood in the Jordan River Basin and have left tells. Perhaps the best known of these is Jericho.

The Transjordanian Highlands

East of the Jordan River Basin is much higher ground, consisting largely of rolling hill country and plateaus. Along the western edge of this higher ground, where it parallels and overlooks the Jordan River Basin, is an escarpment riddled with wadis (valleys) that drop rapidly westward from the rolling hills and plateaus above to the basin below. These wadis separate ridges and knolls that project out over the basin and offer some amazing panoramic views. The same Mediterranean wind and rain patterns described above also bring annual rainfall to this escarpment and the western side of this higher ground, thus producing some very productive agricultural land. As the winds continue eastward, however, the rainfall slackens, and the agricultural land gives way to desert terrain. The result is a north-south strip of good agricultural land sandwiched between the Jordan River Basin to the west and the desert on the east. This is the fourth geographical zone enumerated above: the Transjordanian Highlands. It varies in width depending on other topographical features, but averages around thirty-five miles.

In addition to the many wadis that lace its western escarpment, the Transjordanian Highlands are interrupted by four major valley systems that make their way westward from the desert toward the Jordan River Basin. From north to south, these valley systems are Nahr Yarmouk, Nahr Zarqa, Wadi Mujib, and Wadi Hesa. *Wadi*, in Arabic, generally refers to a dry streambed—anything from a small gully to a major canyon. Many wadis become rushing torrents during rainy season, however, and some of the canyon-size wadis harbor river streams at their base throughout the year. In the latter case the canyon may be called *Nahr*.

Human settlement in the Transjordan has tended throughout history to concentrate in the Transjordanian Highland zone, with these four major valley systems often serving as boundaries. Wadi Hesa (biblical Zered) seems to have been a traditional boundary between Moab and Edom. The ancient Israelites claimed possession of the territory between Wadi Mujib (biblical Arnon) and Nahr Zarqa (the biblical Jabbok River) on the grounds that their ancestors had conquered it from the Amorite king Sihon (Num 21:24–26), but both the Ammonites (Judg 11:12–28) and the Moabites (Mesha Inscription) disputed their claim. Nahr Yarmouk seems to have been a boundary between biblical Gilead and Aram, and marks segments of the present-day political boundaries between Jordan, Israel, and Syria.

The Syria-Arabian Desert

Jordan's desert is actually part of the vast Syria-Arabian Desert, which is relatively flat land, more rocky than sandy, and home to Bedouin. The desert classification has to do primarily with rainfall—less than five inches a year. The *Bedouin*—an Arabic term for the desert nomads—raise sheep and camels and move in seasonal cycles from one area to another, often across political frontiers, seeking pasture. Nowadays it is not uncommon to see a pickup truck and mobile water tank parked at a Bedouin tent, which itself may have a television antenna attached. Many Jordanians who have abandoned the desert and the lifestyle of their ancestors are proud nevertheless of their Bedouin heritage. A visit to southern Jordan, such as an excursion to Petra or into the Wadi Rum, will be your best opportunity to observe Bedouin life.

Note that the map above depicts the lay of the land during biblical times. Comparison with a modern map or satellite photograph will reveal two notable differences. Lake Huleh, which appears as a small lake on biblical maps, was more of a marsh or lagoon than a lake. It was drained during the early 1950s. In addition, the water level of the Dead Sea has dropped over the past half century, and the southern part of the sea, which was always shallow, has been partitioned into shallow segments in order to extract minerals from the water. As a result, the Dead Sea no longer has its historic shape—long, oval, with Lisan Peninsula.

3

Jordan

It is important to distinguish the Transjordan as a geographical region from the present-day political state of Jordan, whose boundaries correspond approximately to the region. The former has a centuries-long history of settlement. The latter was established after World War I as the Emirate of the Transjordan, but the name changed later to the Hashemite Kingdom of Jordan, which usually is shortened simply to Jordan. *Transjordan* clearly reflects a Western perspective (the "other side" of the Jordan River as opposed to "this side"). And for many Westerners it conjures images of sand dunes, palm trees, Bedouin tents, and camels. But not all of the Transjordan is desert, none of it has desert dunes, and most of the Jordanians that you meet will be city dwellers or villagers.

One of the main draws for tour groups to the Transjordan is its spectacular natural scenery—especially the Great Rift Valley to the west, the Syria-Arabian Desert to the east, and Wadi Rum hidden away in the south. One gains spectacular views of the Great Rift Valley/Jordan River Basin from either Israel or Jordan, but by far the most dramatic and pristine views are from the Jordanian side. The view from Mount Nebo is surpassed only by that from Petra. Then there is the desert side of Jordan and the truly amazing landscape of Wadi Rum. Amman itself is situated near the desert edge, which will be especially obvious if you arrive by air in the daytime. My first excursion into Wadi Rum was with archaeologist friends in 1972. We followed vaguely marked desert trails and depended on a compass for directions. Wadi Rum is more tourist friendly today but no less beautiful. Several camps offer rustic facilities where travelers (even tour groups) can spend the night. Sunset in the cool desert air, brilliant stars with no competing artificial lights, and a sense of the stillness of the centuries. There is nothing else like it.

The Transjordan offers a rich menu of historical sites, monuments, and memories. Tell Hesban and nearby Tell Jalul represent ancient cities from the Bronze and Iron Ages. Jerash is an outstanding example from the Roman provinces. Castles at Kerak and Shaubak hark back to the Crusades. Wadi Rum and Aqaba call forth memories of T. E. Lawrence and the Arab Revolt.

Finally, the region abounds in biblical sites. A considerable portion of the pentateuchal narrative—the stories in the first five books of the Hebrew Bible/Old Testament—unfolds while the Israelites are camped in Moab. Gilead makes a frequent appearance in the so-called historical books, especially Judges and 1–2 Samuel. The prophetical books of Amos, Isaiah, and Jeremiah include maledictions against the Ammonites, Moabites, and Edomites. Ruth was from Moab. John baptized Jesus in Bethany Beyond the Jordan.

Amman (Rabbath-Ammon, Philadelphia)

Almost certainly, Jordan's capital city, Amman, will be the hub of your visit to Jordan. Amman is a booming city with an ever-expanding metropolitan area that covers a cluster of hills overlooking an upper branch of Nahr Zarqa. Its recorded history goes back to the Iron Age, Old Testament times, when it was the chief city of the Ammonites and known as Rabbath-Ammon ("chief city" or "capital" of the Ammonites). Later it would follow the pattern described in the segment above, *Keeping up with place-names*. Rabbah was rebuilt by Ptolemy II Philadelphus during the Hellenistic Period, who changed the city's name to Philadelphia, and it continued to thrive under that name through the Roman and Byzantine Periods. With the coming of the Arabs, the older name Rabbath-Ammon reemerged as Amman.

Present-day Amman's Iron Age predecessor, Rabbath-Amman, was confined largely to the most prominent of the hills, the so-called Citadel. This city with surrounding villages represented the core of the Ammonite kingdom, but the Ammonite kings often claimed more—all of Gilead and the region south from there to the Arnon (Wadi Mujib). The claim was disputed by their Israelite neighbors, however, and no doubt by their Aramaean and Moabite neighbors as well.

The Israelites, Judahites, Ammonites, Moabites, and Edomites spoke dialects of the same language, which linguists classify as Canaanite. And their material cultures were similar. But they also went to war with each other from time to time, and the conflicts often had to do with their loosely defined and often disputed frontiers.

Second Samuel 10–11 describes sporadic warfare between the Israelites and Ammonites during the reign of King David. It was on one such occasion, while the Israelites were attacking Rabbath-Ammon, that David had his affair with Bathsheba. David had remained in Jerusalem, Joab was commanding the Israelite troops, and Bathsheba's husband, Uriah, was with Joab and the troops laying siege to Rabbath-Ammon. When David realized that Bathsheba was pregnant, he arranged for Uriah to have some leave time in Jerusalem in order to cover for their misdeed. But Uriah, perhaps suspicious, chose not to spend any private time with Bathsheba while on furlough. David arranged for Uriah's death and then married Bathsheba.

Uriah said to David, "The ark and Israel and Judah remain in booths; and my lord Joab and the servants of my lord are camping in the open field; shall I then go to my house, to eat and to drink, and to lie with my wife? As you live, and as your soul lives, I will not do such a thing." . . .

In the morning David wrote a letter to Joab, and sent it by the hand of Uriah. In the letter he wrote, "Set Uriah in the forefront of the hardest fighting, and then draw back from him, so that he may be struck down and die." . . .

When the wife of Uriah heard that her husband was dead, she made lamentation for him. When the mourning was over, David sent and brought her to his house, and she became his wife, and bore him a son. (2 Sam 11:11, 14–15, 26–27)

One of the responsibilities of prophets in ancient times was to issue maledictions against enemies. Israel's prophets did this as well, and the biblical books of Amos, Isaiah, and Jeremiah include collections of maledictions directed against Israel's enemies. The book of Amos, for example, includes the following malediction against the Ammonites.

This says the LORD:
"For three transgressions of the Ammonites,
    and for four, I will not revoke the punishment.
because they ripped open pregnant women in Gilead
    in order to enlarge their territory.
So I will kindle a fire against the wall of Rabbah,
    fire that shall devour its strongholds,
with shouting on the day of battle,
    with a storm on the day of the whirlwind;
Then her king shall go into exile,
    he and his officials together,"
says the LORD. (Amos 1:13–15)

The Hebrew Bible/Old Testament ranges in content from such prophetic rituals to stories of primeval giants who populated the earth along with human beings. One intriguing passage refers to an iron bedstead preserved in Rabbath-Ammon that had belonged to the last of the Rephaim, the giants of old.

Now only King Og of Bashan was left of the remnant of the Rephaim. In fact his bed, an iron bed, can still be seen in Rabbah of the Ammonites. By the common cubit it is nine cubits long and four cubits wide. (Deut 3:11)

Ptolemy II, who rebuilt and renamed the city Philadelphia during the third century BCE, was one of the rulers who came to power in Egypt after the conquests of Alexander the Great. Attracting many new settlers of Greek heritage, the city spread out beyond and around the citadel, and came to be closely associated with a loose cluster of other cities known as the Decapolis. (More about these Decapolis cities can be found below.) Philadelphia continued to flourish under Roman administration, especially during the second century CE. A major temple to Hercules was erected on the Citadel during the reign of Marcus Aurelius. The remains of a Roman theater, also from the second century but extensively reconstructed, stand at the foot of the Citadel. Continuing as an active city through the Byzantine Period, Philadelphia was the seat of a bishopric and sent representatives to the Councils of Nicaea (325 CE) and Chalcedon (451 CE). One of the Umayyad caliphs built a palace complex on the Citadel, but the city declined under Arab rule and eventually was left mostly unoccupied.

Amman's modern history began in 1878 in connection with the Russo-Turkish War. As a result of this war, Russia gained control of several former Ottoman provinces in the western Caucasus region, which produced a flood of Circassian refugees back into territory that remained under Ottoman rule. Abdulhamid II, the Ottoman sultan, resettled some of these Circassians at various places in the Transjordanian Highlands: at Naur, Suweilih, Jerash, and the site of ancient Rabbath-Ammon/Philadelphia, now to be called Amman.

Amman remained a small Circassian village until 1921 when Abdullah I selected it as the administrative center of the newly established Emirate of the Transjordan. It reemerged as a town of importance and continued to grow, especially with the flood of Palestinian refugees from Israel and the West Bank in 1948–1949 and 1967. Today Amman is a booming city whose population consists largely of Palestinian descendants. Its ever-expanding metropolitan area now encompasses both Na'ur and Suweilih. The Citadel offers a panoramic view of this modern bustling city, the Roman theater, and several mosques.

Theater from the Roman Period when Amman was called Philadelphia

Remains of a Roman Period temple, second-century CE, on the Amman Citadel

Restored palace from the time of the Umayyad Caliphate, on the Amman Citadel

Gilead and the Decapolis

From Amman I suggest a full-day excursion to Jerash. The drive will take you deep into the region of ancient Gilead. Later, during Hellenistic and Roman times, essentially the same region came to be called the Decapolis. It appears as Gilead in the Hebrew Bible/Old Testament, but as the Decapolis in the New Testament.

> Is there no balm in Gilead? Is there no physician there?
> Why then has the health of my poor people not been restored? (Jer 8:22)

> And great crowds followed him from Galilee, the Decapolis, Jerusalem, Judea, and from beyond the Jordan. (Matt 4:25)

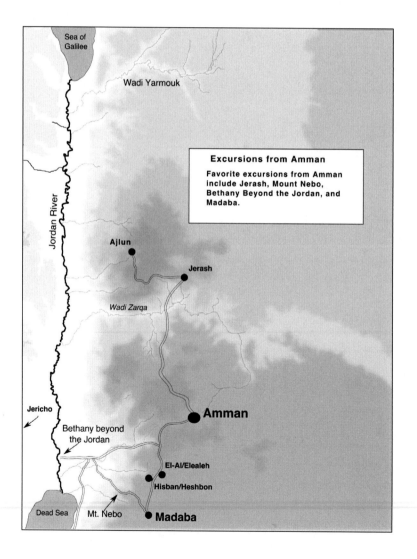

Gilead

Virtually all of our written information about ancient Gilead comes from the Hebrew Bible, thus from an ancient Israelite perspective during the Iron Age. While the name Gilead is used rather loosely in the biblical materials, clearly the heartland of Gilead was the highland region between Nahr Zarqa (the biblical Jabbok River) and Nahr Yarmouk. These highlands consist of modest mountains that reach their highest elevation near present-day Ajlun, northwest of Jerash. Beyond the Yarmouk, which is not mentioned in the Hebrew Bible, was the land of Bashan.

One can understand from its geographical location why Gilead would have been a tempting frontier and a frequent battleground between the Ammonites, Aramaeans, and Israelites. The prophet Amos's malediction against the Ammonites quoted above accuses them of ripping open pregnant women in Gilead in order to extend their borders. His malediction against Aram (Amos 1:2–5) accuses the Aramaeans of "threshing Gilead with threshing sledges of iron." Israel's military actions in Gilead were not only aimed at territorial expansion but apparently involved tribal connections and claims as well. Especially the city Jebesh-Gilead seems to have been a pro-Israelite enclave in Gilead. Ramoth-Gilead served as an Israelite stronghold during Israel's wars with the Aramaeans. The prophet Elijah is referred to as "the Tishbite" in the Hebrew Bible, and the Septuagint (Greek translation of the Hebrew Bible) clarifies that he was from a place called Tishbe in Gilead.

During ancient times, Gilead seems to have been forested. We read in 2 Sam 18, for example, that Absalom led a rebellion against his father, David, and while both armies were encamped in the land of Gilead, "the battle spread over the face of all the country; and the forest claimed more victims that day than the sword" (v. 8). The narrative continues by describing how Absalom, riding on a mule under the thick branches of a great oak, became entangled in the branches and hung there until Joab "took three spears in his hand, and thrust them into the heart of Absalom, while he was still alive in the oak" (v. 14).

Several other dramatic biblical stories also have their settings in the land of Gilead:

- Gen 27–31 tells how Jacob deceived his father, Isaac, received the birthright that belonged to his older brother, Esau, and fled to relatives in Aram. Jacob was kindly received there by Laban, married Laban's two daughters, and prospered. After a time, there was conflict between Jacob and Laban's sons, so Jacob decided to return to Canaan, but he set out with his family, servants, and animals without informing Laban. To make matters worse, Jacob's wife Rachel took one of her family's religious pieces. Laban pursued Jacob and caught up with him in Gilead (Gen 31:22–25). After Jacob managed to convince Laban that he was innocent of any wrongdoing, they negotiated a covenant, marked the spot with a heap of stones, and called it Galeed. This, so the narrative implies, was the origin of the name Gilead.

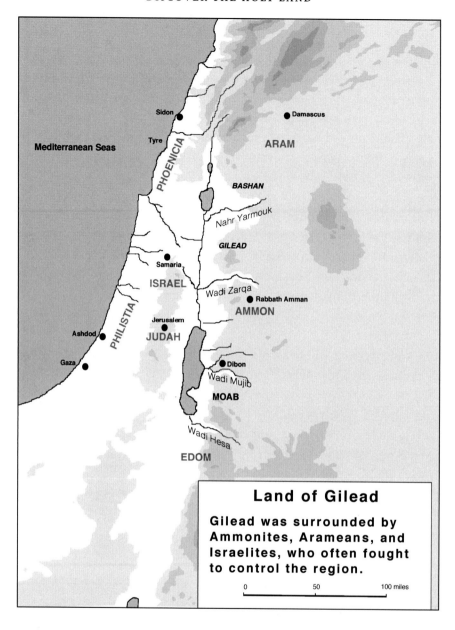

Sidon

Damascus

Tyre

Mediterranean Seas

PHOENICIA

ARAM

BASHAN

Nahr Yarmouk

GILEAD

Samaria

ISRAEL

Wadi Zarqa

Rabbath Amman

AMMON

Jerusalem

PHILISTIA

Ashdod

JUDAH

Gaza

Dibon

Wadi Mujib

MOAB

Wadi Hesa

EDOM

Land of Gilead

Gilead was surrounded by Ammonites, Arameans, and Israelites, who often fought to control the region.

0   50   100 miles

So Jacob took a stone, and set it up as a pillar. And Jacob said to his kins-folk, "Gather stones," and they took stones, and made a heap; and they ate there by the heap. Laban called it Jegar-sahadutha: but Jacob called it Galeed. Laban said, "This heap is a witness between you and me today." Therefore he called it Galeed, and the pillar Mizpah, for he said, "The LORD watch between you and me, when we are absent one from the other. If you ill-treat my daughters, or if you take wives in addition to my daughters, though no one else is with us, remember that God is witness between you and me." (Gen 31:45–50)

Jacob continued on his way southward until he reached the Jabbok River. According to Gen 32, it was on the banks of the Jabbok, with his brother, Esau, approaching from the south, that Jacob wrestled with an angel and received his name Israel. A sanctuary known as Penuel apparently marked that spot during Old Testament times (Gen 32:31; Judg 8:8–9; 1 Kgs 12:25). Somewhere in the same general vicinity was a city named Mahanaim (Gen 32:2; 2 Sam 17–18).

- Judg 11 tells the story of how Jephthah led the Gileadites to victory over the Ammonites, but did so at great price—the sacrificial death of his only child, a little daughter. Jephthah was a son of the Gileadite tribal chief, we are told, but had been expelled from the family by his brothers because his mother was a prostitute. Jephthah nevertheless became a mighty warrior and warlord. Then came a day when the Ammonites were attacking the Gileadites, and Jephthah's brothers, in desperation, appealed to him for help. Jephthah agreed to come to their aid in return for their pledge to recognize him as head and leader over Gilead once the Ammonites were defeated. Meanwhile, Jephthah made a sacred vow: "If you will give the Ammonites into my hand, then whoever comes out of the doors of my house to meet me, when I return victorious from the Ammonites, shall be the Lord's, to be offered up by me as a burnt offering" (vv. 30–31). Jephthah was victorious, but the person who came out to meet him first was his little daughter.

- First Samuel 11 reports yet another occasion when the Ammonites threatened Gilead, this time during the reign of the Ammonite king Nahash. The Ammonites besieged Jabesh-Gilead, the men of the city requested to negotiate terms, but Nahash made demands that seemed unbearable: "On this condition I will make a treaty with you, namely that I gouge out everyone's right eye, and thus put disgrace upon all Israel" (v. 2) Then the men of Jebesh sent appeals for help to Israelite tribes west of the Jordan River. The young Saul took up their cause, mustered an army, and delivered the city. Later Saul became Israel's first king, but his reign ended with a major defeat and suicide on Mount Gilboa. The Philistines cut off his head, stripped off his armor, and fastened his body to the wall of Bethshean (1 Sam 31:8–13).

  > But when the inhabitants of Jabesh-gilead heard what the Philistines had done to Saul, all the valiant men set out, traveled all night long, and took the body of Saul and the bodies of his sons from the wall of Beth-shean. They came to Jabesh and burned them there. Then they took their bones and buried them under the tamarisk tree in Jabesh, and fasted seven days.

- Gilead continued to play a major role in Israelite affairs through the reign of King David—Absalom's rebellion and death were only one instance—and presumably through the reign of Solomon. Second Kings 9 reports another Gilead-related incident that occurred during the time of the separate kingdoms. The Israelite army was encamped at Ramoth-Gilead defending against the Aramaeans while the current king of Israel—Joram, son of Ahab and Jezebel—was recovering from a wound under Jezebel's care at the royal palace in Jezreel. Jehu was in command of the Israelite troops and the prophet Elisha challenged him to seize upon the occasion, overthrow the royal family, and claim the throne of Israel for himself. Jehu accepted the challenge and massacred the royal family. The description of the regal manner in which Jezebel met her brutal death is one of the most powerful scenes in the Hebrew Bible (2 Kgs 9).

Jerash and the Decapolis

Many historic cities scattered throughout the eastern Mediterranean world followed the pattern described for ancient Rabbah of the Ammonites, present-day Amman—cities that were founded or rebuilt and named or renamed during the Hellenistic Period, flourished through the Roman Period, and continued as vital urban centers through the Byzantine Period. Jerash offers another interesting example with much better-preserved archaeological remains. Also, it was one of the Decapolis cities.

While visiting Jerash, be mindful that you are walking among the remains of a city that spanned three historical periods: Hellenistic, Roman, and Byzantine. These three periods transitioned gradually from one to the next, so the dates that historians apply to the periods should be understood as useful benchmarks only. Keep in mind also that many of the other places that you will visit during your Holy Land tour were active cities, towns, or villages during the same time frame and followed the same or similar occupational patterns.

Hellenistic Period (323–67 BCE)

The benchmark dates provided here are from Alexander the Great's death (323 BCE) to Pompey's eastern campaigns (67–63 BCE). As explained above, Alexander's conquests gave rise to Hellenist states that dominated the eastern Mediterranean world for the next two and half centuries. Palestine was disputed frontier between two of these states, the Ptolemies of Egypt and the Seleucids of Syria. The Ptolemies generally managed to hold Palestine through the third century BCE, during which time Ptolemy II rebuilt ancient Rabbah of the Ammonites and renamed it Philadelphia. Then the Seleucid king Antiochus III gained the upper hand with a battle fought in 198 BCE at Paneas (also known as Caesarea Philippi).

The site of Jerash was ideal for habitation. But while artifacts from the Neolithic and Bronze Ages have been found in the immediate vicinity, the first settlement of consequence on the site itself seems to have emerged during the Hellenistic Period. Also, the earliest name recorded for Jerash, Antioch on the Chrysorhoas, suggest that it was founded by Antiochus III or one of his Seleucid successors. *Chrysorhoas* means "Golden (River)," referring to the Nahr Zarqa tributary on which Antioch was located.

The early habitants would have been mainly of Hellenistic background and representing a considerable Hellenistic population that found its way to Palestine under the Ptolemies and Seleucids. They came as soldiers, administrators, and merchants, often married locally, and settled permanently among the indigenous Ammonites, Gileadites, Moabites, Samaritans, and Jews. New cities such as Antioch emerged with predominantly Hellenistic inhabitants and styled after Greek city-states. Pre-existing cities were increased in size and transformed by settlers with Hellenistic ideas and practices. Approximately ten of these Greek-style cities were clustered in the northern Transjordan and came to be known as the Decapolis cities. The region itself was called the Decapolis.

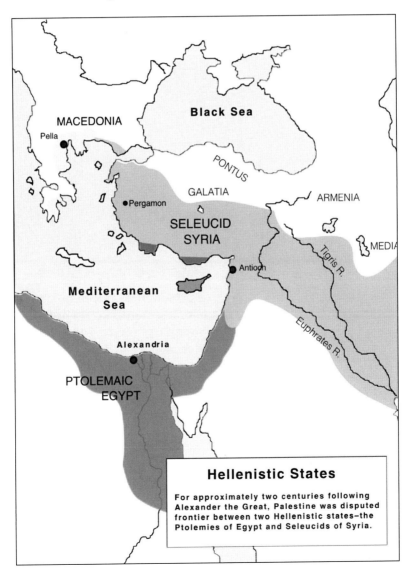

Hellenistic States

For approximately two centuries following Alexander the Great, Palestine was disputed frontier between two Hellenistic states–the Ptolemies of Egypt and Seleucids of Syria.

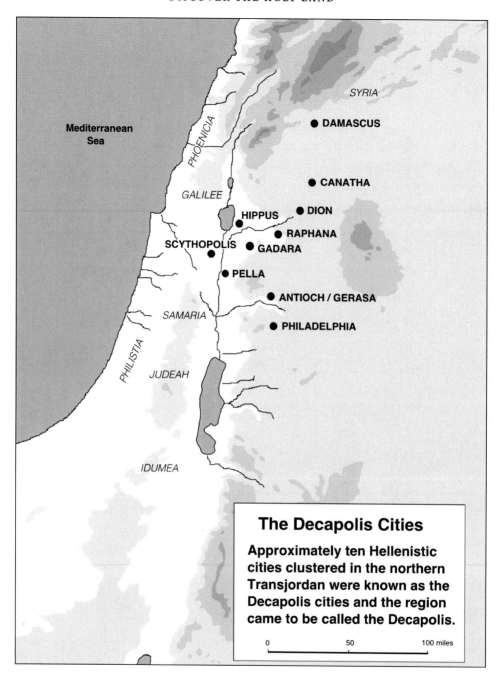

Mediterranean
Sea

SYRIA

● **DAMASCUS**

PHOENICIA

GALILEE

● **CANATHA**

● **DION**

HIPPUS

● **RAPHANA**

SCYTHOPOLIS ● **GADARA**

● **PELLA**

● **ANTIOCH / GERASA**

SAMARIA

● **PHILADELPHIA**

PHILISTIA

JUDEAH

IDUMEA

The Decapolis Cities

Approximately ten Hellenistic cities clustered in the northern Transjordan were known as the Decapolis cities and the region came to be called the Decapolis.

0   50   100 miles

Meanwhile, having defeated Carthage during the Second Punic War (218–201 BCE), Rome began exerting its power eastward. By the mid-second century BCE, Rome overshadowed both the Ptolemies and the Seleucids, as well as two essentially independent dynasties that had emerged in Palestine. These were the Nabatean kings of Petra and Hasmonean kings of Jerusalem. The Nabateans were caravanners of Arab stock, and Petra served as the hub of their extensive trade routes. The Hasmoneans were a Jewish dynasty that established itself in Jerusalem during the mid-second century and expanded its reach under two energetic kings—John Hyrcanus (134–104 BCE) and Alexander Jannaeus (103–76 BCE)—to include most of Palestine west of the Jordan River and some parts of the Transjordan. This Hasmonean expansion enabled Jews to spread beyond their Judean homeland to other areas such as Galilee. Following a practice that would not have seemed so unusual at the time, John Hyrcanus and Alexander Jannaeus sometimes forced the inhabitants of conquered regions to convert to Judaism or leave their homelands. Antioch on the Chrysorhoas fell to Alexander Jannaeus in 83 BCE.

Roman Period (67 BCE—324 CE)

These benchmark dates have the Roman Period beginning with Pompey's eastern campaigns in 67–63 BCE, although Rome had already been the real power overshadowing the eastern Mediterranean world long before that. But Pompey inaugurated more direct Roman control and made significant administrative changes that affected Syria-Palestine. (1) He ended the Seleucid state, creating in its place the Roman province of Syria. (2) He settled a squabble between two claimants to the Hasmonean throne, authorizing Hyrcanus II to serve as the high priest and ruler of the Jews in Palestine. (3) He released the Decapolis cities and certain other predominantly Hellenistic cities from Hasmonean and Nabatean interference, allowing them to function essentially as autonomous city-states connected loosely to the province of Syria. The Decapolis cities may have organized a formal Decapolis League at this point, although that remains uncertain. They clearly developed a distinctive cultural and commercial network.

Change came again to the Transjordan in 106 CE when Trajan created the Roman province of Arabia Petraea. All of the Decapolis cities except for Scythopolis and Damascus were included in this new province and subjected to more direct Roman administration. Trajan also constructed a paved road that ran north-south through this new province, from Bostra (Busra in present-day Syria) to Aela (present-day Eilat/Aqaba). It was called Via Nova Traiana ("Trajan's New Road"), or simply the Via Nova. Also, at some point during the Roman Period, the name of Antioch on the Chrysorhoas was changed to Gerasa.

Archaeological excavations at Jerash have revealed some remains of the Hellenistic city. But the really spectacular and photogenic structures date from Roman Gerasa, especially from the second century CE after Trajan attached it to the province of Arabia Petraea and completed the Via Nova. Situated in good position to benefit from traffic that moved along this important thoroughfare, Gerasa enjoyed almost two centuries of peace and security (Pax Romana). The wealth of the city enabled its inhabitants to build out Gerasa in truly impressive fashion. Moreover, Gerasa is one of the best-preserved examples of a city from the Roman provinces. Other Roman Period sites may offer good or better examples of temples, theaters, colonnaded streets, public baths, or residential areas. But rarely does one find all of these typical features of a Roman city so well preserved at the same place. Visitors are awed by two major temples, one dedicated to Zeus and the other to Artemis; two theaters; a broad colonnaded forum; a main street (*cardo maximus*) that traversed the city from north to south; and monumental intersections (*tetrapyla*) where the main street was joined by perpendicular side streets (*decumani*) with monumental crossings

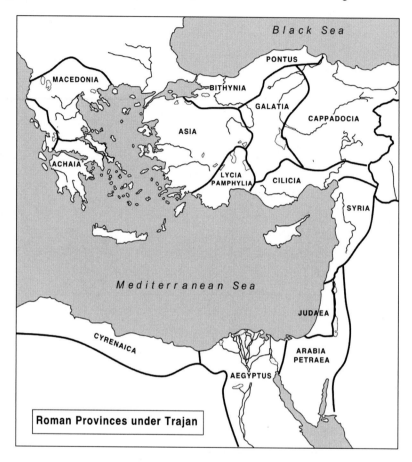

Trajan's successor, Hadrian (117–138 CE), traveled extensively throughout the Roman Empire and spent at least part of the 129/130 CE winter at Gerasa. In anticipation of his visit, the city fathers erected an impressive monumental arch some distance south of the south gate. Perhaps the plan was to expand the walled city that far south, but if so, it never happened. Continuing the same journey, Hadrian visited Jerusalem, which had been sacked by Titus's troops during the First Jewish Revolt sixty years earlier (66–73 CE). Hadrian's decision to rebuild Jerusalem as a proper Roman city may have been the chief cause of a second Jewish revolt, better known as the Bar Kochba Revolt, that erupted in 132 CE. This second revolt also was easily crushed.

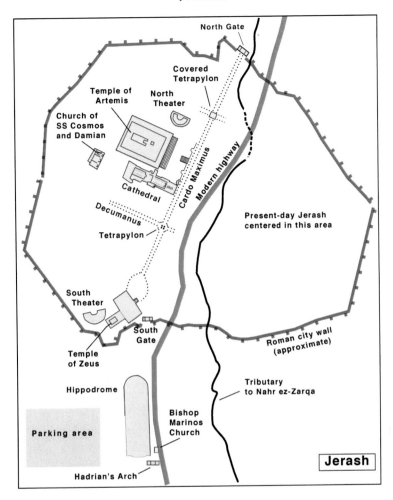

Map labels:

North Gate

Covered Tetrapylon

Temple of Artemis

North Theater

Church of SS Cosmos and Damian

Cathedral

Cardo Maximus

Modern highway

Decumanus

Tetrapylon

Present-day Jerash centered in this area

South Theater

South Gate

Temple of Zeus

Roman city wall (approximate)

Hippodrome

Tributary to Nahr ez-Zarqa

Parking area

Bishop Marinos Church

Hadrian's Arch

Jerash

Jerash: Hadrian's Arch

Jerash: Forum and Cardo Maximus

Jerash: Temple of Artemis

The name Gerasa calls to mind an incident in Jesus' ministry that is reported in three parallel accounts (Matt 8:28–34; Mark 5:1–13; Luke 8:26–39). According to the

NRSV translation of Mark 5:1–3, "They [Jesus and his disciples] came to the other side of the sea, to the country of the Gerasenes. And when he had stepped out of the boat, immediately a man out of the tombs with an unclean spirit met him. He lived among the tombs; and no one could restrain him anymore, even with a chain." The manuscripts behind the three gospel accounts provide alternate readings for "Gerasenes" (for example, "Gergasenes), which makes it difficult to know the original reading. Note that the setting of the incident was not a city in any case, but somewhere along the shore of the Sea of Galilee.

Byzantine Period (324–622 CE)

The beginning of Constantine's reign over a reunified Roman Empire in 324 CE serves as a useful benchmark date for the beginning of the Byzantine Period. Muhammad's flight to Mecca in 622 (year 1 of the Islamic calendar) serves as the end of the period. Constantine was responsible for two important changes that help define the Byzantine Period: (1) He chose as his residency and capital the ancient Greek city of Byzantium, changing its name to Constantinople. (2) He made Christianity the favored religion of the Roman Empire.

Also at the end of that fourth century, the Roman Empire separated into two parts. Actually, the Roman west and Roman east had been drifting apart even before Constantine's rise to power. This drift continued under Constantine's successors and was formalized at the death of Theodosus I in 395 CE. Henceforth there would be two Christian Roman empires—one with its capital at Rome, the other with its capital at Constantinople. The eastern half would be more politically successful over the centuries ahead, and its emperors claimed to represent the true continuation of Imperial Rome. They adopted Greek as the official language of their realm, and it came to be known as the Byzantine Empire, recalling the earlier Greek name of Constantinople.

From Constantine until the arrival of Arab armies during the seventh century, all of Palestine belonged to the Byzantine Empire, and Christianity was the official religion of the realm. Roman cities such as Gerasa continued on without significant changes in their layout, except that pagan temples and other religious structures were abandoned or retrofitted to serve as churches or for other Christian purposes. Also, many new churches were erected within the former Roman cities.

According to Eusebius and Epiphanius, Christians fled from Jerusalem to Pella during that First Jewish Revolt (66–73 CE). Pella was one of the Decapolis cities, not far from Gerasa, and Christianity probably reached Gerasa about the same time. In any case, a Christian community flourished at Gerasa by 359 CE, when a bishop represented the city at the Council of Seleucia (present-day Silifke in Turkey).

The first church most visitors encounter when exploring Gerasa is the Church of Bishop Marianos, situated just north of Hadrian's Arch and across from the Hippodrome. Recently excavated, it dates from 570 CE. The Church of Saints Cosmos and

Damian is reached by a trail that leads from the South Theater toward the Temple of Artemis. This is one of three churches that were built side by side, sharing the same courtyard and apparently part of the same sixth-century building project. The other two churches of the triad were dedicated to Saint George and Saint John the Baptist.

The Church of Saints Cosmos and Damian offers an especially interesting mosaic floor, which fortunately escaped an iconoclastic purge during the early eighth century CE. The inscription at the west end of the mosaic, in front of the chancel step, is flanked by portraits of two major benefactors: Theodore and his wife, Georgia. This inscription is typical of those found at other churches on the site:

> Pray now, while venerating the beautiful pair of victors. In truth, they are saints who own the art allaying suffering. From now on those who make offerings will benefit through the elimination of misadventure in their lives. (B. McDonald, *Pilgrimage in Early Christian Jordan*, 58)

According to legend, Cosmos and Damian were twin brothers who practiced medicine without charging fees and were put to death during a time of persecution because of their Christian faith. They were called "the moneyless holy ones," were invoked as the patron saints of physicians, and widely venerated especially during the fifth and sixth centuries.

Jerash: Church of Saints Cosmos and Damian; arrow points to the inscription

Also of special interest from the Byzantine Period is the Cathedral complex, accessed by a broad stairway from the *cardo maximus*. At the top of the stairway and embedded in the exterior wall of the cathedral apse is a small shrine with a painted inscription to Saint Mary and the archangels Gabriel and Michael. The Cathedral itself was built on the podium base of a dismantled Roman temple, and beyond it on the west is a colonnaded courtyard with a fountain. Beyond that is the Church of Saint Theodore.

Jerash dwindled in importance under the Umayyad caliphs, suffered massive destruction from an earthquake in 747 CE, and became a virtual ghost town thereafter. The temple of Artemis was converted to a fort and badly damaged during the Crusader Period. Centuries later, in 1878, the site was resettled by Circassians who reused stone from the Roman and Byzantine buildings for their own houses. Soon after World War I, during the early years of the Emirate of the Transjordan, the archaeologists arrived, beginning with John Garstang in 1925. Garstang's work was sponsored jointly by the emirate's newly organized Jordanian Department of Antiquities, the British School of Archaeology, the American School of Oriental Research, and Yale University. Excavations and reconstruction have continued off and on at the site since then.

Mount Nebo, the Jordan River, and the Dead Sea

From Amman, consider also a day trip to Mount Nebo, the Jordan River, and the Dead Sea. This will take you into the ancient land of Moab. In addition to Mount Nebo, highlights for the day will be the Madaba Mosaic Map and Bethany Beyond the Jordan.

Madaba Mosaic Map

The Greek Orthodox church dedicated to Saint George in present-day Madaba was rebuilt in 1896 on the ruins of an older, sixth-century church. The mosaic floor of the sixth-century church is partially preserved and provides a colorful map of the land of the Bible. Because this is the earliest map of the Holy Land in existence, it is extremely useful to geographers and archaeologists. As with a number of other Byzantine mosaics that we see in Jordan, however, this Madaba mosaic shows evidence of iconoclastic censoring. Images of animals and two men have been disfigured by rearranging the tesserae, which are the small stone cubes that compose mosaics. This censoring probably occurred during the 720s CE when both Pope Leo III and the Umayyad Caliph Yazid II issued iconoclastic edicts.

Madaba: Detail of the sixth-century-CE mosaic map preserved in the Church of Saint George

Yazid's edict may have been the driving force in this case. The papal edict banned only representations of holy persons, whereas animals are also disfigured in this Madaba mosaic. But before imagining Muslim zealots crashing into Christian churches and vandalizing their precious mosaic floors, note how carefully the images have been removed. Rather than being hacked out with axes and picks, the defaced images have been disfigured carefully without disturbing the surrounding mosaic context—not unlike the way faces are sometimes obscured on television today in order to preserve anonymity. Some evidence suggests that Islam and Christianity were not always sharply distinguished from each other during the early Byzantine Period, especially at the popular level in frontier regions. Perhaps we should imagine a local congregation that included Muslim Christians and Christian Muslims responding to an edict that they remove all images of humans and animals from their church. They did what they had to do, whether or not they favored Yazid's edict, but were careful not to destroy more of their precious mosaic than necessary.

Mount Nebo

A secondary road leads northwest from Madaba to one of the mountain ridges of the escarpment that overlooks the Jordan River Basin. The crest of this ridge (Ras al-Siyagha) provides a marvelous view of the Dead Sea, the Jordan River, Jericho, and the Judean highlands. The ancient name Nebo has been preserved in this vicinity through the centuries, and early Christians believed this crest to be Mount Nebo from which

Moses viewed the promised land (Deut 32:49; 34:1). Consequently, this spot became a sacred destination for early Christian pilgrims.

Ras al-Siyagha (Mount Nebo) viewed from the northeast

The place-names Nebo and Pisgah seem to be closely related in the Hebrew Bible/ Old Testament, especially in several passages that speak of the "top of Pisgah" (Num 21:20; 23:14; Deut 3:27; 34:1). Were Pisgah and Nebo different names for the same place? Or did Pisgah perhaps refer to the mountain spur and Nebo to the crest? Or did Pisgah refer to another vantage point farther down the slope from Nebo?

Several biblical passages indicate another vantage point overlooking the Jordan Valley, called Peor, which was separate from Nebo/Pisgah but nearby (see especially Num 23:28). Apparently it had a shrine or worship center of some sort dedicated to the deity (or Baal) of Peor, thus the biblical references to Beth Peor (Deut 3:29; 4:46; 34:36) and Baal of Peor (Num 25:1–9; Deut 4:3; Ps 106:28; Hos 9:10). The mountain spur paralleling Nebo/Pisgah on the north seems the most likely candidate for Peor, in which case the valley mentioned in Deut. 34:6 may be the one that separates Nebo/ Pisgah from that mountain spur.

> Then Moses climbed Mount Nebo from the plains of Moab to the top of Pisgah, across from Jericho. There the LORD showed him the whole land . . . Then the LORD said to him, "This is the land I promised on oath to Abraham, Isaac and Jacob when I said, 'I will give it to your descendants.' I have let you see it with your eyes, but you will not cross over into it." And Moses the servant of the LORD died there in Moab, as the LORD had said. He buried him in Moab, in the valley opposite Beth Peor, but to this day no one knows where his grave is. (Deut 34:1–6)

Nestled in this valley is a spring with the local name Ain Musa (Spring of Moses). Visible in the farther distance, to the northeast from Nebo/Pisgah, is Tell Hesban.

View west from Mount Nebo toward the land of Canaan

Much of the Hebrew Bible/Old Testament narrative takes place within the panoramic view from Nebo/Pisgah. The Israelites, having escaped from Egypt (book of Exodus), received laws and ritual instructions at Mount Sinai (Leviticus through Num 12) but failed to enter Canaan from the Negeb and wandered forty years (Num 13–19) before resuming their journey toward Canaan by way of the southern Transjordan (Num 21–22; 33). Avoiding the Edomites, they crossed the Arnon (Wadi Mujib) and eventually reached "the valley lying in the region of Moab by the top of Pisgah that overlooks the wasteland" (Num 21:20). While camped there, the Israelites did battle with Sihon king of Heshbon and Og king of Bashan (Num 21:21–35). Then they moved down into the Jordan River Basin itself and camped on the eastern side of the river—on the plains of Moab where their tents spread "from Beth Jeshimoth as far as Abel Shittim" (Num 22:1; 33:49). The "wasteland" mentioned in Num 21:20 is a translation of Hebrew *Jeshimon*, which refers in that context to the barren southern end of the Jordan River Basin where it approaches the Dead Sea. The name Beth Jeshimoth, from which their tents spread as far as Abel Shittim (Num 33:49), might be rendered "the Jeshimon sanctuary" or "the wilderness sanctuary." There the Israelites remained encamped, on the plains of Moab, through the end of the book of Numbers, through Deuteronomy, and into the book of Joshua. Several notable episodes are reported to have occurred while they were camped there.

- Num 22–24 provides a comical story of how the Moabite king, Balak, engaged the prophet Balaam to place a curse on the Israelites. But each time Balak took

Balaam to a high place (such as Kiriath-Huzoth, Bamoth Baal, the top of Pisgah, or the top of Peor) from which they could look upon the Israelites on the plains of Moab below, Balaam was moved to pronounce a blessing.

- Num 25 describes how Israelite men angered God by engaging sexually with Moabite and Midianite women; some even participated in the Baal of Peor cult. God sent a plague, commanded Moses to impale the apostates, and lifted the plague only when this gruesome task was finished. Later (Num 31) God commanded the Israelites to avenge the Midianites by essentially wiping out their population (see especially vv. 17–18).

- It was from the encampment in the plains of Moab that Moses climbed up to Mount Nebo/Pisgah, viewed the promised land, and died. Finally, it was from the encampment in the plains of Moab, specifically from Shittim, that Joshua sent spies to reconnoiter Jericho (Josh 2:1) and from which all the Israelites later crossed over the Jordan River into Canaan.

Christians had already built a church dedicated to Moses on Nebo when the pilgrim Egeria visited there in the late fourth century. This church would be modified and enlarged over the next two centuries, and facilities were added for a monastic community that continued well into the ninth or tenth century. With the expansion of Islam during the seventh century, however, fewer Christian pilgrims ventured to the holy sites east of the Dead Sea, and only a daring few will have reached Nebo after Saladin's overwhelming defeat of the Crusaders at Hattin in 1187. Eventually the church and monastery on Mount Nebo were abandoned.

Franciscan archaeologists began work at Nebo in 1933 and uncovered several building phases of the early church and monastery with impressive mosaic floors. They erected a modest new church on the old foundations during the 1960s that preserved and exhibited the mosaics. Now the 1960s church has been replaced by a new one that offers a much more appealing and informative presentation of the mosaics. But the main reason to visit Mount Nebo is to experience the amazing view across the Dead Sea and Jordan Valley toward Canaan.

Bethany Beyond the Jordan

John 1:24–28 reports that John was baptizing in "Bethany across the Jordan" when priests and Levites came from Jerusalem and challenged his credentials: "Why then do you baptize if you are not the Messiah, nor Elijah, nor the Prophet?" The qualifying phrase "beyond the Jordan" distinguishes this Bethany on the eastern bank of the Jordan River from another place with the same name near Jerusalem—Bethany the home of Lazarus, Mary, and Martha (John 11:1).

The mention of Elijah also directs attention to the eastern side of the river. Second Kings 2 tells how Elisha, aware that Elijah was about to be taken up into heaven, followed him closely from Bethel to Jericho and finally to the Jordan River, where "Elijah took his mantle and rolled it up, and struck the water; the water was parted to the one side and to the other, until the two of them crossed on dry ground" (v. 8). Once across the Jordan, on its eastern bank, Elijah "ascended in a whirlwind into heaven" (v. 10).

Early Christians identified what they believed to be the location of Bethany Beyond the Jordan. And it too, like Mount Nebo, flourished as an active pilgrimage destination from the fourth until the thirteenth century. Then, after the end of the Crusades, the place was abandoned and its exact location forgotten.

The approximate location could be ascertained by biblical scholars and explorers, however, based on clues derived from the Madaba Mosaic Map and surviving pilgrimage reports. Depicted on the map, for example, is a place marked (in Greek) "Ainon where now is Sapsaphas." Sapsaphas, known also from early pilgrimage sources, was a sixth-century monastery where pilgrims commemorated Jesus' baptism. Also, located at approximately where Ainon appears on the Madaba Map, is a small hill known locally as Jebel Mar Elyas (Saint Elijah's Hill). According to local tradition, this was the hill from which Elijah ascended into heaven. The tradition may or may not go back to early Christian centuries, but since early Christians recognized a close theological connection between Elijah and John the Baptist (Matt 17:10–13; Mark 9:11–13; Luke 1:17), it makes sense that they would have venerated Elijah's ascent into heaven in close proximity to where they believed that John baptized Jesus.

Elijah's Hill near Bethany Beyond the Jordan

Archaeological explorations before 1947 identified some meager remains of a monastery and church near Jebel Mar Elyas. More extensive excavations were impossible between 1947 and 1994 when this part of the Jordan Valley was an inaccessible military zone. But soon after the Oslo peace agreement in 1994, and with the urging and guidance of Franciscan archaeologist Michele Piccirillo, a new search led to the discovery of what almost certainly is the site that early pilgrims believed to be Bethany Beyond the Jordan. Near the mouth of Wadi al-Karrar where it joins the Jordan River, approximately opposite Jericho and near Jebel Mar Elyas, archaeologists recovered remains of a riverbank church with steps leading down to the water. Probably this is where thousands of devout Christian pilgrims were baptized during the early Christian centuries, at the same spot where they believed John had baptized Jesus. Remains of a large monastery have been verified nearby.

Jordan River from the Jordanian side at Bethany Beyond the Jordan

Probable early baptism site at Bethany Beyond the Jordan

Bethany Beyond the Jordan: Baptisms performed on the Israeli side of the river

Through Moab and Arabia Petraea to Petra

After Amman and its vicinity, the next most popular destination in Jordan is Petra. It is possible to make a one-day excursion from Amman, though unsatisfying because you must leave Amman very early in the morning and spend most of the day driving to Petra and back. Your time at Petra will be so brief that you hardly get a taste of that magnificent place. And if you do the one-day-trip in summer, your brief time at Petra will be during the midday heat when the sun is high and colors less brilliant. Petra is most beautiful and photogenic either in the early morning light or with late afternoon shadows. The same is true for one-day excursions to Petra from cruise ships docked at Eilat or Aqaba. Think of Petra as an experience for a full day and at least one overnight.

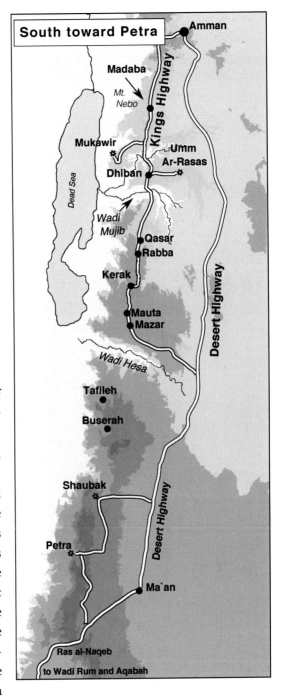

Another reason to avoid a one-day trip to Petra out of Amman is that it requires a hurried drive there and back along the so-called Desert Highway. This is essentially a terribly boring bypass highway that skirts around some of the most interesting and historic parts of Jordan. Consider taking the older and more historic route—the so-called King's Highway, approximated by Highway 35—through the heartland of ancient Moab, Arabia Petraea, and Crusader Oultrejourdain. Allow most of a day to enjoy the scenery and sites along the way. Arrive at Petra in the late afternoon, spend the night in one of Petra's many hotels, and begin exploring this amazing place early the next morning.

The King's Highway

Two international thoroughfares passed through Palestine during ancient times: the Via Maris and the King's Highway. The former passed through western Palestine and will require attention later on in these travel notes. The latter passed north-south through the Transjordanian Highlands connecting Mesopotamia with the Gulf of Aqaba and western Arabia. Highway 35 between Amman and Petra roughly follows a segment of this Transjordanian route—the segment that would have passed through Moab and into Edom during Old Testament times. Travelers along this route would have had to negotiate two large canyons: Wadi Mujib and Wadi Hesa. Wadi Mujib is the River Arnon mentioned several times in the Old Testament, and Wadi Hesa almost certainly is the River Zared. Num 20:14–18 and 21:21–22 may refer to this age-old thoroughfare by the name King's Highway, but more about that below. Centuries later, Trajan's Via Nova followed the same route through the Roman province of Arabia Petraea.

Detail of the Palestinian List of cities conquered by Tuthmosis III.
Each city is depicted as a captive prisoner.

An Egyptian source from the Late Bronze Age may pertain to this early Transjordanian thoroughfare. Inscribed on the walls of the Temple of Amun in ancient Thebes (present-day Luxor, in Egypt) is a list of Syro-Palestinian cities that the pharaoh Tuthmosis III (reigned ca. 1457–1425 BCE) claimed to have conquered. It is known as the Palestinian List and is sometimes called the Megiddo List with reference to a coalition of Syro-Palestinian kings that Tuthmosis claims to have defeated at Megiddo. A leading Egyptologist, Donald Redford, has identified a sequence of names on the list that possibly corresponds to place-names along the ancient Transjordanian thoroughfare. The names on the list are rendered in hieroglyphics, sounded out as the Egyptians would have heard them, which makes it difficult to correlate the hieroglyphic names with locations in Syria-Palestine. But if Redford is correct, Tuthmosis III must have campaigned along this ancient route during the fifteenth century BCE.

Two other inscriptions from the Luxor Temple, also in ancient Thebes, suggest that Ramesses II (reigned ca. 1279–1213 BCE) may have campaigned in this same general region some two centuries later than Tuthmosis III. Both of the Ramesses II inscriptions are brief and not very informative, except that one of them, inscribed on the base of a statue of Ramesses that stands before the northern pylon of the Luxor Temple, provides the earliest known reference to the name Moab. It is interesting to note also that the earliest known written reference to Israel appears in an inscription left by Ramesses's son and successor, Merneptah.

Did Tuthmosis III campaign east of the Dead Sea?

The so-called Palestinian List, inscribed on the walls of the Temple of Amun in Thebes, records the names of cities that Tuthmosis III conquered during the fifteenth century BCE. The following sequence of names in the list may correspond to places along the north-south route through the Transjordan.

#96	*kurmin*	= Tell el-Umeiri, an archaeological site south-southwest of Amman
#97	*beta'e*	= Tell Jalul, an archaeological site east of present-day Madaba
#98	*tipun*	= Tell Dhiban, at the present-day town Dhiban, where the Mesha Inscription was discovered
#99	*'ubir*	= Wadi Mujib, biblical Arnon
#100	*yarutu*	= Khirbet Yarut, at the present-day village el-Yarut north-northwest of present-day Rabba
#101	*harkur*	= Kerak

According to the biblical account of the exodus from Egypt, Moses requested permission first from the king of Edom (Num 20:14–18) and later from the Amorite king of Heshbon (Num 21:21–22) to pass through their lands. In both cases he promised that the Israelites would remain on the *derek hammelek,* which often is translated "King's Highway."

> Then Israel sent messengers to King Sihon of the Amorites, saying, "Let me pass through your land; we will not turn aside into field or vineyard; we will not drink the water of any well; we will go by the King's Highway until we have passed through your territory." But Sihon would not allow Israel to pass through his territory. Sihon gathered all his people together, and went out against Israel to the wilderness; he came to Jahaz, and fought against Israel. Israel put him to the sword, and took possession of his land from the Arnon

to the Jabbok, as far as to the Ammonites; for the boundary of the Ammonites was strong. (Num 21:21–24)

The term *derek hammelek* appears nowhere else in the Hebrew Bible, and biblical scholars debate whether it should be translated as a common noun or as a proper noun. As a common noun, it would refer generically to a "royal road" or "main road." A modern-day Moses leading a convoy across the U.S. might promise various state authorities to stay on their main state highways. Understood as a proper noun, on the other hand, *derek hammelek* would refer to a particular road by that name, which often is rendered the "King's Highway" as in the NRSV translation above. And if the Israelite request to both kings had to do with the same King's Highway that passed through both their kingdoms, then this King's Highway must have followed that same age-old north-south thoroughfare through the Transjordan.

Luxor Temple: The earliest known reference to Moab in ancient written sources appears in a brief inscription on the base of the standing statue of Ramesses II at the far right of the photograph.

Moabites

The area east of the Dead Sea was known as Moab during Old Testament times and its inhabitants were known as Moabites. The Israelites regarded both the Ammonites and Moabites as close relatives, descendants of Abraham's nephew Lot, and Gen 19:30–38 tells how that kinship originated. Fleeing from Sodom and Gomorrah, and his wife having been turned into a pillar of salt, Lot took refuge with his two daughters in a hillside cave. Then the daughters, realizing that their father was old and their intended husbands had perished with the destruction of Sodom and Gomorrah, worried that the family line would come to an end. To avoid this fate, they got their father drunk on two different nights and, each in turn, conceived with him a child.

> Thus both the daughters of Lot became pregnant by their father. The firstborn bore a son, and named him Moab; he is the ancestor of the Moabites to this day. The younger also bore a son and named him Ben-ammi; he is the ancestor of the Ammonites to this day. (Gen 19:36–38)

The book of Ruth provides a more satisfying story about a Judean mother-in-law, Naomi, and her two Moabite daughters-in-law. When all three were widowed, one of the younger women returned to her family, but the other, Ruth, chose to leave her Moabite homeland and live with Naomi in Judah. There, under Naomi's guidance, Ruth married Boaz. The story ends with a genealogical note, raising the possibility (although Boaz may have had other wives) that this Moabite Ruth was King David's great-grandmother: "Boaz [was the father] of Obed, Obed of Jesse, and Jesse of David" (Ruth 4:21–22).

David is reported to have defeated the Moabites on at least one occasion, and he showed no mercy regardless of what family connections there may have been. "He also defeated the Moabites and, making them lie down on the ground, measured them off with a cord; he measured two lengths of cord for those who were to be put to death, and one length for those who were to be spared. And the Moabites became servants to David and brought tribute" (2 Sam 8:2).

We have noted already how the book of Amos opens with maledictions against the Ammonites and other neighboring peoples along with comparable warnings to Judah and Israel. Moab's punishment was to result from an evil deed committed against Edom, who also faced an impending punishment because of some unspecified transgression against "his brother" (probably either Judah or Moab). For more Israelite maledictions against Moab, see especially Isa 15 and Jer 48.

> Thus says the LORD:
> "For three transgressions of Moab,
>> and for four, I will not revoke the punishment;
> because he burned to lime
>> the bones of the king of Edom.
> So I will send fire on Moab,
>> and it shall devour the strongholds of Kerioth,
> and Moab shall die amid uproar,
>> amid shouting and the sound of the trumpet;
> I will cut off the ruler from its midst,
>> and will kill all its officials with him,"
> Says the LORD. (Amos 2:1–3)

Thus says the Lord:

For three transgressions of Edom,

    and for four, I will not revoke the punishment;

because he pursued his brother with the sword,

    and cast off all pity;

he maintained his anger perpetually,

    and kept his wrath forever.

So I will send a fire on Teman,

    and it shall devour the strongholds of Bozrah." (Amos 1:11–12)

Along with these voices from the Old Testament that reflect ancient Israelite perspectives on the Moabites, we are fortunate to have a lengthy inscription from a Moabite king. This is the Mesha Inscription, also called the Moabite Stone. More about it below.

El-Al, Tell Hesban, Madaba

Most of the drive from Amman to Petra will be along Highway 35. But leave Amman to Madaba by way of Naur instead, and about ten miles before reaching Madaba pass two towns that have grown up around two archaeological sites. Watch first for el-Al, situated on a hill left of the road, the present-day town having grown up around Khirbet el-Al. Then pass through Hesban, a larger town surrounding Tell Hesban, which itself is clearly visible to the right of the road. Khirbet el-Al and Tell Hesban are the sites of two ancient Moabite towns, Elealeh and Heshbon, often mentioned together in the Hebrew Bible (Num 32:3, 37; Isa 15:4; 16:9; and Jer 48:34).

Tell Hesban, biblical Heshbon

According to Num 21, Heshbon was the chief city of King Sihon, an Amorite whom the Israelites defeated upon their return from Egypt. Archaeological excavations at Tell Hesban between 1968 and 1978 produced no evidence of occupation during the Middle or Late Bronze Ages, when the exodus from Egypt presumably would have occurred. Only after 1200 BCE did Heshbon emerge as a Moabite town of some prominence (Num 21:30; Isa 15:4). Herod the Great fortified the site centuries later. It reemerged as a flourishing settlement called Esbus during late Roman times.

Madaba is better known today for its Late Roman and Byzantine mosaics, especially the Madaba Mosaic Map discussed above. But it also had been a prominent Moabite city during Old Testament times (Num 21:30; Isa 15:2; 1 Chr 19:7). It was surrounded by rich tableland and is mentioned in the Mesha Inscription. Join Highway 35 at Madaba and continue south toward Dhiban and eventually Petra.

Dhiban

Situated between Wadi Hidan and Wadi Mujib is Dhiban, another Jordanian town that surrounds the tell and preserves the name of its ancient Moabite predecessor. The ancient name was Dibon, mentioned in Egyptian sources as well as in the Old Testament (see Num 21:27–30 and Isa 15:1–9).

In 1868, before the present-day town existed, a German missionary, Frederick Klein, visited a Bedouin encampment near the tell. His host, the Bedouin sheik, called Kline's attention to a large black stone with strange markings on it. Klein recognized this as an ancient inscription, made drawings, and later reported it to authorities and scholars in Jerusalem. Clearly it was an important discovery, which prompted an international race to examine the stone and retrieve it for a European museum. But this part of the Transjordan was not safe to outsiders during the 1860s. There was a dispute among the local Bedouin regarding the stone's ownership. Before the stone could be examined closely or retrieved, it was broken to pieces.

Fortunately, a French scholar named C. S. Clermont-Ganneau had managed to obtain a squeeze (a papier-mâché impression) of the inscription before it was damaged. With this squeeze and surviving pieces of the stone that he was able finally to collect, Clermont-Ganneau reconstructed most of the inscription and published a translation in 1870. The last part of the inscription was badly fragmented and the concluding lines missing altogether.

Excerpts from the Mesha Inscription

I am Mesha, Son of Chemoshyatti, king of Moab, the Dibonite. My father reigned over Moab thirty years and I reigned after my father. And I built this sanctuary to Chemosh at Qarhoh . . . because he saved me from all the kings and caused me to triumph over all my adversaries. Omri, king of Israel, oppressed Moab for a long time because Chemosh was angry with us. His son succeeded him and said, "I too will oppress Moab!" During my reign he said this; but I have triumphed over him and over his house and Israel has perished forever.

Omri had occupied the whole land of Madaba and controlled it during his reign and during half the reign of his son—forty years. But Chemosh controls it during my reign.

And I built Baal-meon, and I made in it a reservoir. And I built Qaryaten. And the men of Gad had dwelt in the land of Ataroth always and the king of Israel had fortified Ataroth for them. But I fought against the town and took it. And I slew all the people of the town as intoxication for Chemosh and Moab. And I brought from there the official altar [translation uncertain] and dragged it before Chemosh at Kerioth. And I settled there [i.e., in Ataroth] men of Sharon and men of Maharith.

And Chemosh said to me, "Go, take Nebo from Israel," and I went by night and fought against it from the break of dawn until noon. And I took it and I slew all 7,000 men and boys and women and girls and maidservants because I had vowed to sacrifice [literally: devote them as *herem*] to Ashtar-Chemosh. And I took from there the official altars [translation uncertain] and dragged them before Chemosh.

And the king of Israel built Jahaz and dwelt there while fighting me. But Chemosh drove him out from before me. And I took from Moab 200 men, all of them noblemen, and established them in Jahaz; thus I took possession of it and attached it to the district of Dibon. And I built Qarhoh, the wall of the forests and the wall of the citadel. And I built its gates and I built its towers. And I built the palace, and I made both of its reservoirs for water inside the town . . .

The inscription was written in Moabite dialect, using the early Canaanite alphabetic script, on the face of a large basalt stele (monumental stone), approximately 44 inches high. Apparently, the stele once stood in a sanctuary built by King Mesha, who ruled Moab from Dibon during the ninth century BCE. This is the same Mesha whom we encounter in 2 Kgs 3. He is introduced there as a sheep breeder, and the chapter goes on to describe Jehoram's unsuccessful attempt to restore Israelite control over Moab.

> Now King Mesha of Moab was a sheep breeder, who used to deliver to the king of Israel one hundred thousand lambs, and the wool of one hundred thousand rams. But when Ahab died, the king of Moab rebelled against the king of Israel. So King Jehoram marched out of Samaria at that time and mustered all Israel . . . (2 Kgs 3:4–6)

Apparently Mesha erected the stele to commemorate completion of the Qarhoh sanctuary, which was dedicated to the Moabite god Chemosh. But he used the inscription also to publicize other major accomplishments of his reign. Mesha was especially proud of having recovered Madaba and its surrounding tableland from Israel. Mesha claims that King Omri of Israel had encroached on this part of Moab at some time in the past, but that he had restored Moabite control during his own reign.

Mukawir (Machaerus)

Soon after leaving Dhiban one reaches the edge of the steep Wadi Mujib. But before exploring the Mujib and beyond, you should visit two important sites accessible by secondary roads between Madaba and Dhiban. These are Mukawir and Umm ar-Rasas, both of which take us again to the Hellenistic, Roman, and Byzantine Periods.

Mukawir is the site of Machaerus, a mountaintop fort founded around 90 BCE by Alexander Jannaeus, the same Hasmonean ruler whom we encountered at Jerash. The fort was destroyed by Pompey and rebuilt later on during the first century BCE by Herod the Great. Rome had a firm grip on Syria-Palestine by that time, but allowed the Herodian rulers and their neighboring Nabatean kings to govern under loose Roman oversight. Relations were not always friendly and, given its strategic location, Machaerus figured prominently in Judean-Nabatean disputes.

Josephus, for example, recounting how Herod the Great's son, Herod Antipas, imprisoned and eventually executed John the Baptist at Mechaerus, mentions a battle between Herod Antipas and his Nabatean contemporary, King Aretas IV. Herod Antipas had been married to Aretas' daughter, but he abandoned her for Herodias, his bother Philip's wife. Naturally this act angered Aretas, which led to the battle and Herod's defeat, an outcome that some Jews saw as divine punishment.

> Now some of the Jews thought that the destruction of Herod's army came from God, and that very justly, as a punishment of what he did against John, that was called "Baptist"; for Herod slew him, who was a good man, and commanded the Jews to exercise virtue, both as to righteousness towards one another, and piety toward God . . . Herod, who feared lest the great influence John had over the people might put it into his power and inclination to raise a rebellion . . . thought it best, by putting him to death, to prevent any mischief he might cause, and not bring himself into difficulties, by sparing a man who might make him repent of it when it should be too late. Accordingly he was sent a prisoner, out of Herod's suspicious temper, to Machaerus, the castle I mentioned, and was there put to death. Now the Jews had an opinion that the destruction of this army was sent as a punishment upon Herod, as a mark of God's displeasure with him. (Josephus *Ant.* 18:116–19)

For the New Testament account of John's execution, see Mark 6:17–29 and Matt 14:1–12.

Mukawir/Machaerus provides an awesome view of the Dead Sea nestled in the Great Rift Valley. And beyond the Dead Sea, although neither is visible from Mukawir, stood two other spectacular mountaintop Herodian forts—to the northwest was the

Herodium and farther to the southwest was Masada. The Romans destroyed Machaerus again in 71 CE—during the First Jewish Revolt, after having sacked Jerusalem and before moving on Masada. A joint Hungarian-Jordanian archaeological team has been excavating the fort since 2009. Among their notable findings are a huge underground cistern almost sixty feet deep, and a large Mikva (Jewish ritual bath and immersion pool).

Mukawir, Machaerus

The Dead Sea viewed from Mukawir

Umm ar-Rasas (Kastron Mefaa)

This is probably Mephaath mentioned in Josh13:18 and 21:37, where we read that Moses assigned it and certain other nearby villages to the tribe of Reuben. Also Mephaath appears along with other Moabite villages in Jer 48: "Judgment has come upon the tableland, upon Holon, and Jahzah, and Mephaath, and Dibon, and Nebo, and Beth-diblathaim" (v. 21–22). The visible archaeological remains at Umm ar-Rasas date from late Roman through early Islamic times.

Trajan's creation of the province of Arabia Petraea and construction of the Via Nova called for additional frontier defenses. Later Roman emperors, especially Diocletian (ruled 284–305 CE), strengthened and increased these defenses. They were known collectively as the *limes arabacus* and included a number of enclosed Roman camps. Among these was Kastron Mefaa, erected on the site of ancient Mephaath, present-day Umm ar-Rasas. Kastron Mefaa was built during the late third or early fourth century CE, probably under Diocletian, and would have served as base camp for a locally recruited cavalry. Its walls can still be traced for a considerable length, but most of the site remains to be excavated.

Umm ar-Rasas: Roman wall in the background

By the fifth century CE, this military settlement had grown into a town approximately twice the size of the original camp, the Roman Empire had split between Roman West and Byzantine East, and Christianity was the official religion of both. Byzantine Mefaa could boast an unusually large number of churches and at least two towers for pillar monks. What remains of the towers are a short distance north of the main Umm ar-Rasas site—one tower almost completely preserved, the other marked only by its nearby base. The holy man who occupied the best-preserved tower would have found solitude forty-five feet above the ground. Possibly these stylite monks, or perhaps one especially renowned holy man, would have attracted many Christian pilgrims to Mefaa, which helps explain the unusually large number of churches.

Umm ar-Rasas: Pillar monk towers in the distance, photo center

Mefaa continued to flourish as a predominantly Christian town with a strong monastic tradition well into the ninth century CE, long after the region had come under Muslim rule. Saint Stephen's Church, which offers the most spectacular mosaic floor to be seen at Mefaa/Umm ar-Rasas, was dedicated in 785 CE. This was thirty-five years after the Abbasid Caliphate had displaced the Umayyads, who themselves had ruled for almost a century. The dedication inscription, located in the nave of the church, mentions "John, son of Isaac, deacon and chief of the people and camp of Mephaon." Apparently, the Muslims of Mefaa, which they called Mephaon, were sufficiently tolerant to allow Christians to hold public positions.

This Church of Saint Stephen belongs to a complex of four churches on the northeast side of the Umm ar-Rasas ruin. Its mosaic, the largest in Jordan, is one of the main reasons that Umm ar-Rasas has been named a UNESCO World Heritage site. Especially interesting are its depictions with names in Greek of seventeen Palestinian towns and villages, eight from west and seven from east of the Jordan River. These depictions of Palestinian towns and villages are located along the north and south sides of the mosaic center, which itself depicts ten more cities from the Nile Delta.

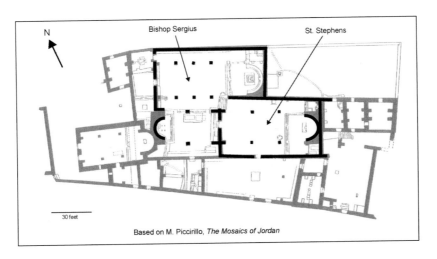

Based on M. Piccirillo, *The Mosaics of Jordan*

Detail of Saint Stephen's mosaic. Depicted are Jerusalem (HAGIA POLIS) and NEAPOLES, present-day Nablus.

Bordering the Church of Saint Stephen on the north is the Church of Bishop Sergius. Its dedication panel reads:

> In the good times of our lord, the most holy and most blessed Bishop Sergius, the whole work of this most holy church was paved with mosaics by the priest, Procopius, in the month of Gorpiaus in the sixth indiction of the year 482 of the Province of Arabia. (trans. M. Piccirillo, *The Mosaics of Jordan*)

Wadi Mujib (Arnon River)

We return our attention now to Wadi Mujib, which one reaches soon after leaving Dhiban and continuing southward. This steep canyon with a stream at its base was known as the River Arnon in ancient times.

Wadi Mujib, biblical Arnon River

According to Num 21, the Israelites camped alongside the Arnon during their exodus from Egypt, having already crossed the Zered Valley and approaching Moab from the south.

> From there they set out, and camped in the Wadi Zered. From there they set out, and camped on the other side of the Arnon, in the wilderness that extends from the boundary of the Amorites; for the Arnon is the boundary of Moab, between Moab and the Amorites. Wherefore it is said in the Book of the Wars of the LORD,

"Waheb in Suphah and the wadis.

The Arnon and the slopes of the wadis that extend to the seat of Ar,

and lie along the border of Moab." (Num 21:12–15)

The modern road across the Mujib/ River Arnon follows the approximate route of the Via Nova, so watch for the Roman milestones approximately halfway up the southern ascent. South of the Mujib, between it and Wadi Hesa (River Zered), is mostly rolling plateau. This was the heartland of Moab during Old Testament times, but it is rich in archaeological remains from virtually every historical period. The road passes through two historic towns on its way to Kerak—Qasr and Rabba. The name Qasr, which means "castle," derives from temple ruins that stood isolated at this spot well into the nineteenth century. This was a Nabatean temple, similar in design to Qasr el-Bint at Petra, and is obscured now by modern buildings. The name Rabba probably harks back to an even earlier time when this would have been regarded as the chief Moabite city,

Roman milestones at Dhiban, biblical Dibon

Rabbath Moab, similar to Rabbath Ammon. It was known as Areopolis during Roman times. Watch for the remains of a Roman Period temple on the right (west) side of the road as you drive through Rabba. Inscriptions indicate that this temple was dedicated to Diocletian and Maximinian. But the city that dominates the region between the Mujib and the Hesa today is Kerak.

Kerak

Situated on a high hill surrounded by steep valleys, Kerak has from earliest times been a key defensive position. Bible atlases often identify it as biblical Kir-heres (or Kir-heseth) featured in 2 Kings 3. We read there how the kings of Israel, Judah, and Edom laid siege to Kir-heseth but withdrew when King Mesha sacrificed his oldest son on the city walls. But this identification of biblical Kir-heseth with present-day Kerak is uncertain. *Kir* simply meant "city" in the ancient Moabite language, and was a common element in Moabite place-names—e.g., Kir (Isa 15:1) and Kerioth (Amos 2:2).

Kerak became an important Christian center during the Byzantine and Early Islamic Periods, as evidenced by its appearance in both the Madaba map and the Saint Stephen's Church mosaic at Umm ar-Rasas. It appears as [Char]achmoba on the Madaba map, the first four letters now missing, and as Charach Mouba on the Saint Stephen's mosaic. Kerak also figured prominently during the Crusader Period, and fortifications from Crusader times dominate the city still today.

The years 1095–1302 serve as convenient dates for the beginning and end of the Crusader Period—from 1095 when Pope Urban II proclaimed the Crusades until 1302 when the Knights Templar attempted, unsuccessfully, to make a last stand on Tartus Island off the coast of present-day Syria. The military actions generally are reckoned as eight separate Crusades, but there was almost constant military activity throughout the period. The first wave of Crusaders captured Jerusalem in 1099 and elected Godfrey of Bouillon to serve as the first ruler of their Kingdom of Jerusalem. He chose the title Defender of the Holy Sepulchre, ruled approximately a year before his death, and was succeeded by his brother Baldwin. Baldwin took the title king, and it was during his reign (1100–1118) that the Crusaders built Montreal (present-day Shaubak) to protect Jerusalem's southeast flank.

The Kerak castle was built a little later, during the reign of Fulk (1131–1144), who appointed his butler, Pagan, to serve as Lord of Montreal and Oultrejourdain. Pagan then built the original Kerak castle, which came to be known as Crac des Moabites, and resided there. Meanwhile, Fulk constructed a line of castles along the northeastern frontier of the Jerusalem Kingdom and a ring of castles around Ashkelon (in Fatimid hands at the time).

Perhaps the most infamous character to inhabit Crac des Moabites was Raynald de Châtillon, who became lord of the castle in 1176 by marriage to the recently widowed lady of the castle, Stephanie of Milly. Raynald seemed unable to contain himself, regardless of peace treaties between the Crusaders and Saladin, from attacking Muslim caravans along the ancient trade route (King's Highway/Via Nova) that passed immediately east of his castle. He also launched ships on the Dead Sea, raided along its coasts, and on one occasion attempted to march on Mecca. The situation came to a head in 1186 when Raynald broke yet another recently signed truce between the Kingdom of Jerusalem and Saladin by attacking a large Muslim caravan as it passed near his castle. This time Saladin marched on Tiberius, presumably with Jerusalem as his intended goal, and a Crusader army met him in battle at the Horns of Hattin (in July 1187) near the Sea of Galilee. Saladin soundly defeated the Crusaders and personally beheaded Raynald on the spot. Kerek, Jerusalem itself, and most other Crusader strongholds except those along the Mediterranean coast, fell to Saladin within a year. Montreal held out until the spring of 1189.

Kerak Castle

Kerak would remain in Muslim hands from that time on, first under the command of Saladin (1188–1193), then of the Egyptian Ayyubids (1193–1416), the Egyptian Mamluks (1260–1516), the Ottoman Turks (1516–World War I), and finally the Hashemite Kingdom of Jordan (1921–present). The Mamluk sultan Baybars expanded the castle to its present size; much of what one sees now is Mamluk expansion.

Ayyubids, Mamluks, Seljuks, and Ottomans

Saladin's defeat of a combined Crusader army at Hattin in 1187 was a threshold moment in the history of the Holy Land. Crusaders would linger on in the land for more than a century, but the tide shifted. For the next seven centuries, Palestine would be dominated by Ayyubids, Mamluks, and Ottoman Turks, each in turn.

Ayyubids. At Saladin's death in 1193, his sultanate included both Egypt and Syria excluding a Crusader foothold along the Palestinian coast. It would soon fragment into smaller sultanates around major cities (Cairo, Damascus, Aleppo) but continue to be ruled by members of Saladin's family until the mid-thirteenth century. Although better known by the honorific title Salah ad-Din, which becomes Saladin in English, Saladin's actual name was Yusuf ibn Ayyub. He family name, in other words, was Ayyub, and the sultans that dominated Egypt, Palestine, and Syria after Saladin are known as the Ayyubids.

Mamluks. The Ayyubids of Egypt followed an earlier practice of buying young boys on the slave market and training them to serve as trusted administrators and soldiers for the sultan. Over time these *Mamluks* (which means "slaves") organized what amounted to fraternities, became a powerful force in Egypt, and eventually replaced the Ayyubid sultanate with Mamluk rule. The transition occurred in 1250, but the first really powerful Mamluk sultan was Baybars (ruled 1260–1277), whom we will encounter later on in these notes. The Mamluk Sultanate was eclipsed by Ottoman Turks in 1517, but the Mamluks would continue to play an important role in Egyptian affairs until the early nineteenth century.

Ottomans. The homeland of the Turkish-speaking peoples was the vast steppeland of Central Asia. A largely nomadic people, they spread from there over time in different directions. One group, called the Seljuk Turks, established an expansive territorial state centered in what is now Iran, and also the Seljuk sultinate of Rum in Anatolia. They attacked and raided cities in Syria-Palestine during the eleventh century, capturing Jerusalem in 1077, and this Seljuk threat was one of the major factors that prompted the Crusades. A Mongol sweep through Anatolia in 1243 meant the end of Seljuk Rum and left in its wake an assortment of remnant states and warlords. Among the latter was an emir named Osman, who attracted a following of soldiers and supporters.

These Osmanlis (or Ottomans, as the followers of Osman came to be known) also included many recent converts from Christianity who had grown disaffected with Byzantine rule. Gradually Osman and the Ottoman sultans that followed secured control of virtually all the former Seljuk and Byzantine territories except for the city of Constantinople. Then Constantinople itself fell to the Ottoman sultan Mehmed II in 1453. A later Ottoman sultan, Selem II, defeated the Mamluks of Egypt in two major battles (1516–1517), which enabled him to annex Syria, Palestine, and the Mamluk Sultanate of Egypt to the Ottoman Empire. The empire reached its peak under Selem's son, Suleiman the Magnificent, who built Jerusalem's Old City walls. It ended with World War I.

Mauta and Mazar

These twin towns are situated seven and eight miles south of Kerak. The first clash between Islamic and Byzantine forces occurred near Mauta in 629 CE, where the Islamic army was defeated and three of its Arab leaders were killed. They are buried in the mosque at Mazar.

The main destination beyond this point for many travelers will be Petra, which can be reached by continuing south by way of Tafila toward Aqaba. This road leads across the Wadi Hesa, probably the Zered of Old Testament times, and through the heartland of ancient Edom. Wadi Hesa is another massive canyon comparable to

Wadi Mujib, but its cliffs, crags, and rock faces are less dramatic. The Israelites considered the Edomites as both relatives, descendants of Esau, and hated enemies (Num 20:14–21; Amos 1:11–12; Jer 49:7–22; and Obadiah). The Edomite capital was Bosra, represented today by ruins near the little Arab village Buseira south of Tafila (Amos 1:11–12; Isa 34:5–12; Jer 49:13, 22).

This road to Petra requires another three hours at best, so many travelers choose to cross over from Kerak or Mauta to the much faster Desert Highway (Route 15), which skirts around Edom's eastern frontier. Either way, it will be possible and worthwhile to stop at Shaubak before reaching Petra.

Shaubak

The Crusaders built this castle, which they called Montreal, to protect the southeastern flank of their Jerusalem Kingdom. It fell to Saladin in 1188, was rebuilt by the Mamluks in the fourteenth century, and then was almost totally demolished by Ibrahim Pasha in 1832. Restorations are underway, but still the castle is much more photogenic from an opposite ridge than from inside.

Shaubak Castle

57

Petra

On approaching Petra, you encounter one of the first landmarks, a copious spring that the Arabs call Ain Musa, or the Spring of Moses. It is covered by a small building now but was more easily accessible in earlier years and always good for a cool drink of water. Tradition holds that this is the spring that Moses and Aaron produced upon striking a rock in the wilderness. Read the biblical account in Num 20, remembering that there is also a Spring of Moses near Mount Nebo/Pisgah that early Christians associated with the water-from-rock event. Looming above Petra in the distance is Jebel Haroun, Aaron's Mountain, where, again according to tradition, Aaron is buried. The shrine to Aaron on top receives occasional visits from local Bedouin.

From Ain Musa, Wadi Musa works its way westward through the present-day town of Wadi Musa (same name) toward the Arabah/Ghor, which it reaches south of the Dead Sea. Although usually a dry riverbed, this wadi can become a destructive torrent during heavy rains unless the water is carefully routed. Over the course of geological time, its water flow has cut a narrow and steep-sided canyon, called the Siq, through the red (Nubian) sandstone west of the present-day town. But before reaching the Arabah, this Siq opens into a broad, isolated valley. And it is in this isolated valley, difficult to reach except through the Siq, that the Nabatean-Roman city of Petra once flourished.

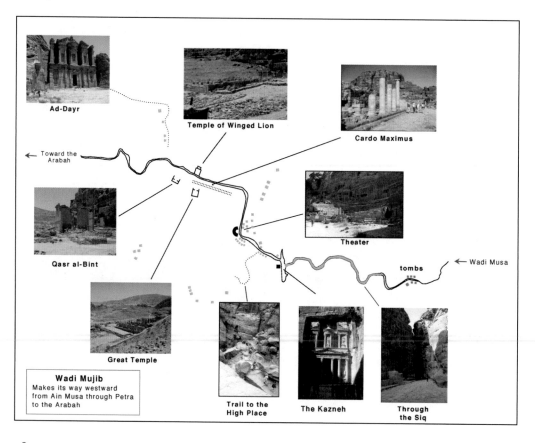

Ad-Dayr

Temple of Winged Lion

Cardo Maximus

← Toward the Arabah

Qasr al-Bint

Theater

← Wadi Musa

tombs

Great Temple

Wadi Mujib
Makes its way westward from Ain Musa through Petra to the Arabah

Trail to the High Place

The Kazneh

Through the Siq

Petra: A drink from Ain Musa during the 1980s before the spring was covered

Jebel Haroun (Aaron's Mountain) viewed from Petra. Note the shrine of Aaron on top

Petra: Through the Siq

The Siq itself, approximately three-quarters of a mile long, is perhaps the most beautiful and dramatic part of Petra. Plan to enter early in the morning when its colors and shadows are at their best. And *do not hurry through*. Walking through the Siq probably will be the most memorable part of your visit to Petra. Eventually, signaling that you are reaching the end of the Siq where it opens into the secluded valley, the Khazneh Fir'awn comes into partial view, peeking through the narrow canyon walls ahead. Khazneh Fir'awn ("Treasure of the Pharaoh") is a local name based on a folk tradition that it was built by a pharaoh and that the decorative urn on its façade contained the pharaoh's treasure. Probably this magnificent facade with an inner chamber carved out of a red sandstone cliff had a funerary function related to the burial of the Nabatean king Aretas III.

After the Khazneh and around a bend in the trail, one enters the isolated Petra Valley, site of the Nabatean-Roman city. Petra flourished as a caravan crossroads inhabited by an early Arab people known as Nabateans. The city and region (Nabatea) were ruled by a local Nabatean dynasty until Trajan created the province of Arabia Petraea to include both the Decapolis and Nabatea. Petra's Nabatean phase peaked under Obodas III (30–9 BCE) and Aretas IV (9 BCE—40 CE), the latter of whom we have encountered already in connection with Machaerus.

Khazneh Firawn approached from the Siq

The archaeological remains of the free-standing city are not particularly impressive at first. What really catches the eye are the numerous monumental facades and chambers carved into the sandstone cliffs that surround the former free-standing city. Most of these, like the Khazneh, were tombs or were otherwise funerary. The city itself has long since collapsed into rubble, but these tombs carved into the cliffs that surrounded the city remain as evidence of the impressive society that once flourished in this isolated valley.

Soon after passing the Khazneh and walking farther into the valley, one reaches the city theater, also carved out of a natural stone cliff. Beyond the theater are the remains of a paved and colonnaded street that made its way alongside the Wadi Musa streambed toward Qasr el-Bint at the opposite (western) side of the valley. This would have been the main street through the city, and it must have been a beautiful sight with water flowing in the stream. Qasr el-Bint, or "Palace of the (Pharaoh's) Daughter," is the only free-standing structure that has survived through the ages, and it has survived only in part. The name also derives from local folklore. Actually, this was a temple dedicated to Petra's chief god and goddess, Dushara and Allat.

Khazneh Firawn

Petra: The theater

Before reaching a gateway into the sacred precinct (*temenos*) of Qasr el-Bint, the colonnaded street passed between two other temples that archaeologists have excavated and partially restored. These are the Temple of the Winged Lions on the right (north) side of the street and the Great Temple on the left side. All three temples date from about the first century BCE, with the Temple of the Winged Lions (so named by archaeologists) probably the earliest. Qasr el-Bint probably dates from the reign of Obodas III, and the Great Temple from the time of his successor Aretas IV, but expanded still further during the first century. The colonnaded street probably was constructed during the late first and early second centuries CE, with the gateway added toward the end of that second century or during the early third century.

Overlooking the Petra Valley from the southwest is a huge rock formation, on top of which archaeologists have excavated Iron Age remains. This rock formation is called Umm el-Biyara ("Mother of Cisterns"), and some scholars identify it as Edomite Sela mentioned in 2 Kgs 14:7. Sela means "rock" in Hebrew, and Petra means "rock" in Greek. It was under the Nabateans that Petra achieved its golden age and eventually covered the entire valley.

Walking west along the Cardo Maximus; Umm el-Biraya in the background

Gateway to Qasr el-Bint temple

Qasr el-Bint, temple to Dushara and Allat

The Nabateans

These were an Arab people of nomadic origin who developed a far-flung caravan network centered in Arabia and the southern Levant. Over time they established several permanent settlements in what is now southern Jordan and the Israeli Negev. Diodorus Siculus, writing during the first century BCE, provides the first known reference to them in ancient written sources. He describes an event that occurred in 315 BCE, soon after Alexander the Great's death, when Alexander's generals were fighting among themselves for control of his recently conquered empire. According to Diodorus, a contingent of Greek soldiers raided and looted a Nabatean settlement on Um el-Biyara in Petra while most of the Nabatean men were away. But it appears that the Nabatean men were not far away, because they were alerted and returned in time to chase down the Greeks and recover their goods.

By the mid-second century BCE, a Nabatean city ruled by a dynasty of Nabatean kings was filling out the secluded valley below Umm el-Biyara. The earliest known of these kings was Aretas I (160s BCE), mentioned in 2 Macc 5:8 and known also from an inscription discovered at Halutza in the Israeli Negeb. His successors would become client kings to Rome after Pompey's eastern campaigns (67–63 BCE), which occurred toward the end of the reign of Aretas III (87–62 BCE). Then Malichus I (reigned 59–30 BCE) made the unwise decision to support the Parthians when they invaded Syria-Palestine in 40 BCE. After expelling the Parthians, Rome increased the Nabateans' tribute requirement and confiscated their Red Sea harbors.

Petra continued to flourish nevertheless, and it enjoyed its peak of commercial power and prosperity under Obodas (Avdat) III (reigned 30–9 BCE) and Aretas IV (reigned 9 BCE—40 CE). Obodas III was a contemporary of Herod the Great and Aretas IV of Herod Antipas. Herod Antipas was married to Aretas' daughter before taking Herodias as his wife, and Paul mentions Aretas in 2 Cor 11:32–33: "In Damascus, the governor under King Aretas guarded the city of Damascus in order to seize me, but I was let down in a basket through a window in the wall, and escaped from his hands."

Trade routes were beginning to shift toward the end of that first century CE, rendering Petra's location less commercially advantageous. Perhaps it was with this in mind that Rabble II (reigned 70–106 CE) transferred the Nabatean capital from Petra to Bozrah (in present-day Syria). Soon after Rabble's death, Trajan annexed the Transjordan including Petra to the Roman Empire as the province of Arabia Petraea.

Nabatean-Roman Petra would continue as a city of importance for yet another hundred years, but it declined during the third century and following.

Christianity reached Petra during the city's declining years, as evidenced by the excavated remains of a church that dates to the mid-fifth century and was remodeled a half-century or so later. It exhibits beautiful mosaics from both building phases. Discovered in a small side room at the northeast corner of the church were 152 papyrus scrolls, extensively carbonized, apparently due to a fire. Although barely legible, they appear to be the family archives of an archdeacon of the congregation during the mid-sixth century CE. A young American archaeologist, Kenneth W. Russell, discovered the church and began excavating it in 1990. He died two years later and is buried at Petra. The excavation continued under the auspices of the American Center of Oriental Research between 1992 and 1998.

Again, what makes Petra so fascinating and photogenic are the hundreds of tombs and other funerary monuments carved into the cliffs that surrounded the Nabatean-Roman city, along with the dramatic and scenic trails among the cliffs and rocks. Two of these trails are breathtaking, both because of the steep climbs required, and because of the spectacular views to be gained. The trail to the so-called high place begins near the theater, leads to a cultic place high above, and offers a stunning overview of the Petra Valley. A trail from the west side of the valley leads to ed-Deir and offers a panoramic view of the Great Rift Valley. Ed-Deir ("the Monastery") is another towering architectural achievement comparable to the Khazneh, except that it is older and probably was intended as a temple. It is thought to have been carved out of the rock in honor of Obodas I (reigned 90–87 BCE), but the project was probably undertaken by a later Nabatean king. Allow approximately an hour for the trail to ed-Deir, depending on how often you stop to rest. After exploring ed-Deir, follow one of the trails over the next rise from there to gain an unforgettable view of the Rift Valley.

Trail to the High Place

Ed-Deir

Wadi Rum and Aqaba

The scenic route from Petra to Aqaba reconnects with the Desert Highway (Route 15) between Maan and Ras an-Naqab and continues from Ras an-Naqab south to Aqaba. Ras an-Naqab itself is situated at the southern end of the Transjordanian Plateau and affords a panoramic view of the unusual terrain ahead. The elevation drops immediately to a desert-like base interrupted here and there by brownish-red, stand-alone mountains with steep, ragged cliffs. The word *moonscape* comes to my mind, although that has to do more with the seemingly otherworldly character of the terrain rather than its actual similarity to the surface of the moon.

Wadi Rum

As the Desert Highway approaches Aqaba, there are mountains that become steep and difficult to negotiate. Through the centuries, unless Aqaba was their specific destination, caravans from Damascus through the Transjordan to places like Mecca in the Hejaz (western Arabia) tended to bypass Aqaba on the east. This meant passing through Wadi Rum, an especially scenic part of the region made famous by T. E. Lawrence in his post–World War I memoir, *The Seven Pillars of Wisdom*.

> We were riding for Rumm, the northern water of the Beni Atiyeh: a place which stirred my thought, as even the unsentimental Howeitat had told me it was lovely. The morrow would be new with our entry to it . . .

Wadi Rum: Jeep on a desert track

Wadi Rum: Camel riders

They were not unbroken walls of rock, but built sectionally, in crags like gigantic buildings, along the two sides of their street. Deep alleys, fifty feet across, divided the crags, whose plans were smoothed by the weather into huge apses and bays, and enriched with surface fretting and fracture, like design. Caverns high up on the precipice were round like windows: others near the foot gaped like doors. Dark stains ran down the shadowed front for hundreds of feet, like accidents of use. The cliffs were striated vertically, in their granular rock; whose main order stood on two hundred feet of broken stone deeper in colour and harder in texture. This plinth did not, like the sandstone, hang in folds like cloth; but chipped itself into loose courses of scree, horizontal as the footings of a wall. (Ch. 62)

When the Hashemite tribal sheik of Mecca and his four sons led an Arab revolt against the Ottoman government during the First World War, T. E. Lawrence served as British liaison officer with the Hashemites, and among other adventures he participated in the Bedouin capture of a Turkish held fortress at Aqaba. The Bedouin army approached Aqaba by way of Wadi Rum, slipped through the mountains that shield Aqaba, and caught the Turks by surprise. It was a small fortress, five or six hundred defenders, attached to the equally modest port village of Aqaba. Aqaba today is a sprawling city with a busy port.

4

Israel and the Palestinian Areas

As with the Hashemite Kingdom of Jordan, present-day Israel is a relatively young nation situated in an ancient land. The connection between the modern state and ancient land is more complicated in two respects. Present-day Israel claims the legacy of ancient Israelites who inhabited much of the land over two thousand years ago. And it shares space with another people of related but different (Arab) heritage who also have roots, but more recent roots, in the same land. We will return to these and other matters pertaining to present-day Jordan, Israel, and the Palestinian areas toward the end of this travel guide. First, let us give attention to ancient Israel, Jerusalem through the centuries, and places west of the Jordan River typically included on Holy Land tours.

Biblical Israel

According to Genesis, Abraham was the father of many nations through three family lines: descendants of his oldest son Ishmael through Sarah's handmaid Hagar (Gen 16); descendants of a second son Isaac through Sarah (Gen 21:1–21); and other descendants through another wife Keturah (Gen 25:1–6). As the biblical narrative continues, God's promises to Abraham were passed down through Isaac's line to Judah. Specifically, we read that Isaac had two sons, Esau and Jacob. Although Jacob was the younger, he managed to gain the "birthright"; God gave him a second name, Israel (Gen 32:22–32); and blessed him with twelve sons who become the ancestors of the twelve Israelite tribes. One of the twelve sons was Judah, from whom descended the tribe of Judah (Gen 29:31—30:24; Exod 1:1–7; Josh 15; and so forth), and it is through this line of descent that Jews are connected to God's promises to Abraham.

Arab Muslims, drawing upon the Arabic Quran, see it differently. They believe that it was their ancestor Ishmael rather than Isaac whom Abraham was commanded to sacrifice and, accordingly, that God's promises to Abraham were passed down to them through Ishmael.

As the biblical narrative continues through the books of 1–2 Samuel and 1–2 Kings, the twelve Israelite tribes are united into a single monarchy under David and Solomon. This monarchy may have been called Israel, although that is not entirely clear—read 2 Sam 19:41–43, for example, where there seems to be some tension among David's subjects between "the men of Israel" and "the men of Judah." In any case, the united monarchy split apart at Solomon's death with most of the tribes establishing a separate kingdom under the name Israel, with its capital first at Shechem and then at Samaria. What was left, mainly the tribe of Judah, became the kingdom of Judah with Jerusalem as its capital (1 Kings 12 through 2 Kings).

The two kingdoms existed alongside each other for two centuries until the Assyrians conquered Samaria in 722 and annexed the territory that had belonged to the Kingdom of Israel. The remnant population of that kingdom continued to be called Samaritans after the name of their former capital city. The Kingdom of Judah survived almost another century and half as a vassal first of Assyria and then of Babylon until the Babylonians destroyed Jerusalem in 586 BCE. Remnants of the tribe of Judah and later the Kingdom of Judah were called Jews.

Note that *Israelite* and *Jew* were not originally synonymous terms, even though they have come to be regarded as such over time. Neither is present-day Israel—a modern Jewish state that has taken the name Israel—a direct and exclusive descendant of biblical Israel, although many Jews and Christian Zionists take this even a step further by insisting that God's promises to Abraham belong now to present-day Jewish Israel.

It should be mentioned also that while God's promises to Abraham and Joshua's allocation of the land of Canaan to the twelve tribes seem to pertain to the whole of western Palestine, close reading of the biblical narratives suggests that the ancient Israelite tribes and the two kingdoms, Israel and Judah, were confined largely to the Central Hill Country. The two possible exceptions would have been during the reign of Solomon in the mid-tenth century BCE, and during the reigns of Omri and Ahab in the mid-ninth century. First Kings 4:24–25 credits Solomon with an expansive empire that extended from Gaza to the Euphrates. But there is no firm evidence of this, written or archaeological, outside the Bible. A better case can be made for Israelite expansion under Omri and Ahab.

Jerusalem through the Centuries

Jewish, Muslim, and Christian pilgrims have been making their way to Jerusalem through the centuries in order to worship at three separate spots that are surprisingly near to each other. Jews come to pray at the Western Wall (traditionally called the Wailing Wall), which is a remnant of the western side of the retaining wall that surrounded the Second Temple compound built by Herod the Great. Muslims pray at the Dome of the Rock and al-Aksa Mosque, both within the area surrounded by the retaining walls of the Herodian temple compound. Christian pilgrims collect not far away at the Church of the Holy Sepulchre, built over the traditional sites of Jesus' crucifixion and tomb. Herod's temple often is referred to as the Second Temple because it was rebuilt on the site of Solomon's temple. Jews and Christians generally refer to this elevated site as the Temple Mount. Arabs refer to it as the Haram ash-Sharif (the Holy Enclosure).

Behind the special role that Jerusalem has played in all three religions is a long and fascinating history—much longer and more fascinating than can be examined properly during a Holy Land tour. But the better sense one has of Jerusalem's long history, the more meaningful will be a visit to the Holy Land. The following is a summary of the highlights, and perhaps now is a good time to review the timeline in chapter 1, "The Long Sweep of History" (see p. 2 above).

Jerusalem during the Bronze Age

Earliest Jerusalem was confined essentially to Ophel, the mountain spur immediately south of the Temple Mount/Haram ash-Sharif. The Gihon Spring, located near the base of Ophel's eastern slopes, provided water. Pottery sherds (fragments) indicate occupation of the site as early as the Chalcolithic Period. The settlement was fortified with a stone wall about 2.5 meters thick during the Middle Bronze Age, and it continued as an active city of modest size through the Late Bronze Age. This Bronze Age phase of Jerusalem's occupation would have been contemporary with most of the tells that you will see during the course of your Holy Land tour. It is mentioned in Egyptian sources, including the Amarna Letters, from which we know the name of a king who ruled Jerusalem during the mid-fourteenth century BCE. His name was Abdi-Heba, which suggests a Hurrian origin. Israelite traditions from later centuries suggest that early Jerusalem had a pluralistic population. Ezek 16:45 mentions Hittites and Amorites: "You are the daughter of your mother, who loathed her husband and her children; and you are the sister of your sisters, who loathed their husbands and their children. Your mother was a Hittite and your father an Amorite."

The city's name itself, Jerusalem, is based on that of a Canaanite god, Shalem. Gen 14:17–21 describes an occasion when Abraham paid tribute to one Melchizedek of Salem—where Salem is possibly an abbreviated form of Jerusalem. Some scholars date Abraham to approximately 2000 BCE, which would be at the beginning of the Middle Bronze Age. But neither Abraham nor any of the other biblical patriarchs or matriarchs are mentioned in written records outside the Hebrew Bible, so any dates applied to them are largely guesswork. A somewhat better case can be made for dating the Hebrew exodus from Egypt toward the end of the Late Bronze Age, but that too is much debated among biblical historians and archaeologists.

Davidic-Solomonic Jerusalem (10th century BCE)

Most of the stories in the biblical books of Joshua, Judges, and 1–2 Samuel are set in the early centuries of the Iron Age. Second Samuel 5:6–10 states that David conquered

Jerusalem from Jebusites and built a palace there, and 1 Chr 11:4 implies that Jerusalem was called Jebus at that time. David is thought to have lived around 1000 BCE, and his son Solomon to have lived during the early to mid-tenth century. Renowned for his wealth, wisdom, and international influence, Solomon is reported to have built another palace and the temple in Jerusalem (1 Kgs 6–7), which would have expanded the walled city northward from Ophel on to the present-day Temple Mount/Haram ash-Sharif. But archaeological evidence for David and Solomon's time period is ambiguous and much debated. More about that can be found below.

Separate Kingdoms: Israel and Judah (ca. 925–586 BCE)

Solomon's death was followed by a division of the tribes into two separate kingdoms that continued alongside each other for two centuries. Israel, with its capital at Samaria, was the stronger of the two and played a more consequential role in international affairs until it was conquered and annexed to the Assyrian Empire in 722 BCE. Judah continued as a satellite state first to Assyria and then to Babylon until the Babylonians seized Jerusalem in 586 and took its last king into exile.

A single dynasty, the House of David, ruled from Jerusalem throughout the kingdom of Judah's history. Archaeological evidence pertaining to Jerusalem during the early years of this dynasty is meager until the late ninth century BCE. It is during the ninth century also that Jerusalem and its kings begin to make occasional appearances in ancient written sources outside the Bible. The relevant sources are as follows:

- The Dan Inscription from the mid-ninth century seems to refer to a king of the "House" (Dynasty) of David. That king probably was Ahaziah, who ruled from Jerusalem ca. 840 BCE. (More about this inscription is given below in connection with Tell el-Qadi/Tel Dan.)

- The Assyrian conqueror Tiglath-pileser III (reigned 744–727 BCE) reported tribute from Jehoahaz (also called Ahaz). Esarhaddon (reigned 680–669 BCE) and Ashurbanipal (reigned 668–627 BCE) reported Judean tribute without naming the Judean kings involved.

- Three almost duplicate accounts from Sennacherib's reign report his 701 BCE invasion of Palestine and siege of Jerusalem. This occurred during the reign of Hezekiah (ca. 727–699 BCE) and inspired Lord Byron's poem "The Destruction of Sennacherib." The Siloam Tunnel and Siloam Inscription may have been prepared in anticipation of this Assyrian threat. (More about the Siloam Inscription is below.)

- A Babylonian Chronicle reports the first surrender of Jerusalem to Nebuchadrezzar's army in "Year 7, month of Kislimu." This corresponds to March 15 or 16, 597 BCE.

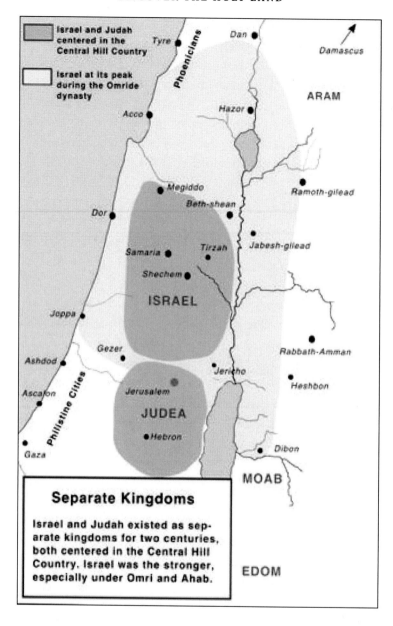

Israel and Judah
centered in the
Central Hill Country

Israel at its peak
during the Omride
dynasty

Separate Kingdoms

Israel and Judah existed as separate kingdoms for two centuries,
both centered in the Central Hill
Country. Israel was the stronger,
especially under Omri and Ahab.

After the Babylonian exile, Jerusalem and the people of Judah would linger on, subject to a parade of foreign powers, for another four centuries. The book of Lamentations reflects the situation in Jerusalem soon after its destruction by the Babylonians, while the books of Ezra and Nehemiah have their setting in the Persian Period. After Alexander the Great, Jerusalem came under the control of the Ptolemies of Egypt for a time, then of the Seleucids of Syria.

Hasmonean Jerusalem (160–40 BCE)

Between 167 and 160 BCE, with Rome now casting its shadow over both the Ptolemies and the Seleucids, Judas Maccabaeus and his brothers led a successful revolt that resulted in an independent Jewish dynasty ruling in Jerusalem—independent, that is, except for ever-increasing Roman oversight. These are known as the Maccabean Revolt and the Hasmonean Dynasty. The Hasmonean rulers eventually expanded their realm to include virtually all of Palestine west of the Jordan River and a considerable portion of the Transjordan. Much of this expansion occurred under John Hyrcanus (ruled 134–104 BCE) and Alexander Jannaeus (ruled 103–76 BCE). Many non-Jews in the conquered territories, such as Herod the Great's Idumean family, were forced to adopt Judaism at this time.

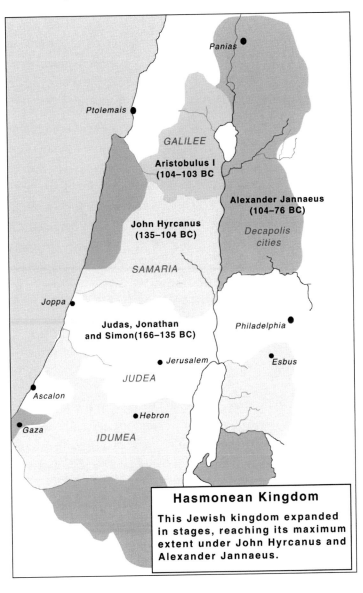

Hasmonean Kingdom

This Jewish kingdom expanded in stages, reaching its maximum extent under John Hyrcanus and Alexander Jannaeus.

Roman-Herodian Jerusalem (1st century BCE—3rd century CE)

Jerusalem and Judea were subject to Rome for approximately four centuries. This subjection unfolded in three stages:

- Pompey affirmed and exercised Roman authority over the Hasmonean Dynasty toward the end of his eastern campaign (67–63 BCE). Two brothers, Aristobulus II and Hyrcanus II, claimed the Hasmonean throne at that time. Pompey settled the squabble in favor of Hyrcanus but removed a number of cities with largely non-Jewish populations from Hasmonean control. These included several of the so-called Decapolis cities, including Gerasa/Jerash and Scythopolis/Beth-shean.

- Julius Caesar's assassination in 44 BCE triggered a decade of political instability from which Herod the Great emerged as king of Jerusalem and Judea. His successors, the Herodian Dynasty, would continue to rule at least parts of Palestine until the First Jewish Revolt (66–73 CE). This revolt, crushed by the Romans, was a disaster for the Jews and a significant event in the development of both Judaism and Christianity. Jerusalem was sacked and the temple destroyed in 70 CE. The last of Jewish resistance ended with the fall of Masada in 73 CE.

- Sixty years later (in 130 CE), during a visit to Rome's eastern provinces, the Roman emperor Hadrian decided to rebuild Jerusalem as a proper Roman city, to change its name to Aelia Capitolina, and to erect a temple to Rome's Capitoline gods. *Aelia* honored Hadrian's family name; *Capitolina* referred to Capitoline Hill in Rome on which stood a temple dedicated to Rome's three Capitoline gods—Jupiter, Juno and Minerva. Probably this is what triggered a Second Jewish Revolt (132–135), also known as the Bar Kochba Revolt. Hadrian crushed the revolt, expelled Jews from Jerusalem, proceeded with his plans for the city, and combined Judea with the Roman province of Syria under the new name Syria Palaestina. Jerusalem's city walls would be rebuilt perhaps a century later and seem to have followed roughly the same lines as the present-day walls.

Early Christian/Byzantine Jerusalem (320s—637 CE)

Christianity gained recognition as a legitimate religion in the Roman Empire under Constantine (reigned 324–336) and soon became the officially favored religion of the empire. Pagan temples were abandoned or converted to serve as churches. Many additional churches were erected, often at places where New Testament events were remembered or thought to have occurred. Christian pilgrims began to arrive from distant regions of the empire. Among the earliest were Constantine's mother Helena (320s CE) and an anonymous pilgrim from Bordeaux (333). Egeria, Jerome and Paula came during the 380s. Another burst of church building, rebuilding, and enhancements occurred during the mid-sixth century under Justinian (527–565). Persian

(Sasanian) invaders, supported by local Jews and Arabs, conquered Jerusalem in 614 and destroyed Christian churches throughout Palestine.

Muslim Jerusalem (637 to World War I)

Arabic-speaking Muslims led by Caliph Omar took Jerusalem in 637 CE. Muslims honor the Jewish prophets including Jesus, and the Arabic name for Jerusalem is al-Quds, which means "the Holy [Place]." Jerusalem would remain under Muslim control until World War I, for almost thirteen hundred years, except for a brief interlude of 88 years when it was held by Crusaders.

- *Caliphate Jerusalem (637–1099).* Three successive Muslim caliphates dominated the Middle East including Jerusalem: the Umayyads, who ruled from Damascus; the Abbasids, who ruled from Baghdad; and the Fatimids, who ruled from Cairo. The Umayyads took the most interest in Jerusalem. Their Caliph Abd al-Malik (685–705 CE) built the domed monument over the rock outcropping on the Temple Mount/Haram ash-Sharif. His son al-Walid (705–715) built the al-Aksa Mosque nearby. Seljuk Turks captured the city in 1077. It changed hands several times after that, and was back under Fatimid control when the Crusaders took the city in 1099.

Dome of the Rock, built by Umayyad Caliphs

- *Crusader Jerusalem (1099–1187).* Crusaders captured Jerusalem, restored it to Christian rule, and held it for eighty-eight years—until Saladin routed the Crusader army at Hattin in 1187 and recovered Jerusalem later that same year. The Roman Catholic (Latin Rite) branch of Christianity gained a foothold in the Holy Land during the Crusades, and Gothic-style architecture became popular. The Crusader Church of Saint Anne is an example from that period of a Roman Catholic Church with Gothic architecture.

- *Ayyubid, Mamluk, and Ottoman Jerusalem (1187 to World War I).* Saladin's Ayyubid successors, who ruled Palestine from Egypt, were displaced by a line of Mamluk sultans in 1250. The Mamluks expelled the last of the Crusaders from Syria-Palestine in 1302 and ruled the region for over two centuries. Then, in 1517, the Mamluks were defeated and Syria-Palestine was annexed to the Ottoman Empire, to which it belonged until World War I. Both the Mamluks and Ottomans were of Turkish heritage rather than Arab. But since they were Sunni Muslim, Jerusalem remained a largely Muslim city. The walls that surround the Old City today were built by the famous Ottoman sultan Suleiman the Magnificent between 1537 and 1542. Many of the buildings inside these walls and still in use also date from the Ottoman Period.

Damascus Gate and Old City Walls, built under Ottoman rule and refurbished during the British Mandate of Palestine

British Mandate Jerusalem (World War I to 1948)

After World War I, the area west of the Jordan River and Dead Sea became the Mandate of Palestine, administered by Great Britain. The Zionist movement had been underway since the late nineteenth century, and Jewish immigrants, in hopes of establishing a Jewish state, were arriving in Palestine already before the war. The mandate arrangement bypassed these hopes, but Jewish immigrants continued to arrive through the Mandate Period, especially with the rise of Nazi Germany. Jerusalem's population, both Arab and Jewish, expanded beyond Jerusalem's Old City walls, which the British refurbished.

Divided Israeli-Jordanian Jerusalem: (1948–1967)

Britain withdrew from Palestine in May 1948. Israel declared itself a nation and managed during the fighting that followed to defend a corridor that reached eastward into the West Bank as far as Jerusalem's walled Old City. The Old City itself remained in Jordanian hands after the fighting, along with the West Bank. Two years after the 1949 armistice, Emir Abdullah annexed Old City Jerusalem and the West Bank to the Emirate of the Transjordan and changed the name of the latter to the Hashemite Kingdom of Jordan. Over the next two decades under separate Israeli and Jordanian administrations, Jerusalem's population continued to expand beyond the Old City walls. Israeli Jews filled in the corridor west of the Old City while Arabs under Jordanian administration expanded north, east, and south of the Old City.

Israeli Jerusalem (1967 to the present)

Israel gained control of Arab/Jordanian Jerusalem during the Six Day War (1967) and officially annexed it to Israel in 1980. This annexation has not been recognized by the international community, however, and Jerusalem's two main population groups—Jewish-heritage Israelis (living primarily in Western Jerusalem) and Arab-heritage Palestinians (living primarily in Eastern Jerusalem)—remain in bitter conflict.

Israeli guards at the Lion's Gate

Hundreds of Christian Holy Land tour groups come each year, most arriving at the Ben Gurion Airport, but others by way of Jordan, and some by way of Egypt. Israel is a relatively small country, and there are many itinerary options. My travel notes will begin with Nazareth and nearby Sepphoris, both of which Jesus would have known as a youngster. Next come places around the Sea of Galilee, center stage of his Galilean ministry. After an excursion to Caesarea Philippi and sources of the Jordan River, the notes assume a journey through Samaria to Jerusalem. Since we have already reviewed Jerusalem's long history, my notes will focus at that point on things to see in and around the city. From Jerusalem, these travel notes project excursions to Bethlehem, Jaffa, Caesarea Maritima, and the Dead Sea area.

Lower Galilee

Jesus' boyhood home was Nazareth, one of the several small Jewish farming villages that dotted Lower Galilee during the first century CE. Approximately five miles northwest of Nazareth was Sepphoris, residency of Herod Antipas and administrative center of his tetrarchy of Galilee. Your Holy Land tour almost certainly will include Nazareth. But for historical background to Galilee at the time of Jesus' ministry, the place to begin is Sepphoris.

Sepphoris

Herod Antipas's family was of Idumean (Edomite) origin, his forebears having converted to Judaism when John Hyrcanus I annexed Idumea to the Hasmonean kingdom in approximately 125 BCE. Presumably Herod Antipas was named after his grandfather, Antipater, who had served as chief advisor to Hyrcanus II. Anitpas is short for Antipater. While serving as chief advisor to Hyrcanus, the grandfather Antipater gained Julius Caesar's confidence and friendship to the extent that Caesar granted him Roman citizenship and eventually appointed him proconsul in Palestine. Antipater then appointed his two sons, Phasael and Herod (future Herod the Great), to serve as governors over Judea and Galilee respectively. No doubt there was resentment among the Jews, and within a year after Julius Caesar's assassination in 44 BCE, Antipater too was assassinated.

The so-called Second Triumvirate—Mark Antony, Octavian, and Lepidus—dominated Roman politics during the turbulent decade that followed. Mark Antony took responsibility for the eastern territories, reaffirmed Phasael and Herod in their administrative positions, and granted both the title tetrarch. But Parthians invaded Syria-Palestine in 40 BCE and were bribed to name Antigonus as king over the Hasmonean realm in place of Hyrcanus II. Antigonus represented another branch of the Hasmonean family, and there had been long-standing animosity between the two branches. Also, there was considerable Jewish opposition to the two Roman-appointed, Idumean tetrarchs—Phasael and Herod. Antigonus attacked Jerusalem in order to claim the throne, while Phasael and Herod led the defense. Antigonus managed to capture Hyrcanus and Phasael before actually taking the city. Phasael committed suicide in order to avoid a tortured death. Herod escaped from Jerusalem to Masada, from there to Nabatea, then to Egypt, and finally to Rome (*War* I.248–62; 274–81).

Octavian and Mark Antony were still on reasonably good terms when Herod reached Rome. With the support of both, the Roman senate designated Herod king of Judea, Samaria, and western Idumea, then sent him back to Palestine with a Roman army to make good on the appointment. Herod's first major victory was at Sepphoris, which he captured from Antigonus during the winter of 39–38 BCE in a battle fought during a snowstorm. Herod took Jerusalem the next year, thus marking the beginning of Herod's reign. Sepphoris served as his northern headquarters.

Conflict between Octavian and Mark Antony soon split the Second Triumvirate and ended with Octavian defeating Mark Antony in the sea battle of Actium (31 BCE), and with the suicides of Mark Antony and Cleopatra. Octavian, who was actually Julius Caesar's nephew and adopted son, was now the most powerful man in the Roman Empire, and the Roman senate confirmed his authority in 27 BCE by granting him the title Augustus. Thus began Octavian's long and remarkable reign as Caesar Augustus (27 BCE—14 CE). Herod, who had remained loyal to Mark Antony until Actium, promised to show the same loyalty to Augustus, and then he made good on that promise throughout his own long and eventful reign (37–4 BCE). His reign

LOLoops

overlapped that of Caesar Augustus by twenty-three years, during which time Augustus expanded Herod's domain to include virtually all the area west of the Jordan River and considerable territory in the Transjordan.

When Herod died in 4 BCE, Augustus honored Herod's request that his kingdom be divided among his three surviving sons: Herod Archelaus, Herod Philip, and Herod Antipas. Archelaus received Judea, Idumaea, and Samaria with the title ethnarch. Philip received territories in the northern Transjordan with the title tetrarch. Antipas received Galilee and Perea also with the title tetrarch. Herod Antipas set about immediately to rebuild Sepphoris as his residence and capital. Later he would build a new capital city at Tiberias.

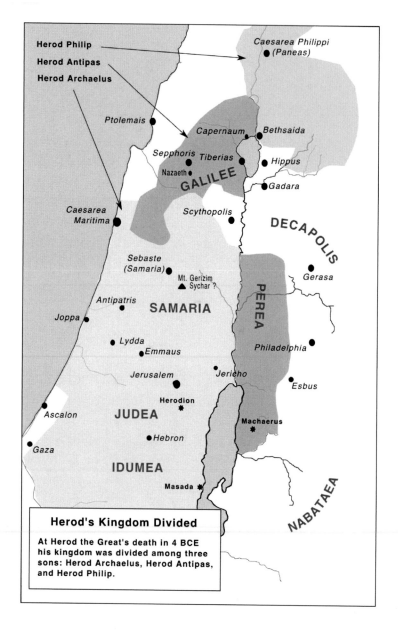

Herod's Kingdom Divided

At Herod the Great's death in 4 BCE his kingdom was divided among three sons: Herod Archelaus, Herod Antipas, and Herod Philip.

Sepphoris's population must have been six thousand or more during the first century, thus considerably larger than the population of Nazareth and of surrounding villages. The residents in Sepphoris would have been both Jewish and Gentile but generally more affluent and more Roman in character than the surrounding villagers. Since Sepphoris was only about five miles from Nazareth, it must have been well known to Jesus' family. There is an early tradition that Mary was from Sepphoris, and it has been suggested that Joseph might have found work in Sepphoris. Surely Jesus and his boyhood friends would have explored the streets of the city on occasion.

Sepphoris wisely remained loyal to Rome during the First Jewish Revolt (66–73 CE). Its role in the Bar Kochba Revolt (132–135 CE) is less clear. The Sanhedrin and center of Jewish learning shifted from Jerusalem to Galilee after the Bar Kochba Revolt—first to Beth-Shearim, then to Sepphoris, and eventually to Tiberias. Rabbi Judah ha-Nasi ("the Prince"), who completed compiling the Mishnah at approximately the beginning of the third century CE, spent his last years at Sepphoris. The city was almost completely demolished by an earthquake in 363 CE. Quickly rebuilt, it continued as an active, predominantly Jewish city through the early Christian centuries. The Hebrew form of the name is Zippori, which means "bird." According to the Talmud, it was called that because the city was perched like a bird on the top of a low mountain surrounded by fertile countryside.

Sepphoris/Zippori declined during the early Arab Period. Then Crusaders arrived in 1099 and held Sepphoris through most of the twelfth century. A Crusader tower still overlooks the city's ruins. After the Crusaders, an Arab village called Saffuriyyeh occupied the Sepphoris site until 1948.

Several archaeological teams have excavated at Sepphoris/Saffuriyyeh/Zippori since Leroy Waterman of the University of Michigan first probed the site in 1931. These include two other American groups—from the University of South Florida (directed by Jim Strange) and Duke University (directed by Eric Meyers and Carol Meyers). Your visit to the site will include some of the following highlights.

- *The Theater.* Built toward the end of the first century or in the early second century CE, so not long after the First Jewish Revolt, the destruction of Jerusalem, and the fall of Masada. Most of the New Testament books (except for the authentic letters of Paul, written during the 50s CE) were being written about the same time that the theater was being built. The theater continued to be in use throughout the later life of the Roman-Byzantine city.

- *Roman streets and buildings.* Typical Roman city planning called for a main street (*cardo maximus*) and several cross streets (*decumani*; sing. *decumanus*). Excavations at Sepphoris have revealed a long section of its *cardo* and one *decumanus.* These apparently were laid out and built during the early second century, thus roughly contemporary with the theater, and like the theater these streets continued in use throughout the later life of the Roman-Byzantine city.

There would have been shops and other structures along each side of the streets. Over time these Roman Period structures were replaced with structures from the Byzantine Period.

Sepphoris: Cardo Maximus

- *A palatial villa with a Dionysus mosaic.* The beautiful Dionysus mosaic adorned the formal dining room (*triclinium*) of a palatial villa built during the third century CE and apparently destroyed during the 363 CE earthquake. The Roman Empire began its decline during that century, and Christianity was spreading rapidly. Early in the fourth century, while this villa was still in use, Constantine and Lucinius issued the Edict of Milan (313), and Constantine sponsored the first international convocation of Christian leaders (the Council of Nicaea in 325). The anonymous Pilgrim of Bordeaux reached Palestine during the 330s.

Sepphoris: Triclinium, the *Mona Lisa* of Galilee

- *The Orpheus House/Western Church.* Situated midway along the northern side of the *cardo* are the remains of a Roman villa, which was replaced during the Byzantine Period with a church. The villa probably was built toward the end of the third century CE, thus is roughly contemporary with the villa described above featuring the Dionysus mosaic. Not much of the villa remains except fragments of the mosaic floor from the dining room. The mosaic depicts Orpheus playing a stringed instrument to calm wild animals and birds that surround him. A church replaced the villa toward the end of the fifth or early in the sixth century, by which time Christianity was firmly established as the official religion of the land and church leaders were embroiled in theological controversies.

- *The Nile Building.* This is the largest structure excavated along the *cardo*, and indeed the largest structure excavated thus far at Sepphoris. It may have been a public building, as suggested by its size and the richness of its mosaic floors. It dates to the early fifth century—about the time of the Nestorian Controversy addressed at the Council of Ephesus in 431, An eight-line inscription near the *cardo* entrance refers to two artists, Procopiuis and his son in-law, Patricius, presumably the artists responsible for the mosaic. All the rooms have colorful mosaics, but the most interesting is in the so-called Nile Festival Room, depicting Nile scenes combined with hunting scenes. Compare these fifth-century mosaics with those of the fifth-century church at Tabgha.

- *The Synagogue.* Sepphoris had many synagogues; the Talmud states that it had eighteen at the time of Rabbi Judah ha-Nasi (in the early third century). This one probably was built during the early fifth century, so about two hundred years later than Rabbi Judah and contemporary with the Nile Building and the Capernaum synagogue. Its floor plan is somewhat unusual for early synagogues in that the main hall had only one aisle, on its northern side. But the mosaic floor is rich with such Jewish symbols as the holy ark with a seven-branched menorah on either side. These symbols are combined with biblical scenes and the zodiac to convey the message that God is the center of creation, that God has chosen the people of Israel, and that in the future, fulfilling the promise to Abraham on Mount Moriah, God will rebuild the temple and redeem Abraham's children. The depiction of the zodiac on a synagogue floor may seem a little strange to us today because the zodiac has come to be associated with astrology. In the fifth-century the zodiac was part of the commonly accepted understanding of the heavens.

A tourist center near the synagogue provides bathrooms, a film introducing Sepphoris, and a helpful model of the site. Another brief film that focuses on Rabbi Judah is available for viewing in the synagogue.

Nazareth

Nazareth, Cana, and Nain were among the numerous small farming villages that dotted Lower Galilee at the time of Jesus' ministry. The location of Cana, where Jesus attended a wedding feast and transformed water into wine (John 2:1; 21:2), remains uncertain. Kefar Cana about five miles north-northeast of Nazareth is the traditional site frequented by tour buses. But Khirbet Kana (Kenet el-Jalil) about six miles farther north seems more likely. (More about Nain is given below.)

These were predominantly Jewish villages, yet they were located a considerable distance from Judea. No doubt many of their inhabitants were from families that converted to Judaism when Aristobulus I annexed Galilee to the Hasmonean kingdom in 104/103 BCE. Others would have emigrated from Judea to Galilee at that time or later. According to Luke's Gospel, Mary and Joseph were required to return to Judea and register in Bethlehem because either Joseph or his ancestors had emigrated from there—i.e., he was descended from the house and family of David, who was from Bethlehem (Luke 2:1–5). Matthew makes no mention of the registration and seems to imply that the couple immigrated to Nazareth shortly after Jesus' birth (Matt 2:21–23).

Nazareth can be confusing to first-time visitors because archaeological remains, church traditions, and the embellishments of tour guides run together. Keep in mind that the Nazareth of New Testament times was nothing like the sprawling city one encounters today; it was a small farming village, probably with between two- and four hundred inhabitants. Accordingly, we find no mention of Nazareth in ancient written sources except for the New Testament and an inscription fragment discovered at Caesarea Maritima in 1962. John 1:43–46 is usually is interpreted to mean that Nazareth was considered to be of little consequence:

> The next day Jesus decided to go to Galilee. He found Philip and said to him, "Follow me." Now Philip was from Bethsaida, the city of Andrew and Peter. Philip found Nathanael and said to him, "We have found him about whom Moses in the law and also the prophets wrote, Jesus son of Joseph from Nazareth." Nathanael said to him, "Can anything good come out of Nazareth?" Philip said to him, "Come and see."

The Caesarea fragment and two other fragments excavated with it, all apparently from a third- or fourth-century synagogue plaque, list places where Jewish priests resettled after Hadrian expelled Jews from Jerusalem in 135 CE. Nazareth is among the places mentioned.

Because Nazareth was such a modest settlement, it left little in the way of archaeological remains. The village was situated on a rocky hillside. There were caves among the rocks, and when the villagers constructed their houses from field stones and mud bricks, they sometimes incorporated the caves into their houses. A house might be built over or in front of a cave, with the cave serving as a back room or stable. The mud bricks and field stones disappeared over time so that archaeological excavations reveal little more than rock surfaces and caves.

Pious Christians during the Byzantine Period identified what they thought would have been the house of Joseph and the house of Mary. There is no confirming archaeological evidence in either case. We are dealing here with tradition, albeit tradition that goes back at least as early as the sixth century CE. And not surprisingly, since little is left of New Testament Nazareth except for stone surfaces and caves, both traditional spots—Joseph's house and Mary's house—are represented by caves.

According to Western tradition, the angel Gabriel appeared to Mary at her house. Thus, the cave that represents her house, known also as the Grotto of the Annunciation, has been converted to a shrine that is accessible in the magnificent Roman Catholic Basilica of the Annunciation. The Greek Orthodox tradition says that the annunciation occurred at the village spring, which is accessible in the Greek

Orthodox Church of Saint Gabriel. In short, Nazareth offers two traditional locations of the annunciation.

The Basilica of the Annunciation

Among the early Christian pilgrims who made their way to Nazareth, Jerome visited Jesus' home village during the fifth century with Paula and her daughter Eustochius. The anonymous Pilgrim of Piacenza, who visited in the sixth century, mentioned that Mary's house had been converted to a basilica.

> The house of the Blessed Mary is a basilica, and many cures are wrought in it by her garments. In the city the beauty of the Hebrew women is so great, that no more beautiful women are found among the Hebrews; and this they say was granted them by the Blessed Mary, who they say was their mother. (Palestine Pilgrims' Text Society, Vol. 2, *Antoninus Martyr*, p. 5)

Arculph, a French bishop who traveled in the Holy Land in approximately 670, reported two churches in Nazareth in the seventh century. Then in the twelfth century Crusaders built a large basilica and monastery complex on the traditional site of Mary's house. Louis IX of France, who conducted the Seventh Crusade, attended Mass at the Crusader basilica on March 24, 1251. Twelve years later (in 1263) the basilica was destroyed by the Egyptian Mamluk sultan Baybars.

Franciscans rebuilt a church on the spot in 1730 and enlarged it in 1877. The magnificent Basilica of Annunciation that marks the spot today was consecrated in 1969. During the 1960s, while plans and preparations were underway for building the current basilica, Italian archaeologist Bellarmino Bagatti cleared the site and identified remains of what he interpreted to be the following phases of earlier occupation and building:

- The early village with caves representing the traditional locations of Joseph's house and the annunciation (Mary's house; Grotto of Annunciation)
- Possibly a synagogue from the third or fourth century
- A Byzantine church and monastery from the fifth century
- The Crusader church and monastery complex from the twelfth century.

The modern basilica is built over remains of these earlier building phases, and from inside the basilica visitors can view Mary's house/Grotto of the Annunciation and part of a wall from the Crusader church. Meager remains of the early village extend beyond the basilica on its northern side, and there (outside the basilica on its north side) is to be found a chapel that covers the traditional location of Joseph's house.

Nazareth: Grotto of the Annunciation in the Roman Catholic Church of the Annunciation.
Photo of the church in upper left

The Village Spring and Saint Gabriel Church

Whatever one's views regarding the locations of Joseph's house, Mary's house, or the annunciation, there is one unquestionably historic spot to visit in Nazareth—the village spring. Everyone in the little village including the holy family would certainly have used the spring. The first traveler to mention it was a Russian pilgrim in the eleventh century, an Abbot Daniel. Near the spring he saw a round church dedicated to the archangel Gabriel.

> We afterwards left the town [Nazareth], and going summer sun-rising [north-east], came to a very deep well, with very cold water, to which one descends by several steps. This well is covered by a round church dedicated to the archangel Gabriel . . . It is near the well that the holy Virgin received the first announcement from the archangel. (Palestine Pilgrims' Text Society, Vol. 4, p. 71)

This church is mentioned also in Crusader sources, and its approximate location is marked by the present-day Greek Orthodox Church of Saint Gabriel. This present-day church was constructed in 1750. Its wooden iconostasis, which is noteworthy, also dates from the eighteenth century. The frescoes that decorate the church's walls are from the 1970s.

Until recent times (until the 1960s), water from the spring was available to Nazareth townspeople at a picturesque fountain approximately 150 yards south of the Church of Saint Gabriel. This earlier fountain was replaced by a nonfunctional replica in 2000, but one can reach the spring now at its approximate source through a crypt inside the church. The crypt, although not the ceramic tiles that cover its walls, probably dates from the Crusader Period. Visitors are allowed to enter and view the spring even when worship is underway. But the congregation expects you to exit through their gift shop.

Nazareth: Access to the village spring through the Church of Saint Gabriel.
Photo of the church in upper left

On the southern outskirts of Nazareth is so-called Mount Precipice, or "the Mount of Precipitation," the traditional place where an angry mob was about to throw Jesus off a cliff after his bold reading and interpretation of Isaiah (Luke 4:16–30). This is a mountain spur that extends to the southwest from the Nazareth hills and overlooks the lowlands that separate Galilee from the Central Hill Country. These lowlands are known inclusively, and rather loosely, as the Valley or Plain of Jezreel (Esdraelon in Greek). Whether or not Mount Precipice is the place to which Luke was referring, it offers a panoramic view of the Jezreel/Esdraelon Valley and an excellent vantage point for locating five other important biblical landmarks: Mount Tabor, Mount Moreh, Mount Gilboa, Mount Carmel, and Megiddo. The Jezreel/Esdraelon Valley was fertile and strategically situated for both trade and warfare. Throughout history the landmarks visible from Mount Precipice have been settings for numerous battles.

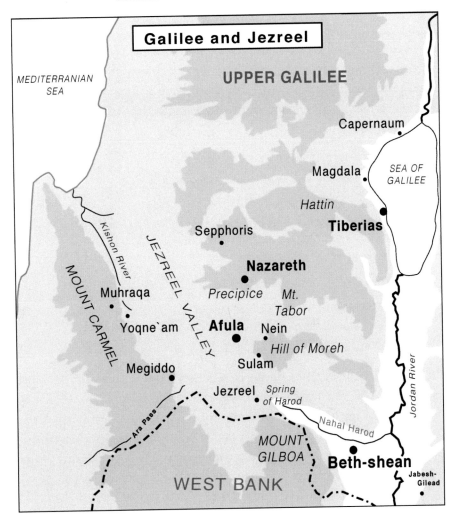

View east-southeast from the Precipice—Mounts Tabor, Moreh, and Gilboa

Mount Tabor

Almost directly to the east of Mount Precipice is Mount Tabor (Jebel et-Tur), which stands majestically apart from the surrounding plain except for a narrow ridge that connects it to the Galilean hills on the northwest. Mount Tabor is mentioned along with Mount Hermon in the Psalms and with Mount Carmel in one of Jeremiah's oracles against Egypt.

> The heavens are yours, the earth also is yours;
>> the world and all that is in it—you have founded them.
> The north and the south—you created them;
>> Tabor and Hermon joyously praise your name. (Ps 89:11–12)

> As I live, says the King,
>> whose name is the LORD of hosts,
> one is coming
>> like Tabor among the mountains,
>> and like Carmel by the sea. (Jer 46:18)

Judg 4 describes an occasion during Israel's early tribal period when the Israelites were oppressed by Jabin, king of Canaan, who ruled from Hazor. Deborah, a prophet serving as Judge for the Israelites at the time, urged Barak to muster an Israelite army on Mount Tabor and challenge Jabin's rule. She assured Barak that the Canaanite army would assemble by the River Kishon and agreed to remain with him during the battle. When Jabin and his commander Sisera heard what was happening, Sisera assembled a massive army with nine hundred iron chariots near the River Kishon. Barak led his army down from Mount Tabor and routed the Canaanites. Sisera fled the battle on foot. Exhausted, Sisera stopped at the tent of Jael, wife of a Kenite. The Kenites were at peace with Jabin's kingdom, so she welcomed him in, gave him water, hid him in the tent, and promised to tell any passersby that no one was there. But once Barak was asleep, Jael drove a tent peg through his temple.

Mount Tabor is not mentioned by name in the New Testament, and there are no geographical clues to support its identification as the mountain of Jesus' transfiguration (Matt 17:1–8; Luke 9:28–36). Since Tabor is the most conspicuous of the Galilean hills, however, it is not surprising that early Christian pilgrims thought it might have been. Churches were erected on Tabor at least as early as the sixth century. The Crusaders built a church and monastery there during the twelfth century. Today there is both a Greek Orthodox monastery and a Franciscan basilica. The latter, the Basilica of the Transfiguration, was built in 1921 and incorporates parts of earlier sixth- and twelfth-century churches. The mountaintop can be reached from the town of Shibli at its base either by taxi or by a winding trail up the north side. Tabor's summit offers another commanding view of Lower Galilee and the Jezreel Valley.

Mount Moreh

Visible to the southeast from Mount Precipice and south from the top of Tabor is a low mountain (or large hill) known traditionally as Little Hermon. This must be the hill of Moreh, mentioned in connection with Gideon's nighttime rout of the Midianites. "Then Jerubbaal (that is, Gideon) and all the troops that were with him rose early and encamped beside the spring of Harod; and the camp of Midian was north of them, below the hill of Moreh, in the valley" (Judg 7:1). At the foot of Little Hermon/ Mount Moreh on its north side, so only about four miles south of Mount Tabor, is Khirbet Endur. Meager archaeological remains confirm only Roman and Arab settlement phases. But the Arabic name (Endur) suggests that it may have been here or somewhere nearby (at biblical Endor) that King Saul consulted a medium on the eve of his last battle with the Philistines (1 Sam 28:3–25).

Two Arab villages situated on the western slope of Moreh, and thus visible from Mount Precipice, call to mind other biblical events. These are Sulam and Nein, which represent the sites of biblical Shunam and Nain. When King David grew old, a beautiful maiden named Abishag the Shunammite was brought to wait on him. Later she would figure in the conflict between Solomon and Adonijah (1 Kgs 1:3; 2:13–25). One of the stories about the prophet Elisha tells how he prophesied that a wealthy Shunammite woman would give birth to a son, which she did. But later her son fell ill and seemed to have died. She appealed to Elisha and he revived her son (2 Kgs 4:8–37). Luke 7:11–17 records a similar incident in Nain, where Jesus revived a widow's son from death.

Mount Gilboa, Jezreel, and the Spring of Harod

Only partly visible from Mount Precipice, peeking from behind Mount Moreh in the farther distance, is Mount Gilboa. Gilboa itself is actually an extension of the Central Hill Country that curves around to the northwest and is separated from Mount Moreh by a broad valley. This valley, while serving as an east-west pass between Mounts Gilboa and Moreh, continues eastward to the Jordan River Valley. At the western opening to the valley was the ancient city of Jezreel (Tel Yizreel). At the eastern end of the valley, where it reaches the Jordan River Valley, was ancient Beth-shean (Tell el-Husn). Less than a mile to the southeast of Tel Yizreel is the Spring of Harod where, according to Judg 7:1 quoted above, Gideon and his troops were camped the night they rousted the Midianites. The Arabic name is Ain Jalut (Spring of Goliath). Nahal Harod/Jalut rises near the spring and flows eastward through the valley past Beth-shean to the Jordan River. It is possible that the biblical name Jezreel Valley applied originally to this valley between the ancient cities of Jezreel and Beth-shean, and was applied only later to the more expansive lowlands west of Jezreel (see esp. Josh 17:16 and Judg 6:33). Be that as it may, this valley route between Jezreel and Beth-shean has been an important thoroughfare throughout history.

Present-day Yizreel is a kibbutz located six miles south-southeast of Afula, at the northeast corner of where Highway 675 crosses Highway 60. It replaced the former Arab village of Zerin, and east of the modern buildings is Tel Yizreel, the archaeological site of ancient Jezreel. David Ussisshkin of Tel Aviv University and John Woodhead representing the British School of Archaeology in Jerusalem conducted six seasons of excavations at this long, low tell between 1990 and 1995. Renewed excavations began in 2012 sponsored by the University of Haifa and University of Evansville.

Tel Yizreel (ancient Jezreel)

King Saul and the Israelite army would have been camped near Jezreel and Ein Harod when he visited the witch at Endor, the Philistines having gathered at Shunem on Mount Moreh (1 Sam 28:4). The Israelites were camped there again on the eve of Saul's last battle with the Philistines (1 Sam 29:1). The battle itself was fought on the slopes of Mount Gilboa, where three of Saul's sons were killed. Then Saul killed himself on Gilboa rather than fall into Philistine hands (1 Sam 31:1–6).

The Northern Kingdom of Israel reached its peak under the Omride Dynasty, which consisted of four kings who ruled in turn during the mid-ninth century BCE. These were Omri, Ahab, Ahaziah, and Jehoram. Their chief city was Samaria, but apparently the family also had a palace in Jezreel. Jezreel was the setting of the story of Naboth's vineyard, which tells how Ahab's wife Jezebel used royal influence to confiscate a poor man's vineyard (2 Kgs 21). Second Kings 9 describes Jehu's rebellion and massacre of the Omride Dynasty, beginning with his assassinations of Jehoram and Jezebel in Jezreel. Its description of how Jezebel prepared for her impending death and met it with dignity befitting a queen is powerful. The book of Hosea opens with a condemnation of Jehu's dynasty because of this horrible deed.

And the LORD said to him, "Name him Jezreel; for in a little while I will punish the house of Jehu for the blood of Jezreel, and I will put an end to the kingdom of the house of Israel. On that day I will break the bow of Israel in the valley of Jezreel." (Hos 1:4)

Ein Harod/Ain Jalut was to be the scene of another momentous battle that occurred in 1260 CE. A Mongol army led by Hulegu, grandson of Genghis Khan, had sacked Baghdad two years earlier, massacred all the members of the Abbasid line that could be rounded up, sacked Aleppo in early 1260, taken Damascus without resistance, and was headed toward Egypt when Hulegu received news that Möngke, the current Great Khan, had died. Hulegu hurried back to Mongolia with most of his army to support his brother's bid to become the next Great Khan. That brother was Khubilai, who did become the next Great Khan—the same Khubilai Khan that Marco Polo would serve for seventeen years (1274–1291). The remainder of Hulagu's Mongolian force continued from Baalbek in present-day Lebanon toward Egypt. They passed east of the Sea of Galilee, crossed the Jordan River to Beth-shean, and were moving toward Ain Jalut when they were confronted by a Mamluk army. Having displaced the Ayyubid sultans in Egypt ten years earlier, the Mamluks were divided by factions, but their sultan Qutuz had managed to assemble a unified army. Commanded by Baybars, the Mamluk army met and defeated the Mongols in the valley between Ain Jalut and Beth-shean in September of 1260. Qutuz was assassinated soon after, and Baybars emerged as the next Mamluk sultan.

Baybars then set about to secure Mamluk control of Syria-Palestine and guard against future Mongol attacks. This required expelling the Crusaders from the land once and for all. After the battle at Hattin in 1187, Crusader presence in Syria-Palestine had been reduced largely to the coastal regions. They remained a threat to Mamluk control of Syria-Palestine, however, and some Christian leaders looked upon the Mongols as potential allies. Nestorian Christianity had reached Mongolia and China by this time. Hulegu's wife was a Nestorian Christian, along with his best general who had commanded the Mongols at Ain Jalut. Bohemond VI, Crusader ruler of Antioch and Tripoli, had allied with the Mongols for their attack on Aleppo, and Crusader leaders in Palestine remained neutral for the battle at Ain Jalut. During the 1260s, therefore, Baybars systematically cleared the Holy Land of Crusaders.

Afuleh

Almost directly south of Mount Precipice is the present-day Israeli city of Afuleh, which began its modern history as a railroad station near a small Arab village and ancient mound (Tell el-Fuleh). On the tell are remains of a fortress from the Crusader and Mamluk Periods. A battle fought in April 1799 and known as the Battle of Mount Tabor actually took place nearer to Afuleh than Tabor. Napoleon, having invaded

Egypt and defeated a Mamluk force at the Battle of the Pyramids, pushed up through the Palestinian coast and besieged Acre (Acco). Monitoring his eastern flank was Jean Babtiste Kléber with approximately two thousand men. Kléber decided to risk a surprise attack on a much larger Ottoman force, which almost failed. But Kléber managed to hold out until Napoleon arrived with additional troops, and the Ottoman army was routed.

Mount Carmel and the Via Maris

In the far distance from Mount Precipice, beyond Afuleh and stretching across the southwestern horizon, is Mount Carmel. It is mentioned often in the Hebrew Bible/ Old Testament (2 Kgs 2:23–25 and 4:18–25; Isa 33:9 and 35:2; Jer 46:18 and 50:19; Amos 1:2; and so forth). Your guide will be able to point out the approximate locations of Muhraqa and Megiddo.

Mount Carmel is actually a mountain ridge that extends northwestward from the Central Hill Country and juts out into the Mediterranean Sea at present-day Haifa. Throughout the ages, this mountain ridge has been a barrier to traffic moving from Egypt through Palestine toward Syria, Mesopotamia, or Anatolia (and vice versa). Caravans and armies have been forced either to squeeze through the few hundred feet that separate Mount Carmel's northwest promontory from the Mediterranean Sea or to go through one of the passes across the Mount Carmel ridge. The Wadi Ara passage, guarded by the ancient city of Megiddo, offered the most convenient route. The ancient city of Jokneam guarded another pass. A third option, which avoided Mount Carmel, veered east, past the ancient city of Dothan toward Gilead in the Transjordan.

Two international thoroughfares passed north-south through Palestine during ancient times. We have already discussed the Transjordanian route, possibly called the King's Highway in earlier times, later the path of Trajan's Via Nova. The other thoroughfare passed through western Palestine, connecting Egypt with Syria and other points north. From Egypt, it followed along the Mediterranean seacost, crossed Mount Carmel ridge at Megiddo, and continued across the Jezreel Valley toward Syria. Because it followed along the Mediterranean seacoast much of the way, and because it seems to fit an enigmatic reference to the "way of the sea" in Isa 9:1, this latter thoroughfare often is referred to as the Via Maris (Way of the Sea). But it may not have gone by that name in ancient times.

Muhraqa

Perched high on Mount Carmel is a Carmelite monastery that marks the traditional site of Elijah's sacrifice contest with the 450 prophets of Baal (1 Kgs 18:7–46). Nearby is a spring known as the Fountain of Elijah.

While the origin of the Carmelite order remains somewhat uncertain, it seems to have begun with European hermits who settled around this spring and built a monastery during the twelfth century. This was during the Crusader Period when the area changed hands from time to time between Christians and Muslims. Accordingly, the monastery chapel served as a mosque at times. The Arabic name el-Muhraqa ("the burning") derives from this early period and refers to Elijah's sacrifice contest.

When the Mamluks expelled the last of the Crusaders from Syria-Palestine, the Carmelites fled also, and their monastery was burned. Four hundred years later, with Syria-Palestine under Ottoman rule, members of the Carmelite order returned, regained possession of the site, and restored the monastery. The core of the present building dates from the nineteenth century, and its roof offers another good view of the Jezreel Valley, this time from the southwest. One can see Mount Tabor, Mount Moreh, and Mount Gilboa in the far distance. Immediately below is Tell Yoqne'am, the stratified archaeological remains of the ancient city of Jokneam.

Megiddo/Armageddon (Tell Mutesellim, Tel Megiddo)

Tell el-Mutesellim, now Tel Megiddo on Israeli maps, is situated a short distance southeast of Muhraqa and Tel Yoqne'am. Archaeological excavations have revealed that people were living at this site as early as the fourth millennium BCE, long before the Egyptian pyramids, and that it continued to be occupied, off and on, until the fourth century BCE, about the time of Alexander the Great. Each phase of human settlement left a layer of occupational debris, each new layer superimposed over that of the preceding phase so that gradually this multilayered (stratified) mound of debris emerged. The Arabic name recorded by early archaeologists was Tell Mutesellim. But geographical clues in the Hebrew Bible and other ancient records indicate that this tell presents the remains of ancient Megiddo (Josh 12:21; 17:11; Judg 1:27; 5:19; 1 Kgs 4:12; 9:15; 2 Kgs 9:27).

Situated on the slopes of Mount Carmel and overlooking the Jezreel Valley, Megiddo was one of the most famous and strategically located fortress cities of Bronze-Iron Age Palestine. It guarded the Wadi Ara passage, which connects the Jezreel Valley with the coastal plain to the southwest. (Highway 65 goes through this pass today.) Megiddo witnessed many historic battles. The earliest recorded one was fought in the fifteenth century BCE between Pharaoh Tuthmosis III and a coalition of Syro-Palestinian kings who had gathered with their armies at Megiddo to defend against him. Tuthmosis claimed total victory and recorded on the walls of the temple of Amun in Luxor, Egypt, the names of the many cities that he conquered during this campaign. This is the so-called Palestinian List (also called the Megiddo List—see pp. 40–41 above), which I discussed earlier.

Tell Mutesellim, now Tel Megiddo

Eight hundred years later, Josiah met his death at Megiddo in a struggle with Pharaoh Neco II (2 Kgs 23:28–30; 1 Chr 35:20–24). Josiah was considered a good and faithful king, and his untimely death at Megiddo raised a serious theological question for ancient Jews: Why had God allowed Neco to triumph? Why had evil overcome good? Eventually Megiddo became the symbol of a great battle anticipated for the future when the forces of evil would again clash with the forces of good. It is in this regard that Megiddo makes its single appearance in the New Testament (Rev 16:16). It appears there, however, as Armageddon. Another word for "hill" or "mountain" in Hebrew is *har*. Thus the Megiddo tell could be spoken of in Hebrew as *har-megiddo*, which becomes *Armageddon* in Greek. (Note that the NRSV translation renders it "Harmagedon.")

Between 1903 and 1905, when archaeological techniques were still in their infancy, German excavators led by Gottlieb Schumacher probed the site. The University of Chicago sponsored more extensive excavations between 1925 and 1939; their dig house serves now as the museum. The famous Israeli archaeologist Yigael Yadin conducted further excavations at Megiddo between 1960 and 1971. A new series of excavations was begun in 1993 under the joint direction of two contemporary Israeli archaeologists, David Ussishkin and Israel Finkelstein.

The site is preserved as a national park. Visitors typically pass through the museum first, giving special attention to a model of Iron Age Megiddo, and then follow a trail onto the acropolis of the tell. After exploring the archaeological features on the tell—which include a high place from the Early Bronze Age, a city gate from the Late Bronze Age, portions of an early Iron Age gate that may date from Solomon's reign, and remains of what some scholars interpret to be horse stables but what others insist are storehouses—one precedes to ancient Megiddo's impressive water system. Believed to date from the time of Ahab and Jezebel, the system consists of a deep shaft and tunnel that provided access from within the city wall to water from a spring outside the wall.

Take the steps down into the shaft, follow the tunnel to the spring, and exit the site beyond the spring. Arrange for your transportation to be waiting there.

It is not easy to understand an archaeological site like Tell el-Mutesellim/Tel Megiddo that was excavated by different archaeological teams over the years. One of the downsides of archaeology is that archaeologists must destroy much of their excavated evidence as they go along. Once an architectural feature has been exposed and recorded, it must be removed, or partially removed, in order to excavate the layers below. Remnants of excavated features left in place after partial removal often make little sense to future visitors, especially if they have been left exposed along with remnants of other architectural features from other periods—all left to weather over the years. In order to make the best of it, take a close look at the model of the Iron Age city in the museum before going to the tell. The site plan provided below will help also. The following notes correspond to the numbers on the site plan.

1. Approaching the tell, you pass on your left the stone foundations and lower courses of the outer gate of the tenth- or ninth-century (Iron Age) fortifications. The main gate tower of this fortification system will be visible farther on (#3). Archaeologists disagree whether this fortification system dates to the time of King Solomon or whether it was built by a later Israelite king, perhaps King Ahab.

2. Rather than entering the Megiddo ruins through the Iron Age gate system, the visitor trail passes beyond it and enters through the earlier Late Bronze Age gate. This Late Bronze Age gate would have been in use during the fifteenth and fourteenth centuries BCE, while Egypt's pharaohs ruled from Thebes and Mycenaean civilization dominated the Mediterranean.

3. After passing through the Late Bronze Age gate, the visitor trail turns back to the left and then to the right, crossing between the northern half of the tenth- or ninth-century main gate tower and the outer gate. The southern half of the Iron Age gate tower is no longer there; archaeologists removed it in order to reach the layers below. You see only the lower courses of the northern half of the tower, because the upper part of the tower did not survive the centuries. Archaeologists refer to this kind of gate as a six-chambered or four-entryway gate because each side had four partitions that separated three chambers and, with the opposing partitions and chambers of the other side, provided four entryways.

4. A *casemate wall* is a partitioned wall. Or one might think of it as two parallel walls separated into rooms by cross walls at regular intervals. Although not as strong as a solid wall, it required less stone to build, the partitioned rooms could be used for storage or other purposes, and a flat roof on the parallel and cross walls provided a platform for defending soldiers. This segment of casemate wall dates from the Iron age, but it is not entirely clear how it relates to the tenth- or ninth-century main gate tower.

Megiddo: Late Bronze Age gateway

5. Even archaeologists have had trouble understanding the various wall lines exposed on this northwestern portion of the tell. Some of them are from a solidly built structure that stood here perhaps as early as the time of Solomon (in the tenth century BCE). Others pertain to stables or storerooms probably dating from the time of King Ahab.

6. From here one enjoys a panoramic view of the Jezreel Valley and beyond. Nazareth, Mount Tabor, and Mount Gilboa (where Saul and Jonathan met their deaths) are visible on clear days. From here also one can look down into the deep sounding (or slice) that archaeologists made into the tell in order to reach its lower layers. This seems to have been a sacred precinct going back as early as the Chalcolithic Period (to the fourth millennium BCE). Look especially for the round platform altar of stone dating from the Early Bronze Age (from the third millennium BCE).

7. After enjoying the view of Jezreel, follow the trail to the southeastern quadrant of the site where another tenth-/ninth-century palace stood, and also another complex of stables or storerooms. (You may want to veer off from the trail in order to see the remains of a more modest Iron Age house in the northeast quadrant.) Marked as number (7) on the site plan is a granary that probably dates from the late eighth century BCE, sometime after 722 when the Assyrians sacked Samaria and converted the Northern Kingdom of Israel to an Assyrian province.

Megiddo: Early Bronze Age platform altar

8. Here are remains of the southeastern stables or storeroom complex. Note the stone mangers for feeding or watering animals, and the holes in some of the stone pillars that could have been used for tethering horses or donkeys.

9. Located at the base of the tell on its south side was a spring, Megiddo's chief source of groundwater. As the tell grew in height over the centuries, maintaining access to this spring must have become increasingly laborious. Because the spring was outside the city walls that circled the crest of the tell, the town also had a problem when the city was under attack. At some point, therefore, probably during the reign of Omri or Ahab, the citizens of Megiddo constructed an ingenious water system that consisted of a deep shaft inside the city wall that connected at its base with a horizontal tunnel leading to the spring. Water flowed from the spring through the tunnel and under the wall to the base of the shaft. From there the water was accessible by stairs around the sides of the shaft. The ancient stairs have been replaced by modern ones, so take them down the shaft and follow the tunnel to the spring. Then exit the site through a turnstile provided; your bus should be waiting in the parking lot nearby.

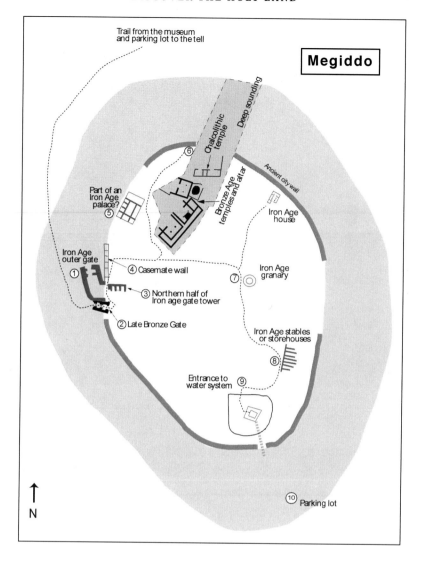

Sea of Galilee

We turn our attention now to the shores of the Sea of Galilee, center stage of Jesus' Galilean ministry. As I explained above, his ministry happened during the second generation of Herodian rulers. Herod Antipas resided and ruled his tetrarchy first from Sepphoris and later from Tiberias. Herod Philip resided and ruled his tetrarchy from Paneas, which he renamed Caesarea after Caesar Augustus. Capernaum seems to have served as the base for Jesus' Galilean ministry, but he would have visited other nearby Galilean towns and villages such as Magdala, home of Mary Magdalene.

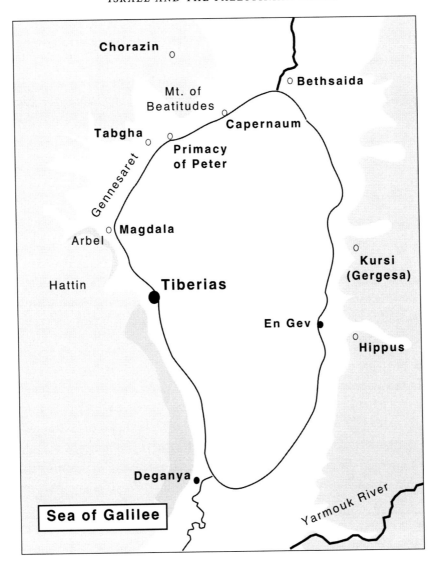

Arbel Cliff

Overlooking the Sea of Galilee and dominating the skyline from the west are two large cliffs. They face each other across the Arbel Stream (Wadi Hamam in Arabic), also called the Valley of the Doves or Valley of the Pigeons. Ancient travelers making their way from Lower Galilee to the Sea of Galilee (from Nazareth to Capernaum, for example) probably would have passed through this valley and reached the seashore at approximately Magdala.

The larger of the two cliffs, the one on the southeastern side of the Valley of Doves, is Arbel. On a clear day one can enjoy from the top of Arbel a glorious view of the northern shores of the Sea of Galilee, scene of much of Jesus' Galilean ministry. Weather permitting, therefore, what better way to begin exploring Galilee than to get bearings on the general landscape from the top of Arbel? The Arbel cliff is maintained as a national park, and your journey to the top will be a leisurely walk up the gradually sloping back side of the cliff, about twenty minutes from a parking area. After reaching the top, find a comfortable spot to sit among the large limestone rocks. There is no need for concern if you have a problem with heights; the cliff looks steep and scary from a distance, but not from above. There is a steep trail down the face of the cliff past caves where Herod annihilated scattered resistance after he took Sepphoris from Antigonus during the winter of 39–38 BCE.

> These caves opened on to almost vertical slopes and could not be reached from any direction except by winding, steep, and very narrow paths; the cliff in front stretched right down into ravines of immense depth dropping straight into the torrent-bed. So for a long time the king was defeated by the appalling difficulty of the ground, finally resorting to a plan fraught with the utmost danger. He lowered the toughest of his soldiers in cradles till they reached the mouths of the caves: they then slaughtered the bandits with their families and threw firebrands at those who proved awkward. (*War* 1:309–311; Penguin ed., p. 63)

The best view is to the north, and immediately below the cliff in that direction is the Plain of Gennesaret. Josephus described this pleasant, fertile plain at length and referred to the Sea of Galilee as the Sea of Gennesar. After feeding the five thousand, according to Matt 14:34 and Mark 6:53, Jesus and the disciples crossed the sea to the land of Gennesaret. A large grey building near the shore at the opposite end of the plain is a museum on the grounds of Kibbutz Nof Ginnosar. The museum's main attraction is a boat dating from New Testament times that was recovered from beneath the Sea of Galilee.

Farther in the distance as your eyes follow the shoreline around to the northeast are the Tabgha Church and Primacy of Peter Chapel. The Tabgha Church is a white building in a clump of trees along the shoreline. The Primacy Chapel is just a little farther to the right (east). Above them is the Mount of Beatitudes. Behind the Mount of Beatitudes (not visible) is Chorazin. Follow the shoreline with your eyes still farther east to find another white building near the shore. This is Capernaum, marked by its Greek Orthodox church (the Church of the Holy Apostles) with several rose-colored domes. Still farther to the east but difficult to make out is where the Jordan River enters the Sea of Galilee from the north. Bethsaida would have been nearby.

Arbel and the Valley of Doves viewed from the northeast. On the horizon beyond is Hattin.

Tiberias

Herod Antipas founded this city in 20 CE, naming it after the Roman emperor Tiberius, who had succeeded Caesar Augustus six years earlier. Soon Tiberias replaced Sepphoris as the chief city of Galilee. Initially few Jews settled there because it was built on the site of a cemetery. But following the Bar Kochba Revolt in the second century CE, Tiberias became an important center for Jewish learning. Rabbi Judah ha-Nasi, compiler of the Mishnah, was a resident during the early third century. The Palestinian Talmud was largely the work of Jewish interpreters active at Tiberias toward the end of the fourth century. Two centuries later, Jewish scholars at Tiberias designed a system of vowel points for the Hebrew Bible. They also developed an extensive set of notes (*massorah*) intended to guard the biblical text against copying errors that sometimes occurred during its transmission from one generation to the next.

Still an important city when the first wave of Crusaders arrived in 1099, Tiberias was granted to the Norman leader Tancred. Later it belonged to the fiefdom of Guy de Lusignan, and in 1187, responding to Lusignan's call for help to defend against a Muslim attack led by Saladin, Crusaders from throughout the Holy Land mustered for war at Sepphoris and marched toward Tiberias.

As discussed above in the notes on Kerak, Saladin's attack on Tiberias had been prompted by Raynald de Châtillon, lord of Crac des Moabitis, who seized a Muslim caravan as it passed near his castle. This was only the most recent of Ranald's outrages against Saladin's subjects, carried out in spite of a recent truce between Saladin and the Crusader kingdom, and the last straw for Saladin. Determined to settle affairs, Saladin mustered his army in Damascus, marched on the Crusader kingdom, and had reached Tiberias when Guy de Lusignan sent out the alarm and appeal for help. The two armies clashed at Hattin on July 4, 1187. Saladin outmaneuvered and demolished the Crusader army.

Hattin was to be a major turning point in the Crusader endeavor. The Crusaders had captured Jerusalem in 1099 and established the Latin Kingdom of Jerusalem, which remained relatively stable and strong for almost a century. But virtually every available fighting man in the kingdom had mustered for this battle at Hattin. Those who were not massacred were sold as slaves. Within a year, Saladin had captured Jerusalem itself and virtually every Crusader castle in the Palestinian interior. The goal of later Crusades, none completely successful, would be to recover Jerusalem and the lost territory. The Battle of Ain Jalut in 1260, discussed above (see page 97), would mark the next major turning point. During the two decades following Ain Jalut, Baybars systematically expelled the last of the Crusaders from the Holy Land. Louis IX of France attempted one more Crusade in 1270, his second, which did not reach Palestine. A last Crusader stand attempted by Knights Templar on Arwad Island, off the coast of present-day Syria, failed in 1302.

Hattin is located just west of Tiberias, but on much higher ground above the Jordan Valley. Highway 77 from Tiberias to the Golani Junction passes near its base and a secondary road from Highway 77 to Arbel provides an even better view of its distinctive shape. It is a flat-topped mountain, slightly raised on either end, thus often referred to as the "Horns of Hattin."

The tombs of several Talmudic scholars and sages are to be found in Tiberias, among them that of the famous scholar Maimonides. He was born in Cordoba where he studied medicine, but he immigrated with his family to North Africa and eventually to Egypt. There he became the chief rabbi in Cairo and served also as Saladin's private physician. (His full name with his title was Rabbi Moshe Ben Maimon; his name is sometimes abbreviated Rambam and is Anglicized as Maimonides.) When Maimonides died in 1204, his students brought his body to Palestine for burial. According to legend, they followed a camel bearing his coffin until the camel knelt just outside the walls of Tiberias. There they buried their master and the tomb is revered by Jews still today. Tiberias was left a desolate ruin at the end of the Crusader Period, the Jews of the city having fled when the Crusaders first arrived in 1099, and the Crusader population having been massacred by Mamluks in 1247. The site remained virtually unoccupied until the eighteenth century when Daher el-Omar, a regional

Bedouin ruler, rebuilt the city walls and sponsored resettlement. The new settlers were primarily Jews, led by Rabbi Hayyim Abulafia from Turkey.

Capernaum

According to the opening chapters of Mark's Gospel, Jesus came to Galilee preaching the gospel soon after John the Baptist was arrested. Passing along the seashore, he called Simon Peter and Andrew, who were casting their nets into the sea, and then James and John, who were fishing from a boat with their father Zebedee and hired servants. Next Jesus and these four disciples went to Capernaum, where he taught in the synagogue with authority and began to perform miracles of healing. "At once his fame began to spread throughout the surrounding region of Galilee" (Mark 1:28).

The first healing occurred in the synagogue and involved a man with an unclean spirit. The second occurred in the house of Simon Peter where Jesus healed Simon's mother-in-law of a fever. Other miracles of healing followed, and after a few days such a large crowd had gathered in and around Peter's house that a paralytic had to be lowered through the roof to be healed by Jesus (Mark 1:14—2:12). Matt 4:13 and 9:1 indicate that Jesus lived in Capernaum for a time. See also Luke 7:1 and John 6:59 for Capernaum's central role in his Galilean ministry. Matt 9:9 explains that the disciple Matthew was a tax collector from Capernaum.

One of the earliest surviving accounts from Christian pilgrims to the Holy Land is that of Egeria, a nun from one of the western provinces of the Roman Empire (possibly present-day Spain). She visited Capernaum during the late fourth century (between 381 and 384 CE) and reported that Peter's house had been converted into a church:

> Moreover, in Capernaum the house of the prince of the apostles has been made into a church, with its original walls still standing. It is where the Lord healed the paralytic. There also is the synagogue where the Lord cured a man possessed by the devil. The way in is up many stairs, and it is made of dressed stone. (John Wilkinson, *Egeria's Travels*, p. 97)

Visitors to the site today walk along a paved driveway to the entrance of an enclosure that surrounds the Franciscan grounds. No shorts or tank tops are allowed inside. Keep in mind that this enclosed area is not the whole of ancient Capernaum, which nevertheless was a small fishing village that probably extended about one thousand feet along the waterfront. A second enclosed area east of the Franciscan grounds also covers part of the ancient village and includes the picturesque Orthodox church with rose-colored domes. This whole area was a disputed frontier between Syria and Israel before 1967, and the Orthodox church remained unused for a time, but it has been restored and worship liturgies reinstated.

As you enter the Franciscan grounds and pass beyond the ticket booth, a modern church is straight ahead. Walk toward the church, but before entering it or examining the remains below it, turn to your left and face the walkway that leads to a partially reconstructed synagogue. To the right of the walkway, between the modern church and the synagogue, are remains of the fishing village that Jesus and his disciples would have known. It is easy to distinguish the earlier village remains (from the first and second centuries CE) from those of the later synagogue because the earlier houses were constructed from dark basalt fieldstones while the synagogue was constructed from white limestone blocks.

Franciscan archaeologists who excavated this part of Capernaum and reconstructed the synagogue dated it to approximately the fifth century CE. Obviously, it is not the synagogue that Jesus would have known, but it may well have replaced the earlier synagogue that served the first- and second-century village, the one in which Jesus "taught with authority."

Capernaum: Reconstructed fifth-century synagogue
overlooks ruins of the first- and second-century village.
Greek Orthodox church with rose-colored domes in the distance.

Among the first- and second-century village ruins between the fifth-century synagogue and the sea, Franciscans uncovered what they interpreted to be a first-century house, which was modified during the fourth century to serve as a house-church (a *domus ecclesia*) and then rebuilt during the fifth century as an octagonal church. If this interpretation is correct, the first-century house may be Peter's house, the fourth-century house-church would be the one visited by Egeria, and the octagonal church would have been roughly contemporary with the synagogue. The modern church, built in 1990 and hovering like a flying saucer above the house, house-church, and octagonal remains was constructed in this fashion to both feature and protect the remains without disturbing them. Visitors may find it difficult to make sense of these remains because remnants of foundation walls from all three building phases are visible at the same time. But the wall lines of the fifth-century octagonal church (contemporary with the synagogue) are clear enough.

Capernaum: Wall lines from a fifth-century octagonal building, which may have replaced a fourth-century *domus ecclesia*, that may have replaced Saint Peter's house

Christianity became the official religion of the Roman Empire during the fourth century, but Capernaum apparently remained a largely Jewish town through the fifth century, by which time the church marking Peter's house must have been receiving many Christian pilgrims. This would have prompted Capernaum's local Christian minority to upgrade the house-church to a more impressive octagonal shrine about the same time that Capernaum's Jews built their impressive new synagogue.

Elsewhere on the Franciscan grounds are various items related to agriculture—basalt mills for grinding grain, presses for olive oil and grapes. There is a Roman milestone from the time of the emperor Hadrian (reigned 117–138 CE). Its inscription can be reconstructed to read:

Imperator Caesar, son of the divine Trajan the conqueror of the Parthians,

Grandson of the divine Nerva,

Trajan Hadrian Augustus

Also on display in a fenced area west of the synagogue are decorative elements from the synagogue and other public buildings from its period. Look for the ark (a small shrine for storing and displaying the Torah scroll), depicted as a miniature colonnaded temple on wheels.

Magdala

Surface remains from another Roman Period fishing village on the Sea of Galilee's western shore have long indicated the site of Magdala, home of Mary Magdalene. The site's identification as Magdala was signaled by its traditional Arabic name, Majdal. But only recently has the site been excavated systematically and gained widespread attention among Jews and Christians alike.

That the current excavations reveal remains of another Galilean village contemporary with Capernaum is a matter of interest in and of itself. But whereas Capernaum offers a fifth-century synagogue that possibly replaced an earlier one that Jesus would have known, the excavations at Magdala have revealed remains of a first-century synagogue that Jesus may have actually visited. Its first-century date seems confirmed by a central feature—a large stone block with detailed carvings that relate to the Jerusalem temple. This strongly suggests that the carvings were made before the temple was destroyed in 70 CE.

Magdala synagogue recently excavated; at the center of the photo is a facsimile of the large stone block with carvings that relate to the Jerusalem temple

The Magdala excavations were prompted and are sponsored by the Pontifical Institute Notre Dame of Jerusalem Center, which is building a retreat center at Magdala also. The chapel, already completed, highlights the role of women in the New Testament and early church. From its sanctuary, one gains a powerful view of the Sea of Galilee.

Kursi (Gergesa)

Three of the Gospels include an account of the "miracle of the swine," according to which Jesus cast out demons from a man (or two men according to Matthew) who lived among the tombs. Jesus allowed the demons to enter a herd of swine, whereupon the swine rushed headlong into the sea (Matt 8:28–34; Mark 5:1–20; Luke 8:26–39). Likewise, these three Gospels place the incident "on the other side of the sea," presumably across Sea of Galilee from Capernaum. As observed above in connection with Jerash, there was uncertainty even in early Christian times about the specific name of the shoreline area where the miracle occurred. According to Mark and Luke, it occurred in "the country of the Gerasenes"; Matthew has "the country of the Gadarenes"; and yet another name "the country of the Gergesenes" turns up as a variant reading in the manuscripts of Matthew, Mark, and Luke.

During road construction in 1969, workers discovered a Byzantine site on the eastern side of the Sea of Galilee near the coast, approximately three miles north of Kibbutz En Gev. The site was excavated between 1970 and 1974, revealing remains of an impressive basilica and monastery dating from the fifth century. This would have been one of the largest monastic churches in Palestine at that time and must have marked a spot that early Christians considered important. Probably they associated it with the miracle of the swine.

Kursi: basilica in the foreground; small cave-chapel on the slopes beyond (center right of photo)

Remains of what appears to have been a small chapel built into a natural cave were discovered on a slope above and southeast of the monastery. Attached to the chapel was a square tower built around a natural rock pillar. The excavator, Vassilios Tzaferis, suggested that early Christians may have associated this cave with the tombs where Jesus encountered the demoniac.

Mount of Beatitudes, Tabgha, Primacy of Peter Chapel

Matthew's Gospel introduces the Sermon on the Mount with the following words: "When Jesus saw the crowds, he went up the mountain" (Matt 5:1). But which mountain? The Scripture provides no clues. We learn from other references that the miracle of the multiplication of the loaves and fishes occurred when Jesus had gone by boat to a deserted place somewhere along the shore of the Sea of Galilee and was followed by the crowds (Matt 14:13ff.; Mark 6:30ff.). But where was this deserted place? We are not told. John 21 reports how Peter and several other disciples went fishing after Jesus' resurrection but caught nothing until daybreak. Jesus appeared to them from the shore and instructed them to cast their nets on the other side of the boat. This resulted in a miraculous catch of fish, and Jesus had breakfast with them. Three times he asked Peter, "Do you love me?" And three times Peter proclaimed that he did. Roman Catholic tradition interprets this event as affirming Peter's primacy among the disciples. But where along the shore of the Sea of Galilee did this happen? The biblical narrative provides no clues.

Christian pilgrims have made their way through the centuries and remembered these events at three traditional places that seem to fit the gospel narrative. These traditional places may not be the exact spots where Jesus taught the Beatitudes, fed the crowds with five loaves and two fish, and appeared to the disciples after his resurrection, but over the centuries they have taken on an authenticity in their own right. When travelers visit the Mount of Beatitudes, Tabgha, and Primacy of Peter, they follow in the footsteps of thousands of pilgrims who have come to these same places and remembered the same biblical events during centuries past. All three are quite near each other and maintained by different Roman Catholic orders.

The Mount of Beatitudes

The traditional Mount of Beatitudes is a peaceful hill overlooking the Sea of Galilee from the north. Franciscan sisters maintain an enclosed portion of the hill. There is a church designed by Antonio Barluzzi and completed in 1938, a hospice for pilgrims, and beautifully kept grounds with semiprivate places where individuals and small groups can meditate and worship. Walk around to the back balcony of the church for a memorable view of the Sea of Galilee and surrounding landscape. Off to your right (southwest) is the lush Gennesaret plain. Looming behind are Arbel and the Valley of Doves. Visible on the farther horizon beyond Arbel are "the Horns of Hattin."

Mount of Beatitudes

Tabgha

At the foot of the traditional Mount of Beatitudes and on the shore of the Sea of Galilee, German Benedictines maintain the traditional site of the miracle of the loaves and fishes. Tabgha, the Arabic name, is derived from Greek *Heptapegon,* which means "Seven Springs." Egeria visited Heptapegon in the late fourth century and mentioned a church in her travel diary.

> And in the same place [not far from Capernaum] by the sea is a grassy field with plenty of hay and many palm trees. By them are seven springs, each flowing strongly. And this is the field where the Lord fed the people with the five loaves and the two fishes. In fact the stone on which the Lord placed the bread has now been made into an altar. People who go there take away small pieces of the stone to bring them prosperity, and they are very effective. (John Wilkinson, *Egeria's Travels,* p. 97)

Other pilgrims that followed over the next two centuries also mentioned a church—among them Saint Sabas toward the end of the fifth century, Theodosius in the early sixth century, and Antoninus Placentinus later on in the sixth century. But when Arculf visited Heptapegon during the latter half of the seventh century, he found the church in ruins.

Archaeological investigations have clarified the story somewhat. Apparently, a small church was erected on the spot during the fourth century—the century during which Christianity emerged as the official religion of the Roman Empire. This original church, approximately 30 x 60 feet, is the one that Egeria would have visited. It was replaced in the fifth century with a larger, basilica-style church and monastery complex that covered approximately 108 x 184 feet. This fifth-century basilical church was decorated with beautiful mosaics that require further comment below, and the associated monastery complex included courtyards surrounded by rooms used as workshops and lodging for monks and pilgrims. Both the fourth-century church and the fifth-century church that replaced it featured a stone upon which, according to tradition, Jesus performed the miracle of the loaves and fishes. Probably during the sixth century a beautiful mosaic was added that depicts a basket of loves with two fish. The basilical church was destroyed sometime during the seventh century, possibly by Persians (Sassanians) who raided Palestine in 614 CE, or by Arab Muslims who invaded Palestine soon thereafter. Thus Arculf found it in ruins toward the end of the seventh century.

The church that stands on the spot today was erected by Benedictines in 1981, styled after the fifth-century basilical church, and incorporates some of the walls and mosaics from that earlier building. An opening in the floor to the left of the altar allows one to view foundation walls of the original fourth-century church, but that segment of the floor often is roped off to visitors.

Tabgha: Altar with detail of loaves and fishes mosaic

At the center of the apse, also usually roped off to general visitors, is an untrimmed stone marking the traditional site of the miracle. In front of the stone is the sixth-century mosaic of Loaves and the Fishes. Mosaics from the fifth-century church are preserved elsewhere in the floor. Those on the right side of the chancel are especially interesting. Note the multi-colored and naturalistic representations of flowers and animals, mainly birds (duck, snipe, heron, goose, dove, swan, cormorant, flamingo and stork). You can also see a "nilometer," a tower marked with bands bearing Greek letters for measuring the water level of a river or lake. Although it is tempting to think that the mosaic represents the Sea of Galilee, more likely the artist had the Nile River in mind. Nile scenes were favored by mosaic artists of the day. Compare, for example, the mosaic of the so-called "Nile Building" at Sepphoris, which also dates from the fifth century, and which presents a similar scene, including a nilometer. No guiding or explanations are allowed in the church.

Primacy of Peter Chapel

Along the seashore and immediately east of Tabgha are the small chapel and grounds of the Primacy of Peter. The chapel was built over another rock known as the Mensa Domini, "the Lord's Table," which marks the spot where, according to tradition, Jesus had breakfast with the disciples after their miraculous catch of fish. The church grounds are shaded with trees and provide access to the sea. In good weather and when the ground is dry, consider walking from the Mount of Beatitudes down the hill to Primacy of Peter and Tabgha. The trail is a bit steep toward the end, but manageable. Primacy of Peter and Tabgha are only about two hundred yards apart along the shore, but to go from one to the other it is necessary to walk around by the main road.

Trail from Mount of Beatitudes to the Primacy of Peter Chapel

Caesarea Philippi and Jordan River Sources

The Jordan River originates from springs and small streams at the foot of Mount Hermon and makes its way through the upper Jordan Valley to the Sea of Galilee. Situated at the headwaters of two of these streams were two ancient sanctuaries, Dan and Paneas. The main road from the Sea of Galilee to the archaeological sites of ancient Dan and Paneas passes through the upper Jordan River Valley with the Galilean Mountains on the west and the Golan Heights on the east. Along the way, it passes Tell el-Qedah, the remains of biblical Hazor.

Hazor (Tell el-Qadeh, Tel Hazor)

Hazor was the largest and most impressive city in Palestine during the Bronze Age, but it had dwindled to a much smaller settlement by the time that the Israelites would have arrived at Canaan (Josh 11:10; Judg 4:2). It was refortified by Solomon according to 1 Kings 9:15, and later expanded, apparently by Ahab. Full-scale excavations at the site during the 1950s revealed settlement phases ranging from Early Bronze Age to Hellenistic. These excavators also discovered an impressive Iron Age water system, probably dating from Ahab's reign. Recent excavations have uncovered and partially restored a Late Bronze Age palace complex. There is a very nice archaeological museum near the site, at the entrance to Kibbutz Ayelet Hashahar. Entrance to the museum must be arranged in advance.

Continuing north from Tell el-Qedah/Hazor, the highway passes near Shmurat Hula Nature Reserve, which preserves the fauna and flora of the Huleh swamps. These swamps, which appear on some historical maps as Huleh Lake, were drained in the 1950s. Finally, as one approaches the sites of ancient Dan and Paneas, and assuming a clear day, Mount Hermon comes into view. Mount Hermon is the southernmost peak of the Anti-Lebanon Mountains and mentioned often in the Old Testament as a landmark (Deut 3:8–9; 4:48; Josh 11:7; 13:5).

Dan (Tell el-Qadi, Tel Dan)

In the Old Testament, the phrase "from Dan to Beersheba" indicates the full extent of the territory that the ancient Israelites claimed as their homeland—from Dan in the north to Beersheba in the south. We read in 1 Sam 3:20: "And all Israel from Dan to Beer-sheba knew that Samuel was established as a trustworthy prophet of the LORD." Originally, according to Judges 18, Dan was named Laish and occupied by "a quiet and unsuspecting" people. But the Israelite tribe of Dan captured the city, massacred its population, and changed the name to Dan.

> [The Danites] came to Laish, to a people quiet and unsuspecting, put them to
> the sword, and burned down the city. There was no deliverer, because it was

far from Sidon and they had no dealings with Aram. It was in the valley that belongs to Beth-rehob. They rebuilt the city and lived in it. They named the city Dan, after their ancestor Dan, who was born to Israel; but the name of the city was formerly Laish. (Judg 18:27–29)

Tell Qadi fits the location of biblical Dan. Both names—*Qadi* in Arabic and *Dan* in Hebrew—mean "judge." Also, a bilingual inscription (Aramaic and Greek) from the Hellenistic Period has been discovered at the site that bears the phrase "god of Dan." Tell Qadi has been renamed Tel Dan under Israeli administration and appears with that name on present-day maps.

Dan figures again in the Old Testament narrative when Solomon died and Jeroboam led the northern tribes in rebellion.

> Then Jeroboam said to himself, "Now the kingdom may well revert to the house of David. If this people continues to go up to offer sacrifices in the house of the LORD at Jerusalem, the heart of this people will turn again to their master, King Rehoboam of Judah; they will kill me and return to King Rehoboam of Judah." So the king took counsel, and made two calves of gold. He said to the people, "You have gone up to Jerusalem long enough. Here are your gods, O Israel, who brought you up out of the land of Egypt." He set one in Bethel, and the other he put in Dan (1 Kgs 12:26–29; see also Amos 8:14)

Israeli archaeologist Avrahim Biran conducted more than twenty seasons of excavations at Tell Qadi/Tel Dan beginning in 1966 with spectacular results. The site was settled already during the Neolithic Period. A strong city had emerged by the Middle Bronze Age that covered approximately fifty acres and was protected by sloping ramparts. A triple-arched, mud brick gate at the southeast corner of the site dates from this period. The Iron Age phase of the city, that of the Danites, was also impressive. Its fortifications were of stone and consisted of a massive city wall and double gateway system. In what appears to have been the city's main sanctuary area, where the Hellenistic "god of Dan" inscription was found, Biran uncovered what he interpreted to be a cultic center dating back to Old Testament times.

Tel Dan: Middle Bronze Age gate

Perhaps the most important discovery of all was made near the entrance to the Iron Age gate. Discovered by accident, not during excavation season, were three fragments of an Aramaic inscription. Known now as the Tel Dan Inscription, it apparently had been placed in Dan by one of the Aramaic kings of Damascus to commemorate his military victory over the Northern Kingdom of Israel. While no complete sentences have survived from the inscription, one of the fragments seems to refer to both a king of Israel and a king of the House of David by their names. The translation "House of David" had been challenged by some scholars but seems fairly certain, and would refer to the Dynasty of David. Both of the kings' names are only partially preserved, but the surviving bits seem to indicate Jehoram of Israel and Ahaziah of Judah, who ruled simultaneously ca. 850 BCE. This inscription provides only an indirect reference to King David himself, who would have lived more than a century earlier. It is an important discovery, nevertheless, because King David now joins King Shishak/ Sheshonq of Egypt as the first two biblical individuals mentioned in both the Hebrew Bible/Old Testament and ancient written sources outside the Bible. The next was King Omri of Israel, mentioned in the Mesha Inscription.

Tel Dan: Iron Age wall

In addition to its strong biblical connections and rich archaeological remains, Tell Qadi/Tel Dan is a pleasant place to visit. It offers beautiful trails under shade trees alongside bubbling brooks.

Caesarea Philippi (Banias)

An imposing rock scarp almost one hundred feet high cuts across a southern slope of Mount Hermon. A cave at its western end opens onto a terrace that stretches some 250 feet across the base of the scarp, and below the cave and terrace are springs and pools of water that feed a mountain stream. This Banias Stream is joined soon by two other streams—first the Guveta, which approaches from the northwest, and then the Saar, which approaches from the east—to form one of the three upper tributaries to the Jordan River. The rock scarp, cave, pools, and streams offer a beautiful natural setting protected today as the Hermon Stream (Banias) Natural Reserve. Not surprisingly, it was associated in ancient times with the god Pan, whose domain was nature, especially uninhabited areas—mountain wilds, woodlands, pasturelands, waterfalls and streams. The cave apparently served as a simple cultic center for sacrifices to Pan during the Hellenistic Period, and was known as the Paneion or Panium. The surrounding area was called Paneas, which became Banias in Arabic.

Paneas, later Caesarea Philippi: Rock scarp and cave

Eventually a city would emerge south of the Paneon cave and terrace. But it is unclear whether this had occurred before 20 BCE when Caesar Augustus annexed territory that included Paneas to the Roman Empire and added it to Herod the Great's domain. Herod then built a temple dedicated to Augustus at the mouth of the cave. This temple was called the *Augusteum* and would have required some permanent personnel. A short distance from the Augusteum are remnants of two walls from a structure with stone masonry suggestive of Herod's reign, so he may have added other buildings in addition to the Augusteum.

When Herod the Great died in 4 BCE, this northeastern part of his kingdom was passed to his son Herod Philip. Philip made Paneas the capital of his tetrarchy, expanded and enhanced whatever settlement existed there already into an imposing city, renamed it Caesarea in honor of the same Caesar Augustus whom his father had already honored with the Augusteum, and gave his tetrarchy three decades of reasonably responsible government. Herod the Great had already built and named another city Caesarea in honor of Caesar Augustus. In order to distinguish one from the other, Philip's Caesarea was called Caesarea Philippi and Herod the Great's Caesarea was called Caesarea Maritima (Caesarea by the Sea).

Both Jesus' hometown, Nazareth, and the northwestern shores of the Sea of Galilee, where much of his Galilean ministry unfolded, fell within the tetrarchy of Philip's brother Herod Antipas. On at least one occasion Jesus and the disciples went into Herod Philip's tetrarchy (not necessarily to Caesarea Philippi itself). It was on this occasion that Jesus posed the question "Who do people say that I am?"

> Jesus went on with his disciples to the villages of Caesarea Philippi; and on the way he asked his disciples, "Who do people say that I am?" And they answered him, "John the Baptist; and others, Elijah; and still others, one of the prophets." He asked them, "But who do you say that I am?" Peter answered him, "You are the Messiah." And he sternly ordered them not to tell anyone about him. (Mark 8:27–30; see also Matt 16:13–20)

When Herod Philip died in 34 CE his tetrarchy reverted to direct Roman administration until Caligula became emperor three years later. Caligula then granted Philip's domain to his own boyhood friend Herod Agrippa with the title king. Agrippa and his sister Herodias—now married to their uncle Herod Antipas (Matt 14:1–12; Mark 6:17–29)—were grandchildren of Herod the Great through a son that Herod had executed before his own death. Agrippa had been sent to Rome as a child to be educated in the royal (Julio-Claudian) court, which is how he and Caligula, two years his junior, became friends. Caligula exiled Herod Antipas and Herodias in 39 CE and added Herod Antipas's tetrarchy to Agrippa's kingdom as well. Then when Caligula was assassinated in 41 CE, Agrippa supported Caligula's uncle Claudius for emperor, and once Claudius was on the throne, he added the remainder of Herod the Great's former territories to Agrippa's kingdom. For a short time therefore, between 41 and 44 CE, Herod the Great's former kingdom was reconstituted under the rule of his grandson, Herod Agrippa I. This is the Herod Agrippa who executed James brother of John the apostle, imprisoned Peter, and died a terrible death described in Acts 12.

Presumably Paneas/Caesarea Philippi served as Agrippa's nominal capital at first, while his kingdom included only Philip's former tetrarchy (37–39 CE). But

Agrippa was really Roman at heart and probably continued to spend considerable time in Rome or in Caesarea Maritima, which served as Roman headquarters for the Palestinian area. This would have been true all the more after Agrippa's territorial domain was expanded to include Galilee and Judea. For official visits to Jerusalem he had the Herodian palace.

With Agrippa's death in 44, most of his extensive kingdom reverted again to direct Roman rule—administered by governors residing in Caesarea. Four years later, Agrippa's son, also named Agrippa and only seventeen or eighteen years old at the time of his father's death, was granted the small principality of Chalcis in Syria. Then, not long before his own death in 54 CE, Claudius granted Herod Philip's former tetrarchy to Agrippa II in exchange for Chalcis. Herod Agrippa II arrived in Paneas/Caesarea Philippi to begin his approximately forty-year reign there at about the same time that Nero ascended the throne in Rome.

Herod Agrippa II, like his father, had grown up in the imperial Roman court and was thoroughly Roman in his sentiments and tastes. But he actually resided in Caesarea Philippi, was more personally invested in its infrastructure and beauty than his father had been, built an impressive palace there, and renamed the city after Nero. Caesarea Philippi became Neronias.

Agrippa's reign coincided with turbulent times for Jews in Palestine, which climaxed with the devastating First Jewish Revolt (66–73 CE). Although most of Galilee and all of Judea were outside of Agrippa's official administrative authority, Rome granted him the prerogative of selecting the high priests of the Jerusalem temple, and Agrippa II showed some concern for the welfare of the Jews. As the revolt began to spread across the land, he went to Jerusalem and urged its inhabitants not to join in. But they ignored his advice. Several other cities, including Agrippa's Caesarea Philippi/Neronias, chose not join the revolt. When Emperor Nero sent Vespasian to crush the resistance, Vespasian took his son Titus along. Agrippa provided military support for the Roman side, accompanied Vespasian and Titus during the fighting, and hosted a victory celebration for them and their troops at Neronias after the fall of Jerusalem.

Better known perhaps than Herod Agrippa II was his sister and close ally, Queen Berenice (also Bernice). She was twice widowed before making the move with Agrippa from Chalcis to Caesarea Philippi/Neronias, having gained the title queen from the most recent marriage. Rumors and suspicions surfaced of incestuous relations between Agrippa and Berenice. Be that as it may, she and the future Roman emperor Titus reportedly became romantically involved while he was in Palestine subduing the Jewish revolt. After the revolt she went to Rome with him, and their relationship continued until Titus assumed the throne in 79 CE. We will encounter Agrippa II and Berenice again at Caesarea Maritima, where they heard Paul make his defense before Felix and Festus (Acts 25:13—26:31). Paneas/Caesarea Philippi/Neronias reverted to direct Roman rule when Agrippa II died (probably in 93 CE), flourished during the next century while the Roman Empire reached its peak, and continued as an important city through the Byzantine Period.

Over time, while the city spread out south of the cave and terrace, temples, shrines, and other religious trappings were added to the terrace itself. Although none of the additions can be dated with absolute certainty, the surviving remnants visible today probably belong mostly to the second century CE. These include (from the cave eastward) a shrine dedicated to Pan and the Nymphs in front of a small, artificial cave; a temple to Zeus; an open-air shrine that archaeologists call the Nemesis Court; and a structure called the Temple of Pan and the Goats. Eventually the city spread out beyond the present-day parking lot and ticketing kiosk, even beyond the paved Kiriat Shemona-Mas'ade road (Highway 99), as far as the Saar Stream. The name Neronias was dropped after Nero's suicide, and the name Caesarea Philippi faded more gradually, while Paneas (or Caesarea Paneas) survived as Banias.

The rock scarp, cave, cultic terrace, and pools of water will command your attention upon arrival, and many tourists explore no farther. But there are pleasant walking trails to follow and more to be seen.

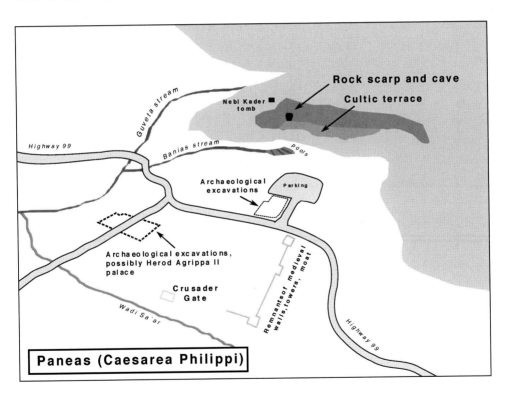

Grave of Nebi Khader

Through the centuries, Saint George and Nebi (Prophet) Khader have been revered as semilegendary and essentially identical figures at the popular religious level in the Middle East. The small domed shrine that overlooks the cave and terrace from the west may have originated during the Byzantine Period as a shrine to Saint George. It played an especially important role in the worship of Sunni Sufis who immigrated to Banias during the tenth century. And it continues as a revered shrine for the Druze, who inhabit this area now.

Crusader Fortifications and Medieval City

South of the Kiriat Shemona to Mas'ade road (Highway 99) are segments of Crusader walls, towers, and moats that mark the eastern and southern margins of the medieval city. Banias declined under the early Arab caliphates (Umayyads, Abbasids, Fatimids), although it was reenergized somewhat during the tenth century by Sunni immigrants mentioned above. Then it figured prominently during the eleventh and twelfth centuries as a strategically situated and fortified city on the frontier between Damascus and the Crusader Kingdom of Jerusalem. Crusaders fortified the city, it changed hands several times, and then it then fell into Ayyubid hands after Saladin's victory at Hattin. It belonged to Saladin and his Ayyubid successors until the mid-thirteenth century, then to the Mamluks of Egypt until the early sixteenth century, and after that to the Ottoman Turks until World War I.

Archaeological Excavations

One of the several areas that archaeologist have excavated will be visible on your left as you pass the ticket kiosk and enter the main parking lot from Highway 99. Among remains uncovered here from the first and second centuries CE were those of a monumental building of uncertain purpose, possibly part of a formal entry to the cultic terrace. This building was replaced during the late third or fourth century with a basilica that probably was used eventually, if not originally, as a church. A much larger excavated area extends westward along the south side of Highway 99 and beyond a secondary road (actually a branch of 99 that rejoins it farther on). The most noteworthy feature here is a massive building complex with remains on both sides of the secondary road. Josephus reports that Agrippa II "built Caesarea Philippi larger than it was before, and, in honor of Nero, named it Neronias" (*Ant.* 20:211). This large building complex may have been Agrippa's palace.

The Banias Waterfall

If you visit during good weather, do not miss the Banias waterfall a short drive farther downstream. It has its own parking area and is included with your entrance ticket to the main site. Better still, walk the trail that follows the Banias stream from the cave and cultic terrace site to the waterfall and arrange for your transportation to meet you there. The walk will take a little more than an hour.

Along the trail from Caesarea Philippi to the Banias Falls

The Druze

The Druze are a small and close-knit religious sect with communities located in present-day Lebanon, Syria, and Israel. They are Arab, and their religion an off-shoot of Shiite Islam, but they are regarded as heretical by mainstream Muslims, both Shiite and Sunni.

The Druze story begins at the turn of the eleventh century CE when the Fatimid Caliphate dominated North Africa and Syria-Palestine from their base in Cairo. The Fatimids had emerged from the Ismaili branch of Shiite Islam. Perhaps their most controversial caliph was al-Hakim bi-Amr Allah, who ruled from 996 to 1021. Al-Hakim was eccentric and issued harsh and erratic decrees, and most of his Ismaili-Shiite subjects probably considered him deranged. But at least a few believed him to be divine, even God incarnate, and encouraged al-Hakim to think so of himself. Among the early proponents of this notion was Muhammad al-Darazi, after whom the name Druze probably derives.

Al-Hakim disappeared mysteriously in 1021, al-Darazi eventually was excommunicated, and the movement soon died out in Egypt. But missionaries spread the Druze teachings to other parts of the Fatimid realm, and the sect gained traction in areas where Druze towns and villages exist still today—in the Lebanon Mountains, in the Golan, in the Mount Carmel range. An early missionary phase ended in the mid-eleventh century, after which converts were no longer accepted and the Druze communities became endogamous and increasingly closed.

The Druze religion is not well known to outsiders and only partially known to most Druze themselves. About 15 percent of Druze individuals make the formal decision to become fully religious, and only these are initiated into full knowledge of the faith. These initiates, men and women, are called sheiks (or 'uqqal). They live a more disciplined lifestyle than other Druze and generally are recognizable by their dress. Religious men often have shaved heads, bristling mustaches, white woolen caps or turbans, and black pants baggy at the crotch. Religious women wear white headscarves.

It can be said that the Druze religion is eclectic—Muslim in origin, but with elements of Judaism, Christianity, Hinduism, and even Greek philosophy. Their belief in reincarnation, for example, is reminiscent of Pythagorean theory. Their most revered saint is Jethro, Moses's father-in-law, who is considered to be their ancestor, spiritual founder, and chief prophet. Jethro's tomb, near Hattin, is one of their chief shrines.

Druze are known to be loyal to whatever government is in charge, which is true of the approximately one hundred fifty thousand Druze that live in Israel. They serve in the Israeli army, for example, but naturally were disappointed by the 2018 Israeli law known as the Nationality Bill, which declares Israel to be a Jewish state.

Nimrod's Castle (Qalat al-Subayba)

Situated in the foothills of the Golan Heights and overlooking Banias from the east are the remains of Qalat al-Subayba, known also as Nimrod's Castle for reasons explained below. Crusaders built an earlier castle on this site, which fell to the Ayyubids after their devastating defeat by Saladin at Hattin in 1187. What one sees today is an expanded Ayyubid fortification that would have been under construction during the Fifth Crusade (1217–1228).

Nimrod's Castle

The Third Crusade (1190–1192), led by King Richard I of England and King Philip II of France, was launched soon after the disaster at Hattin in an effort to recover Jerusalem. Richard managed to reassert and expand Crusader presence along the coast, but failed to take Jerusalem. The Fourth Crusade (1204) never made it to Palestine and sacked Constantinople instead, which brings us to Fifth Crusade (1217–1228). Al-Kamil Naser ad-Din was the sultan of Egypt and senior political figure among the Ayyubs at the time. His younger brother, al-Aziz Uthman, was governor of Banias (governed 1229–1233), and al-Aziz rebuilt Qalat Subayba in order to provide additional protection for Banias. Rebuilding Qalat Subayba and protecting Banias enabled al-Aziz to control the most direct route from Palestine to Damascus.

This Fifth Crusade was led at first by King Andrew II of Hungary, who attempted to invade Ayyubid Egypt but was forced to withdraw. Then the Holy Roman Emperor Frederick II arrived with a fresh army and took charge. Frederick had grown up in Sicily, was familiar with Islam, spoke some Arabic, and had entered the Crusade only under pressure of excommunication. He made a show of force at Acre, then began negotiations with al-Kamil, and in that way secured Christian control of a corridor from Jaffa to Jerusalem, as well as Christian access to Jerusalem itself, Bethlehem, and Nazareth. By negotiation rather than by conquest, and through negotiations conducted by an excommunicated Holy Roman Emperor, the Crusaders managed to regain temporary access to Jerusalem.

Mongols captured and largely destroyed Qalat Subayba in 1260, before suffering their own defeat at Ain Jalut later that year. Baybars, the Mamluk commander at Ain Jalut, seized the Egyptian sultanate for himself soon after the battle. He restored and expanded Qalat Subayba. But as political circumstances changed over the years ahead, the castle's location became less strategically crucial, and eventually it fell into disuse.

An abandoned castle visible from afar was sure to stimulate folk imagination and give rise to folk stories. These stories associate Qalat Subayba with Nimrod the "mighty hunter" mentioned in Gen 10:8. Nimrod turns up also in rabbinic and Islamic traditions, where he is seen as an evil ruler who attempted to kill Abraham or squelch Abraham's voice for monotheism. *Qalat Subayba* means "Castle of the Cliff," and according to one of the folk legends Nimrod would sit high on the castle cliff and reach out his hand to take water from the Banias Stream. Another legend had it that Nimrod built the castle on the cliff so he could shoot his arrows into the sky and prove his might to God. But God sent a fly that entered Nimrod's nose and ate away at his brain until he died in agony. This is a play on *Subayba*, which sounds like the word for "fly" in Arabic and Hebrew.

For good views of the castle and Mount Hermon, continue on Highway 99 from Banias to the Druze town of Mas'ade. After Masada, turn south on Highway 98 to its juncture with Highway 91 and then left on Highway 91 for a view across the Israeli border into Syria. Return to Highway 98 and follow it through the Golan to the Sea of Galilee.

Through Samaria to Jerusalem

In keeping with his Jewish heritage, Jesus would have traveled from Galilee to Jerusalem on various occasions. As a youngster he would have made pilgrimages to Jerusalem with his family (Luke 2:41–52). He was in Judea when baptized by John the Baptist (Matt 3:5–6). He had come to Jerusalem with his disciples to celebrate the Passover when he was crucified. Jews traveling from Galilee to Jerusalem could follow either of two routes. They could go directly through the Central Hill Country to Jerusalem, which meant going through Samaria. Or they could pass east of Samaria through the Jordan River basin to Jericho, and turn west from there to Jerusalem. Jesus and his disciples seem to have followed both routes at different times. They were passing through the Hill Country when Jesus encountered the Samaritan woman at Jacob's Well (John 4:1–6). Luke 18:33–19:10 describes an occasion when Jesus and his disciples passed through Jericho on the way to Jerusalem.

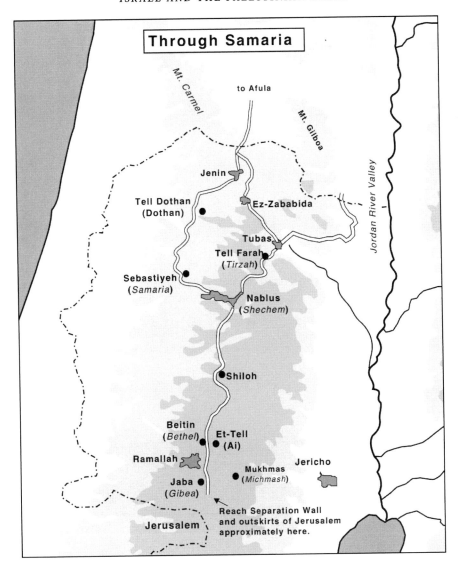

The Hill Country–Samaria route would have taken them through the old tribal territories of Manasseh, Ephraim, and Benjamin. These three tribes became the core of the Northern Kingdom of Israel, often called Samaria after its capital city, and the inhabitants of this region came to be known as Samaritans. Relations between Jews and Samaritans were not good—understandably. Only a century or so before Jesus encountered the woman at Jacob's Well, Jerusalem's Hasmonean rulers had seized military control over Samaria. All of this was background to Jesus' encounter with the Samaritan woman. She would have been referring to Mount Gerizim when she said, "Our fathers worshiped on this mountain" (John 4:20). No doubt the disciples would have preferred to avoid Samaritan territory.

A similar situation exists today in that the drive from Galilee through the Central Hill Country to Jerusalem means passing through the disputed West Bank. Israeli maps and signposts along the way warn Jewish Israelis not to enter certain areas with predominantly Palestinian populations. Yet it is possible for tour buses to make this drive, and I strongly recommend it. The two biblical highlights will be the sites of ancient Shechem and Samaria. Depending on which present-day roads you follow, you probably will also pass near Dothan or Tirzah, Shiloh, and Bethel.

Dothan (Tell Dothan)

Driving south from Jenin on Highway 60 and soon before reaching the Dothan Junction (Tzomet Dotan), watch for Tell Dothan in the distance, east of the highway. Gen 37 tells how Joseph found his brothers grazing their sheep at Dothan, and how they sold him to a caravan of Ishmaelites on their way from Gilead to Egypt. "Then they [Joseph's brothers] sat down to eat; and looking up they saw a caravan of Ishmaelites coming from Gilead, with their camels carrying gum, balm, and resin, on their way to carry it down to Egypt" (v. 25). Tell Dothan was excavated during the 1950s by Joseph Free of Wheaton College, but the findings were never fully published.

Tell Dothan (Dothan)

Tirzah (Tell el-Farah)

Driving south from Tubas on Highway 58, pass through the Mukhayam Fariah refugee camp after about six miles, then watch for Tell el-Farah on the right (west) side of the road. This tell represents a fortified position of some size, comparable to Megiddo, and it was strategically located with respect to traffic between Shechem and the Jordan River basin. Nine seasons of excavations directed by Roland de Vaux between 1946 and 1960 revealed a long history of Bronze and Iron Age occupation. Although its identification remains uncertain, many biblical scholars regard Tell el-Farah to be the best candidate for Tirzah, where early kings of the Northern Kingdom resided before Omri built Samaria (1 Kgs 14:1–18; 15:21, 33; 16:8; 16:15; and 16:23–24).

Tell el-Farah (Tirzah)

Shechem (Tell Balatah)

Nablus and the adjoining Balatah refugee camp dominate the pass between Mounts Ebal and Gerizim. Completely surrounded and almost hidden by present-day buildings is Tell Balatah, the mound of stratified remains from ancient Shechem. Egyptian records indicate that Shechem was a city of more than regional importance during the Bronze Age, and this has been confirmed by archaeological excavations. German archaeologists led by Ernst Sellin conducted excavations at Tell Balatah in 1913–1914, 1926–1927, and 1934. Unfortunately, Sellin's records and many artifacts were destroyed in Berlin during World War II. Then an American team directed by G. E. Wright conducted seven seasons of excavations at Tell Balatah between 1956 and 1968. In addition to probing the largely Middle and Late Bronze phases of the site, Professor Wright and his staff used Tell Balatah as a training school for the next generation of American archaeologists.

Somewhere in the Shechem vicinity, according to Genesis, Abraham built the first of three altars as he entered and passed through the land of Canaan:

> Abram passed through the land to the place at Shechem, to the oak of Moreh. At that time the Canaanites were in the land. Then the LORD appeared to Abram, and said, "To your offspring I will give this land." So he built there an altar to the LORD, who had appeared to him. (Gen 12:6–7)

Further on in the Genesis account, we read that Jacob camped near Shechem, built an altar, and purchased a plot of land:

> Jacob came safely to the city of Shechem, which is in the land of Canaan, on his way from Paddan-aram; and he camped before the city. And from the sons of Hamor, Shechem's father, he bought for one hundred pieces of money the plot of land on which he had pitched his tent. There he erected an altar and called it El-Elohe-Israel. (Gen 33:18–20)

Nablus: Mount Gerizim, overlooking Tell Balata, Middle Bronze Age wall

As the narrative continues, one of Hamor's sons, named Shechem, raped Jacob's daughter Dinah. Hamor then, at Shechem's request, proposed marriage between Shechem and Dinah. Jacob and her brothers agreed, with the stipulation that Shechem and all the men of his city be circumcised. On the third day, when they were still in pain, two of Dinah's brothers, Simeon and Levi, took their swords, came against the city unawares, and killed all the males (Gen 34:25). Jacob moved with the family then to Bethel.

Joshua called the tribes together at Shechem on more than one occasion, including for his farewell address:

> Then Joshua gathered all the tribes of Israel to Shechem, and summoned the elders, the heads, the judges, and the officers of Israel; and they presented themselves before God. And Joshua said to all the people, "Thus says the LORD, the God of Israel: . . . (Josh 24:1–2; see also Josh 8:30–35)

It was at Shechem, following Solomon's death, that the northern tribes rebuffed Rehoboam's arrogant claim upon their loyalty. First Kings 12 tells the story. Rehoboam called the northern tribes together at Shechem to receive their affirmation of loyalty to the Davidic Dynasty in Jerusalem. But when the tribal leaders inquired about his intended policies, and Rehoboam threatened to be even more harsh on his subjects than his father Solomon had been, they sent him packing and formed a separate kingdom. Appropriately, since this new kingdom actually included most of the Israelite tribes, they claimed for it the name Israel. What remained of the Davidic-Solomonic kingdom, basically the tribe of Judah, was centered in Jerusalem and came to be known as Judah.

Nablus: Mount Ebal overlooking Tell Balath, Bronze Age temple area

Shechem may have continued to serve as chief city of the Northern Kingdom of Israel for some time. But its earliest kings seem to have resided at Tirzah for about forty years, until Omri built a new capital and royal residency at Samaria. The Northern Kingdom was sometimes called Samaria after that (Hos 7:1; Amos 4:1; Jer 31:5), and this name continued to be used for the region long after the Kingdom of Israel/ Samaria was no more.

Shechem was situated in the region of Samaria, and a Samaritan temple was built on Mount Gerizim at some point, possibly during the fifth century BCE while Palestine was under Persian rule. The city of Samaria became increasingly Greek in population and character during the Hellenistic Period, prompting many of its native Samaritans to migrate to Shechem, and with them came the priests of the Samaritan religion. So Shechem, and especially the temple on Mount Gerizim, emerged as the real center of Samaritan religion and sentiment. The Samaritans and their temple priesthood stood aside from the conflict when the Seleucid king Antiochus IV (reigned 175–164 BCE) attempted to stamp out traditional Judaism and Hellenize the Jerusalem temple. Later, the Hasmonean ruler John Hyrcanus I conquered the chief cities of Samaria, forced their inhabitants to accept Jerusalem-based Judaism, destroyed the Samaritan temple on Mount Gerizim (in 129 BCE), and eventually destroyed the city of Shechem itself (in 108 BCE).

John 4:1–30 reports the occasion when Jesus and his disciples returned from Judea to Galilee by way of Samaria.

> Now when Jesus learned that the Pharisees had heard, "Jesus is making and
> baptizing more disciples than John" . . . he left Judea and started back to

Galilee. But he had to go through Samaria. So he came to a Samaritan city called Sychar, near the plot of ground that Jacob had given to his son Joseph. Jacob's well was there, and Jesus, tired out by his journey, was sitting by the well. It was about noon. (vv. 1–6)

Sychar is otherwise unknown in ancient sources. But the woman is quoted in verse 20 as saying, "Our fathers worshiped on this mountain," surely a reference to Mount Gerizim where the Samaritan temple had stood until both it and the city of Shechem had been destroyed. So if the well that Jesus visited was not identical to the one known today as Jacob's Well, situated at the foot of Mount Gerizim, that well must have been somewhere nearby.

Jesus' encounter with the woman at the well would have occurred about a hundred years after the Jews destroyed the Samaritan temple. Samaria was still tied politically to Jerusalem—falling within Herod Archaelaus's ethnarchy but administered at that point by Roman procurators. One can imagine the tone of irony and bitterness in the Samaritan woman's voice when she said, "Our ancestors worshiped on this mountain; but you say that the place where people must worship is in Jerusalem" (v. 20).

The well venerated today as Jacob's Well has been covered by churches, built and rebuilt over time, going back to the Byzantine Period. The Crusaders built a church on the site. A late nineteenth-century Greek Orthodox church was destroyed by earthquake in 1927. The current church, also Greek Orthodox, was completed in 2007.

While suppressing the First Jewish Revolt (66–73 CE), the Roman emperor Vespasian and his son Titus built a new city immediately to the west of the ruins of ancient Shechem (Tell Balatah). They named it Flavius Neapolis (after their family name, Flavius), from which the present-day Arabic name Nablus derives. Among the citizens of Flavius Neapolis, born in about 100 CE, was Justin Martyr, an important early Christian apologist. Today, centuries after Justin, Flavius Neapolis has become the expansive city of Nablus. In 1950, the Balatah refugee camp was founded on the eastern outskirts of Nablus. Now Balatah is the largest Palestinian refugee camp in the West Bank and functions much like a suburb of Nablus.

Jacob's Well is reached below the recently restored Greek Orthodox church.

Samaria/Sebaste (Sebastiyeh)

Around 880 BCE, an energetic ruler of the Northern Kingdom of Israel named Omri chose the hill of Samaria (Shomron in Hebrew) as the site for a new capital and began to build a palace there. Apparently Omri made quite a name for himself during his ten-year reign. The ninth-century Mesha Inscription credits him with conquering part of Moab. Assyrian scribes referred to Israel as "the land of Omri" and continued to do so for a hundred years after Omri's death. After the Egyptian pharaoh Sheshonq who appears as Shishak in 1 Kgs 14:25–27, and "House of David" mentioned in the Dan Inscription, Omri is the next biblical character to appear in ancient inscriptions from his own time.

Better known today, however, are Omri's son and daughter-in-law, Ahab and Jezebel. Archaeological evidence suggests that Ahab not only completed but also expanded the palace begun by Omri at Samaria. No doubt Elijah and Elisha walked the streets of the city, and the former may have witnessed the building of the palace. Samaria would serve as the Northern Kingdom's capital for more than a century and half—until 722 BCE when Sargon II conquered Samaria and annexed the kingdom's territory to the Assyrian Empire.

Samaria: Omride palace area

Samaria continued as an administrative center under Assyrian and Persian rule, then took on new life after Alexander the Great's conquest of the east. Apparently, the Samaritans submitted to Alexander at first but then revolted, whereupon Alexander punished them severely and colonized Samaria with Macedonian veterans. The massive circular towers visible at the site probably represent the work of these veterans, although Samaria would be partially destroyed and rebuilt at least twice during the wars between his generals that followed Alexander's death. Samaria became increasingly Greek in character during the Hellenistic Period, and many of the native Samaritans migrated to Shechem. Between 113 and 110 BCE, when John Hyrcanus conquered the region of Samaria, he totally destroyed the city of Samaria and enslaved its population.

Pompey liberated the Samaritans from Hasmonean control in 63 BCE and left Samaria under the general oversight of the newly established Roman province of Syria. Aulus Gabinius was appointed governor of Syria soon thereafter (served 57–55 BCE) and began to rebuild the city of Samaria. Two decades later (in 37 BCE), while still fighting for control of Jerusalem, Herod the Great married his favorite wife, Mariamne, in Samaria (*Ant.* 14:15.14). Ten years later, with Herod in place as king in Jerusalem and Octavian having just been recognized by the Roman Senate as Caesar Augustus, Caesar transferred Samaria to Herod's kingdom. Herod renamed the city Sebaste (the Greek equivalent of *Augustus*) and began to build it out on a grand scale. Where the ancient Omride palace had stood, Herod erected an imposing temple dedicated to Augustus. He added a new defensive wall around the city. Later he would have two of his sons by Mariamne executed at Samaria/Sebaste (*Ant.* 16:11.7).

Samaria: Hellenistic tower, photo center left

Samaria: These steps led to an imposing temple built
by Herod the Great and dedicated to Caesar Augustus

Sebaste refused to support the First Jewish Revolt (66–73 CE), was captured and burned by Jewish rebels, revived after the revolt, and then flourished under Roman rule. Septimius Severus (193–211 CE) elevated the city to colony status, after which it was known officially as Colonia Lucia Septimia Sebaste. He also rebuilt and expanded the Sebaste temple; the massive temple steps visible today belong to this later building phase. Samaria/Sebaste's colonnaded street, basilica, and theater also date from this second- to third-century phase.

Continuing as an important city through the Byzantine Period, Sebaste became an episcopal see: bishops from the city attended the Councils of Nicaea (325 CE), Constantinople (381), and Chalcedon (451). At these councils they shared in theological disputations that determined the official view of the Byzantine Empire and Orthodox Church about the divinity of Jesus. Surviving remnants of paganism gradually were stamped out. Temples and other associated structures were destroyed or converted to churches. The temple to Augustus served as a quarry, and the Roman basilica was converted to a Christian cathedral. A tradition emerged that John the Baptist was buried in Sebaste, and two shrines received pilgrims: a basilica that enclosed what was believed to be John's tomb, and another that marked the place where Herodias supposedly had hidden his head.

The whole region fell under Arab rule in 634 CE, after which Arabic gradually became the dominant language and Islam largely replaced Christianity as the dominant religion. Note that the current name of the village, Sebastiyeh, is the Arabic form of the earlier Greek name, Sebaste, and that the name of the village mosque, Nabi Yahya, is Arabic for "Saint John." This mosque is a rebuild of an eleventh-century Crusader basilica, which itself was a rebuild of the Byzantine basilica that had marked what was believed to be John the Baptist's tomb. This Byzantine basilica had been destroyed by the Persians in 614 CE.

Harvard University sponsored excavations at Samaria/Sebaste/Sebastiyeh between 1908 and 1910. Under the direction first of Gottlieb Schumacher and then George A. Reisner, the excavators discovered more than a hundred ostraca (potsherds with writing on them). These seem to have been used to register shipments of wine and oil to Samaria during the early eighth century BCE, about the time of Jeroboam II (2 Kgs 14:23–29). The site was excavated further between 1932 and 1935 as a joint effort by five British and American institutions. J. W. Crowfoot was director of the overall project, but the person whose work was to have the most significant impact was Kathleen Kenyon, who supervised the excavation of the royal quarter on the summit of the site. She employed and refined a method of excavating and recording that has come to be known as the Wheeler-Kenyon method. She also made important progress toward working out the basics of ceramic chronology (pottery dating) for Iron Age Palestine.

Shiloh (Khirbet Seilun, Shilo)

Leaving Nablus and continuing south toward Jerusalem on Highway 60, watch for the Israeli settlement of Shilo. You will pass the archaeological ruins of ancient Shiloh on the left (east) side of the road immediately before passing the Israeli settlement, which is situated farther back from the road and on higher ground. The archaeological site was known by its Arabic name Khirbet Seilun before the settlement was established during the early 1970s.

Shilo: The Israeli settlement by this name overlooks
the archaeological site of biblical Shiloh, indicated by the arrow

First Samuel begins with a heartwarming story of how Samuel's mother, Hannah, dedicated him as a child to serve Eli at Shiloh (3:3). As the narrative continues in 1 Samuel 3, Samuel heard someone calling him while he is lying in the temple. At first, he thought it was Eli. But not so; this was Yahweh calling, and it was the beginning of Samuel's own career as a prophet. Hear again 1 Sam 3:20–21 cited above in connection with Tel Dan.

> And all Israel from Dan to Beer-sheba knew that Samuel was a trustworthy prophet of the LORD. The LORD continued to appear at Shiloh, for the LORD revealed himself to Samuel at Shiloh by the word of the LORD.

Actually, Shiloh's role in ancient Israel is somewhat puzzling. According to Josh 18, the Israelite tribes gathered at Shiloh soon after entering the land of Canaan and set up the tabernacle there. Several other biblical passages including the story about young Samuel also suggest that Shiloh served as an important center for Israelite tribal affairs (Josh 19:51; 21:1–2; 22:12; and so forth). Yet Judg 21 reports an occasion when the Israelite tribes encouraged the Benjaminites to ambush and kidnap daughters from Shiloh.

Present-day Shilo was one of the first modern Israeli settlements to be established in the Nablus area and is typical of the hilltop settlements that now dominate the West Bank. Its founder, Ira Rappaport, secured permission to excavate the archaeological site, then used the dig as cover to begin the settlement. In 1985 he was found guilty of attempted murder after planting a car bomb that blew the legs off two Palestinian officials. After spending less than a year in prison, he was released and became head of the Shilo settlement. The Israeli government claims that this settlement was built on abandoned land; local Palestinians and Israeli civil rights groups insist that at least a quarter of the settlement, which has grown now to about 2,500 residents, overlaps privately owned Palestinian land.

Benjaminite Villages

After Shiloh, watch next for the more substantial Israeli settlement Bet El, west of the highway. From here until you reach the security wall and checkpoint entry to Jerusalem, you will be passing through the ancient tribal territory of Benjamin.

Before the 1967 Six Day War when Israel gained control of the West Bank, and even through the mid-1970s, this Benjaminite area was dotted with Arab villages. Many of them had Arabic names that correspond to Benjaminite towns and villages mentioned in the Old Testament, and they were located on the same ancient sites. The Arab village Beitin, for example, marked the site of biblical Bethel (Gen 12:8; 1 Kgs 12:29; Amos 7:10); the Arab village Mukhmas marked the site of biblical Michmash (1 Sam 13:5ff. Neh 11:31; Isa 10:28); the Arab village el-Jib marked the site of biblical Gibeon (Josh 9:3ff; 1 Sam 2:12ff; 1 Kgs 3:4ff); the Arab village Jaba marked the site of biblical Geba/Gibeah (Judg 20:10ff; 1 Sam 13:3ff; 1 Kgs 15:22); and the Arab neighborhood Anata marked the biblical site Anathoth (Josh 21:18; 1 Kgs 2:26; Isa 10:30; Jer 1:1).

This area is so fully developed now, crisscrossed with new paved roads, and dominated by post-1967 Israeli settlements, that it is difficult to locate many of these traditional Arab village sites. Also, the more recent Israeli settlements often have taken the names of biblical places whose actual locations are indicated by the Arab villages. Bet El mentioned above, for example, is a modern Israeli settlement that has taken the biblical name Bethel. But the actual location of biblical Bethel corresponds to that of nearby Arab Beitin. You will notice many biblical names on the road signs as you pass through Benjamin, but be aware that they often point to recent Israeli settlements rather than to actual biblical sites.

Through the Jordan Valley to Jerusalem

Jesus' disciples probably would have preferred a route between Galilee and Jerusalem that did not pass through Samaria. The next best possibility for Jesus and his disciples would have been to go south from Galilee through the Jordan River Valley to Jericho and turn west from there into the Central Hill Country toward Jerusalem. This Jordan Valley route passes near the tell of ancient Beth-shean and its Hellenistic-Roman successor city, Scythopolis. The Jordan Valley is well watered and luscious green at that point. But as the river flows from the Sea of Galilee toward the Dead Sea, the valley becomes increasingly dry and barren. On the west side of the river near where it enters the Dead Sea is a major spring—the famous oasis of Jericho. The gospel narratives report an occasion when Jesus and his disciples passed through Jericho, and we know from his parable of the good Samaritan (Luke 10:30–35) that he was familiar with the steep and treacherous trail (along Wadi Kelt) from Jericho to Jerusalem.

Beth-shean/Scythopolis (Tell el-Husn, Tel Beth Shean)

Tell el-Husn is the archaeological site of ancient Beth-shean (appears also as Beth-Shan). Stratified remains from especially the Bronze and Iron Ages rest upon a natural hill, making for a high tell with steep sides. Ancient Beth-shean was strategically located at the southeastern end of the Jezreel Valley, where the Jezreel Valley reaches the Jordan River Valley, and near a place where the Jordan River could be forded. In addition to its easily defensible position, Beth-shean lay at the crossroads of commercial and military routes, including connections between the main coastal route through western Palestine (Via Maris) and the main north-south route through the Transjordan (the King's Highway). Along with the fertility of the soil at this southeastern end of the Jezreel Valley, the small river stream, Nahal Harod/Jalut, flows past Tell el-Husn into the Jordan River.

Excavations on Tell Husn, Jordan Valley and Gilead in the distance

Excavations conducted on Tell Husn under the auspices of the University of Pennsylvania Museum between 1921 and 1933 revealed eighteen occupational layers ranging from Chalcolithic to Byzantine and Arab. More recent excavations during 1983 and from 1989 through 1996, sponsored by the Hebrew University in Jerusalem

143

and conducted by Amahai Mazar, have added new information and evaluations. These excavations and ancient written sources reveal that Beth-shean emerged as an important city during the Early and Middle Bronze Ages, then fell under Egyptian control during the Late Bronze Age.

Beth-shean appears in the Palestinian List of cities that Tuthmosis III claims to have conquered at Megiddo during the mid-fifteenth century BCE, and it appears again about a century later in the Amarna Letters. These letters, written in cuneiform script on clay tablets, are correspondence between various Egyptian vassal rulers in Syria-Palestine and the royal courts of Amenhotep III and Amenhotep IV. Among them are letters from Abdi-Heba, the pre-Israelite king of Jerusalem mentioned above, reporting to the pharaoh that a military garrison from Gath-Carmel had taken position in Beth-shean.

Beth-shean seems to have served as an Egyptian outpost and administrative center toward the end of the Late Bronze Age, and excavations at the site have yielded an unparalleled collection of monuments and inscriptions from the Egyptian Dynasties 19 and 20. Among these are two stelae (inscribed stone slabs or columns) with inscriptions from the time of Seti I (reigned ca. 1294–1213 BCE), one from Ramesses II (reigned ca. 1279–1213 BCE), and a seated statue of Ramesses III (reigned ca. 1184–1153 BCE).

Beth-shean continued as a city into the Iron Age, but we are dependent on the Hebrew Bible/Old Testament for written information at that point. According to Josh 17:11, Beth-shean and its villages were allotted to the tribe of Manasseh. But then Judg 1:27 reports that the inhabitants of Beth-shean, Megiddo, and several other cities were never expelled. First Samuel 31 indicates that Philistines held Beth-shean at the time of King Saul's last battle and suicide on Mount Gilboa nearby.

> The next day, when the Philistines came to strip the dead, they found Saul and his three sons fallen on Mount Gilboa. They cut off his head, stripped off his armor, and sent messengers throughout the land of the Philistines to carry the good news to the houses of their idols and to the people. They put his armor in the temple of Astarte; and they fastened his body to the wall of Beth-shan. (1 Sam 31:8–10)

Across the Jordan River from Beth-shean was Jebesh-Gilead, where Saul was remembered as a hero. Years back, before he became king, the Ammonites attacked Jebesh and were threatening to gouge out the right eye of everyone in the city. Saul raised a militia, hurried across the Jordan River to Jebesh, and saved the day (1 Sam 11:1–11). Now he had fallen in battle and the Philistines were making sport of his body.

> But when the inhabitants of Jabesh-gilead heard what the Philistines had done to Saul, all the valiant men set out, traveled all night long, and took the body of Saul and the bodies of his sons from the wall of Beth-shan. They came to Jabesh

and burned them there. Then they took their bones and buried them under the tamarisk tree in Jabesh, and fasted seven days. (1 Sam 31:11–13)

Archaeological remains of Hellenistic-Roman Scythopolis spread out below Tell Husn.

Centuries later, with the high and steep-sided tell of ancient Beth-shean serving as an acropolis, a Hellenistic-Roman city spread out at its base. Its name was Scythopolis, which suggests a connection with Scythians. Possibly the Ptolemaic rulers deployed Scythian soldiers there. John Hyrcanus I conquered Scythopolis in 107 BCE, and Scythopolis was among the Hellenistic-oriented cities that Pompey released from Hasmonean rule in 63 BCE. Aulus Gabinius, appointed governor to Syria soon thereafter, attached Scythopolis to the Decapolis group. Already an important crossroads city, Scythopolis now enjoyed yet another commercial advantage. As the only Decapolis city located west of the Jordan River, it served as a link between the Decapolis and western Palestine. Scythopolis continued to flourish through the Byzantine Period, but then declined and was devastated by an earthquake in 749.

Jericho (Tell es-Sultan, Ariha)

Tell es-Sultan is situated next to a copious spring and surrounded by a modest-sized Palestinian city in the West Bank, Zone A. This name of the tell is relatively recent, but the Arabic name of the surrounding city, Ariha, corresponds to the ancient biblical name Jericho. Almost certainly, Tell es-Sultan represents the stratified archaeological remains of ancient Jericho, and the spring is the one mentioned in 2 Kgs 2:19–22.

Now the people of the city [Jericho] said to Elisha, "The location of this city is good, as my lord sees; but the water is bad, and the land is unfruitful. He said, "Bring me a new bowl, and put salt in it." So they brought it to him. Then he went to the spring of water and threw the salt into it, and said, "Thus says the LORD, I have made this water wholesome; from now on neither death nor miscarriage shall come from it." So the water has been wholesome to this day, according to the word that Elisha spoke.

Jericho/Ariha does indeed enjoy a good location—tropical climate, lush and green, referred to as "the city of palm trees" in 2 Chr 28:15. Other biblical references to Jericho include 2 Sam 10:5; 1 Kgs 16:34; Luke 10:30; and Heb 11:30.

Remains from Roman Period Jericho are to be seen on the southern outskirts of the present-day city. These include several imposing structures, one of which is a royal palace built by Herod the Great, who died in Jericho. Overlooking Jericho from the west, and accessible now by cable car, is the Monastery of Qurantul (the Forty), perched on the side of the traditional Mount of Temptation (Matt 4:1–11; Mark 1:12–13). Remains of a luxurious winter palace, begun in 724 CE by the Umayyad caliph Hisham but never finished, are on the northwestern outskirts of town, north of Tell es-Sultan and the spring.

Jericho: Tell es-Sultan

Jericho: Monastery of Qurantul

Tell es-Sultan received early attention from archaeologists, beginning with excavations conducted by Earnest Sellin and Carl Watzinger from 1907 to 1911. They were followed by John Garstang between 1929 and 1936, and Kathleen Kenyon from 1952 to 1958. These excavations revealed almost constant human activity at the site from the Epi-Paleolithic (or Mesolithic) Period through the Middle Bronze Age. Especially noteworthy was a Neolithic settlement dating back to 8000 BCE. Defended by a stone wall and tower, this is one of the oldest permanent settlements known to archaeologists. Centuries later, during the Early Bronze Age, a thriving urban center surrounded by a thick mud-brick wall emerged on the site. That phase of the city was destroyed toward the end of the Early Bronze Age and eventually replaced by a Middle Bronze Age phase also protected by a substantial mud-brick wall. This Middle Bronze Age phase ended around 1500 BCE, and the archaeological trail at the site essentially ends at that point.

This is somewhat disconcerting because Jericho is perhaps best known as the city whose walls came tumbling down when the Israelites, commanded by God and led by Joshua, marched around them once a day for six days and then seven times on the seventh day (Josh 6). Yet there seems to be no archaeological evidence that a walled city existed at Jericho during the Late Bronze Age, when Joshua would seem most likely to have lived and the Israelite conquest of Canaan would have occurred. Moreover, excavations at several other cities mentioned in connection with the Israelite conquest of Canaan yield no evidence that they were thriving cities during Late Bronze Age. This was true, as noted above, of Tell Hesban (biblical Heshbon). Two other notable examples are Tell Arad (biblical Arad) and et-Tell (biblical Ai).

Neolithic tower excavated at Tell es-Sultan

Mark 10:32–52 describes an occasion when Jesus and the disciples passed through Jericho on their way to or from Jerusalem. As they were leaving Jericho, a blind beggar named Bartimaeus was sitting by the road, heard that it was Jesus, and began to shout out: "Jesus, Son of David, have mercy on me." The surrounding crowd attempted to quiet him, but he continued to shout out all the more until Jesus answered him and healed him of his blindness.

Matthew and Luke describe the event with minor differences (compare Matt 20:29–34; Luke 18:35–43). Then Luke, who has Jesus healing Bartimaeus while he and the disciples are entering Jericho rather than leaving the city, reports Jesus' encounter with Zacchaeus. A mandatory stop in Jericho for all tour buses is an enormous Sycamore tree reminiscent of the one mentioned in this New Testament story.

> He entered Jericho and was passing through it. A man was there named Zacchaeus; he was a chief tax collector and was rich. He was trying to see who Jesus was, but on account of the crowd he could not, because he was short in stature. So he ran ahead and climbed a sycamore tree to see him, because he was going to pass that way. When Jesus came to the place, he looked up and said to him, "Zacchaeus, hurry and come down; for I must stay at your house today." So he hurried down and was happy to welcome him. (Luke 19:1–6)

Jerusalem

As we return our attention to Jerusalem, perhaps the best place to begin is with the Old City walls and gates. Some of the lower courses of stone date back to Roman times, but basically these walls date from the Ottoman Period, built by Suleiman the Magnificent during the sixteenth century, then refurbished by the British during the Mandate Period following World War I.

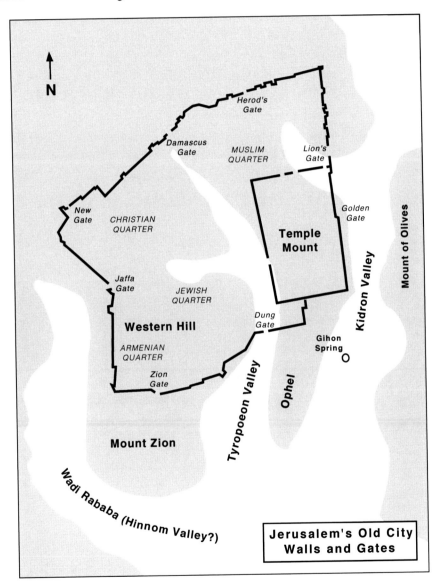

Jerusalem's Old City Walls and Gates

From the west, one enters the Old City through the Jaffa Gate. A section of wall between this gate and the citadel (immediately to the south of the Jaffa Gate) was removed by Ottoman authorities in 1898 in preparation for a state visit by Kaiser Wilhelm II. The New Gate at the northwestern corner of the Old City had been opened shortly before (1887) in order to provide better access to the Christian Quarter. Two other gates provide access to the Old City from the north (the Damascus Gate and Herod's Gate), one provides access from the east (Saint Stephen's Gate, also called the Lion's Gate) and two from the south (the Dung Gate and the Zion Gate).

As long as one understands that the names apply only in a general fashion and that boundaries are not sharply drawn, it is appropriate to think of the Old City as divided into four quarters: the Muslim Quarter (northeast quadrant with close access to the al-Aksa Mosque), the Christian Quarter (northwest quadrant with close access to the Church of the Holy Sepulchre), the Jewish Quarter (south-central quadrant with close access to the Western/Wailing Wall, and the Armenian Quarter (southwest quadrant with close access to Saint James Cathedral).

It is possible to walk on the walls (access at the Jaffa Gate), view the Old City from above, and gain a better sense of the lay of the land. Three valleys separate the higher ground into named hills before joining southeast of the Old City. The Kidron Valley (also called the Valley of Jehosaphat) separates the Old City from the Mount of Olives and Mount Scopus. The Tyropoeon Valley separates the Temple Mount/ Haram ash-Sharif and Ophel from the Western Hill and Mount Zion. Wadi Rababa, usually identified with the Hinnom Valley (2 Kgs 23:10; Jer 7:32), marks the southern end of Mount Zion. The Tyropoeon Valley is no longer clearly discernible, having been largely filled in over time.

Ophel and Mount Zion viewed from the east

Ophel (City of Abdi-Heba, the Jebusites, and David)

This long, sloping hill immediately south of the Temple Mount/Haram ash-Sharif is the site of oldest Jerusalem, the city of Abdi-Heba and other pre-Israelite kings. Their Bronze Age era is represented by remains of Middle and Late Bronze Age fortifications. Situated at the foot of Ophel on the east is the Gihon spring, the main water source for early Jerusalem. An early water shaft provided access to the spring from inside the fortifications.

Archaeological evidence for early Iron Age Jerusalem—when David, Solomon, and the early Judean kings that followed them would have lived—is more ambivalent. According to 2 Sam 5:6–8, David conquered Jerusalem from Jebusites, and an uncertain word in the passage (*tsinnor*) is generally interpreted as a reference to the water shaft:

> The king and his men marched to Jerusalem against the Jebusites, the inhabitants of the land, who said to David, "You will not come in here, even the blind and the lame will turn you back"—thinking, "David cannot come in here." Nevertheless David took the stronghold of Zion, which is now the city of David. David had said on that day, "Whoever would strike down the Jebusites, let him get up the water shaft (*tsinnor*) to attack the lame and the blind, those whom David hates." Therefore it is said, "The blind and the lame shall not come into the house."

The narrative continues to describe how Hiram, king of Tyre, sent cedar trees, carpenters, and masons to build David a palace (2 Sam 5:11–12).

Remains of two architectural structures have been excavated on Ophel that possibly pertain to David's palace. The first, having been known for some

Hezekiah's Tunnel

The Chronicler's account of King Hezekiah's reign includes the following note in 2 Chr 32:30: "This same Hezekiah closed the upper outlet of the waters of Gihon and directed them down to the west side of the city of David." Water still flows through an ancient tunnel that connects the Gihon Spring with the Pool of Siloam, and in 1880 an ancient Hebrew inscription was discovered in the tunnel. Unfortunately, the inscription was badly damaged before scholars had a chance to study it. The damaged text reads as follows:

> . . . the tunneling through. And this is the account of the tunneling through. While (the workmen raised) the pick each toward his fellow and while there [remained] to be tunneled [through, there was heard] the voice of a man calling to his fellow, for there was a split in the rock on the right hand and on [the left hand]. And on the day of the tunneling through the workmen stuck, each in the direction of his fellow, pick against pick. And the water started flowing from the source to the pool, twelve hundred cubits. And the height of the rock above the head of the workmen was a hundred cubits. (See Pritchard, *ANET*, 321)

time, is a stepped stone structure built over a series of terraces on the eastern slopes of Ophel. It is curved, approximately 60 feet high, apparently a retaining wall. The second, excavated recently by archaeologist Eliat Mazar, consists of foundational remains of a large stone structure situated higher up on Ophel and seemingly bonded at one corner with the stepped structure. Mazar dates the large stone structure to Iron Age IIa, the archaeological period during which David probably would have lived, and interprets the structure as part of David's palace. The City of David Foundation, which controls and presents the Ophel archaeological site to the public, takes this a step further. They present an artistic mockup of a hypothetical City of David that was protected by the Bronze Age walls, supposedly still in use, and crowned with David's palace, which was shored up by the stepped structure.

Stepped stone structure excavated on Ophel, photo center

Other archeologists are more cautious about Mazar's dating and interpretation of both the stepped structure and the large stone structure. Perhaps the most surprising thing about early Iron Age Jerusalem is the absence of firm archaeological evidence for Solomon's capital city. First Kings 6–7 states that he spent seven years building the temple, presumably higher up on the Temple Mount, and then thirteen years building his own palace. Admittedly, the Temple Mount and much of Ophel is unavailable for archaeological exploration, but even allowing for that, archaeological evidence of a Solomonic golden age as described in 1 Kings is surprisingly absent.

Evidence of urban settlement on Ophel becomes more perceptible for the ninth century and following, when later Judean kings were ruling Jerusalem. Two assemblages of bullae and seals from the late ninth and early eighth centuries have been recovered from fills in the Kidron Valley near the Gihon Spring. Bullae are lumps of clay, stamped with writing or graphic symbols or both, used to seal rolls of papyrus scrolls. These bullae and seals probably held documents pertaining to the royal Judean administration.

By the late eighth century, Jerusalem's urban settlement had expanded to the so-called Western Hill (present-day Jewish and Armenian Quarters). About that time—almost certainly during the reign of King Hezekiah (ca. 727–699)—a tunnel was engineered to bring water from Gihon to the Pool of Siloam. This is the same Pool of Siloam mentioned in the New Testament where, according to John 9:1–12, Jesus healed a blind man with spit-clay and sent him to wash in the pool.

Another seal impression, recently reported from excavations currently underway on Ophel, dates a century or more later than Hezekiah and was found among the remains of a building that archaeologists believe was demolished and burned when the Babylonians sacked Jerusalem in 586 BCE. This bulla bears the imprint of a seal that belonged to a man named Nathan-Melech, identified as a servant (or "official") of the king. Might this be the same Nathan-Melech mentioned in 2 Kgs 23:11? "He [King Josiah] removed the horses that the kings of Judah had dedicated to the sun, at the entrance to the house of the LORD, by the chamber of the eunuch Nathan-melech, which was in the precincts; then he burned the chariots of the sun with fire."

The Temple Mount/Haram ash-Sharif

The Old City walls incorporate, in the east-southeast corner, a large rectangular compound that Jews and Christians generally refer to as the Temple Mount, and that Muslims call the Haram ash-Sharif ("Noble Enclosure" in Arabic). The walls of this compound trace essentially the outer wall lines of the Second Temple compound.

Presumably Solomon's temple (the First Temple) stood somewhere on this mount until it was destroyed by the Babylonians in 586 BCE. Second Chronicles 3:1 explains that Solomon built this first temple on Mount Moriah, where there had been a Jebusite threshing floor. This brings to mind Gen 22:1–19, which describes how God commanded Abraham to sacrifice Isaac on a mountain in "the land of Moriah." Accordingly, tradition holds that the Temple Mount/Haram ash-Sharif was the mountain on which Abraham was prepared to sacrifice his son.

Another temple was erected on the mount after the exile. Then early in Herod the Great's reign, during the time of the Second Triumvirate, he built a fort on the mount and named it Antonia in honor of Mark Antony. Later Herod lavishly rebuilt the postexilic temple itself, and enclosed it within a massive walled compound defended at its northwest corner by the Antonia. This postexilic temple compound as rebuilt and expanded by Herod the Great is generally referred to as the Second Temple. It is the one that Jesus and Paul would have known and the one that Titus destroyed during the First Jewish Revolt (66–73 CE). The so-called Wailing Wall—more appropriately called the Western Wall—is a remnant of the western retaining wall of the Second Temple compound. Approximately sixty years after the Second Temple was destroyed by Titus, Hadrian erected a temple to the Roman Capitoline gods somewhere in the city, probably on the Temple Mount.

The Temple Mount seems not to have played an important religious role during the Byzantine Period but became important again under Arab-Muslim rule. Muslims regard this as the "distant place" (al-Aksa) to which Mohammed was transported in a dream, and they refer to the Temple Mount as the Noble Enclosure (Haram ash-Sharif). The Umayyad caliph Abd al-Malik (reigned 685–705) built the Dome of the Rock monument over the stone outcropping from which Mohammed is believed to have been transported to paradise during the dream, and al-Malik's son al-Walid (reigned 705–715) added the al-Aksa Mosque. This same al-Walid built the Umayyad Mosque in Damascus and the Great Mosque in Mecca. Crusaders used al-Aksa as a church while they ruled Jerusalem, and the Knights Templar had their headquarters on the Temple Mount. Saladin recovered Jerusalem in 1187 and the Haram ash-Sharif remains under Muslim administration still today

Temple Mount viewed from the southwest

The Golden Gate entry was not original to Herod's Second Temple walls, and when it was added remains uncertain. Possibly it was added by one of the Umayyad caliphs—perhaps al-Malik or al-Walid who built the Dome of the Rock and al-Aksa Mosque—so Muslims could enter the Haram ash-Sharif from the east. But the fact that the Golden Gate entry is positioned almost directly east of the Church of the Holy Sepulchre raises another possibility, suggested by archaeologist Dan Bahat. Perhaps the Byzantine emperor Heraclius added the Golden Gate after defeating the Persians, who invaded and destroyed churches throughout Palestine between 614 and 622. Having defeated the Persians and recovered the relic of the True Cross, Heraclius may have commissioned this grand new gate for his triumphal entry with the cross to the Holy Sepulchre. Neither is it certain when the Golden Gate entry was sealed shut, but certainly no later than the sixteenth century when Suleiman the Magnificent built the current walls around the Old City.

The Western Hill and Mount Zion

The Temple Mount on which Solomon's temple stood during Old Testament times seems to have been known then as Mount Zion. But at some point, apparently by the first century CE, the name Zion shifted to the Western Hill. Today the name Mount Zion generally is used more specifically for the southern end of the Western Hill, where it extends southward outside the Zion Gate.

This latter area had been included within the city walls before Titus destroyed Jerusalem's fortifications in 70 CE. It was left outside the southern wall of Hadrian's Aelia Capitolina. Then during the mid-fifth century CE, with the support of Empress Eutocia, wife of Theodosius II, the city's southern wall was extended to include both Ophel and Zion. Jerusalem's city walls were largely destroyed again in 1219 and rebuilds since that time have left Zion and Ophel outside the southern wall.

A first burst of church building occurred during the fourth century CE. Among the many churches erected at that time was the Basilica of Holy Zion on the Western Hill/Zion in 390 CE. Justinian's reign (527–565) saw another burst of church building. Among the churches built at that time was the so-called Néa Church, also on the Western Hill but north of the Zion Gate in what is now the Jewish Quarter. Consecrated in 543 CE as the New Church of Saint Mary, Mother of God, it is generally known as the Néa Church. (*Néa* means "new" in Greek.). Probably it was Justinian also who extended Jerusalem's main north-south street (*cardo*) so that it connected the Néa Church with the Church of the Holy Sepulchre. A short section of this Byzantine Period street has been excavated, reconstructed, and may be seen in the Jewish Quarter.

Early Christian tradition located the site of the Upper Room (Mark 14:15; Luke 22:12) on Zion. It was believed that the apostles celebrated the first Pentecost in the same room (Acts 1:13), and that Caiaphas's house was located nearby (Matt 26:57; Mark 14:53; Luke 22:54). Another tradition holds that King David was buried in this vicinity. The Cenacle, which includes the traditional Upper Room and David's Tomb, is a fourteenth-century restoration of a Crusader church.

Church of Saint Peter in Gallicantu

From the Mount of Olives to the Church of the Holy Sepulchre

An ideal way for Christian pilgrims to enter Jerusalem is to walk the trail indicated on the map below from the Mount of Olives to the Church of the Holy Sepulchre. Begin with a panoramic view of the Old City from the terraces below the Intercontinental Hotel (1). Then follow the narrow street down the slope, passing a Jewish cemetery on your left, to the Dominus Flevit Church (2). Exit the church grounds and continue down the street and around a corner to the Garden of Gethsemane and Basilica of the Agony (3). Exit Gethsemane, turn left, and within a few steps you will find yourself on a busy street that traces the approximate route of the Kidron Valley. Follow this street to the right for a short way, cross the street (watching for traffic!), and walk up a secondary street to enter the Old City through the Lions' Gate (4). Continue on the same street until you reach (on your right) the entrance to the grounds of the Church of Saint Anne (5). Farther along the street, and again on your right, you reach the entrance to a Franciscan monastery (6). This is the beginning of the Via Dolorosa. Locate and follow the Stations of the Cross along the Via Dolorosa to the Church of the Holy Sepulchre (7).

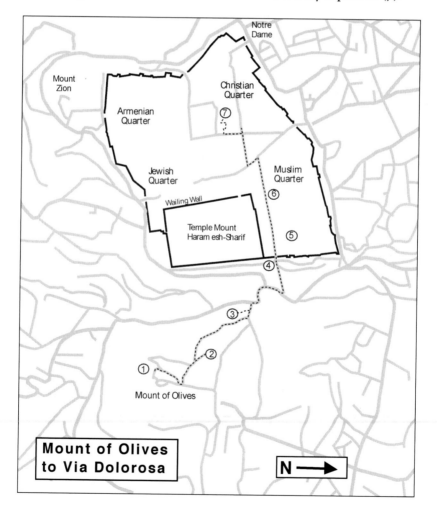

Mount Scopus and the Mount of Olives

Separated from Jerusalem by the Kidron Valley, these two prominent mountain ridges provide an excellent view of the city from the northeast and east. Mount Scopus to the northeast may be Nob, mentioned in Isa 10:32. David is reported to have fled Jerusalem across the Mount of Olives at the time of Absalom's rebellion (2 Sam 15:30). Jesus spent the night on the Mount of Olives, or possibly at nearby Bethany, during his last week in Jerusalem (Luke 21:37).

Mount of Olives: Dominus Flevit Church, Russian Church of
Saint Mary Magdalene, and Church of All Nations

Dominus Flevit Church

The name means "cry of our Lord" and the shape of the church represents a teardrop to symbolize Jesus weeping over the city of Jerusalem (Luke 19:41–44). Built in 1954–1955, this is one of several churches in the Holy Land designed by Antonio Barluzzi. Others include the Church of All Nations in the Garden of Gethsemane (1922–1924), the Church of Transfiguration on Mount Tabor (1924), the Church of Beatitudes (1937–1938), and the Shepherds' Field Chapel in Beit Sahur (1953). The terrace in front of Dominus Flevit offers another wide-ranging view of Jerusalem.

The Garden of Gethsemane

All four Gospels record the incident of Jesus' agonizing prayer and betrayal by Judas. Matt 26:36 and Mark 14:32 relate that the incident occurred in a "field" called Gethsemane (the name Gethsemane probably means "oil press"). The other two Gospels do not identify the place by name: Luke 22:39–40 informs us only that the incident occurred on the Mount of Olives; John 18:1–11 notes that it occurred across the Kidron Valley where there was a garden. Gethsemane (whether it was a field, garden, oil vat, or whatever) must have been located somewhere in the general vicinity of the beautiful garden visited by present-day pilgrims.

The Pool of Bethzatha and Church of Saint Anne

John 5:2–9 describes the Pool of Bethzatha (also called Bethesda) as a pool with five porticoes located near the Sheep Gate. The passage goes on to describe how Jesus healed a man who had been there for thirty-eight years unable because of his illness to get into the pool quickly enough when the waters were troubled. Early pilgrims to Jerusalem spoke of the "twin pools" of Bethzatha, and archaeological excavations conducted northwest of Saint Anne's Church by Conrad Scheck in 1888 revealed what he believed to be the pool of Bethzatha. More recent excavations in 1964 clarified the site further and identified the foundations of a large Byzantine church, a smaller Crusader church, and a second-century temple of Asclepius and Serapis.

Pool of Bethzatha: The deep arch at photo center was one of a line of arches that supported the Byzantine church above the pool. Arrow points to the Crusader church that would have been much smaller

Scholars now believe that a temple to Asclepius and Serapis, both gods of healing, stood on this spot during the Roman Period, and that it featured two large pools surrounded and separated by colonnaded porches. The pagan temple apparently was replaced during the Byzantine Period by a large church that commemorated Jesus' healing miracle. This Byzantine church was followed by the smaller Crusader church. It was the Crusaders also who built the beautiful Church of Saint Anne nearby. Fortunately, after expelling the Crusaders, Saladin converted the Church of Saint Anne into a madrassa (Islamic school). Consequently, it has survived in pristine condition, and with stunning acoustics.

The Via Dolorosa

Christian pilgrims to Jerusalem through the centuries have attempted to discern and follow the stages of Jesus' passion from trial to crucifixion. It has been generally supposed that he was taken before Pilate in the Antonia Fortress for trial, where he was condemned, scourged, and forced to take up the cross. The trail of the cross would have led from there to Golgotha and the nearby tomb, both reclaimed by early fourth-century Christians, as described by Eusebius. After the Crusades, when Latin Christians were less welcome in Mamluk Jerusalem, Christians in Europe began the practice of placing small shrines inside and outside churches and monasteries to serve as remembrances of the stages of Jesus' passion.

Without actually making the long and dangerous journey to Jerusalem, one could make a symbolic pilgrimage, stopping to pray at each of the Stations of the Cross. Gradually, during the seventeenth and eighteenth centuries, the number and sequence of the stations were standardized to fourteen. It would have been about that time also that fourteen Stations of the Cross were marked through Jerusalem's narrow streets—from the approximate location of the Antonia to the Church of the Holy Sepulchre. This trail is known as the Via Dolorosa (Latin for "Way of Sorrow").

The site of the Antonia is covered today by several buildings (al-Omariya Elementary School, Franciscan Biblical School, Sisters of Zion Convent). The pattern of streets between the Antonia and the site of the Church of the Holy Sepulchre has changed since Roman times. Nevertheless, assuming that Jesus was taken to Pilate in the Antonia, and that the early fourth-century Christians remembered correctly where Jesus had been crucified and buried, the Via Dolorosa must represent the approximate route that Jesus carried the cross from condemnation to crucifixion.

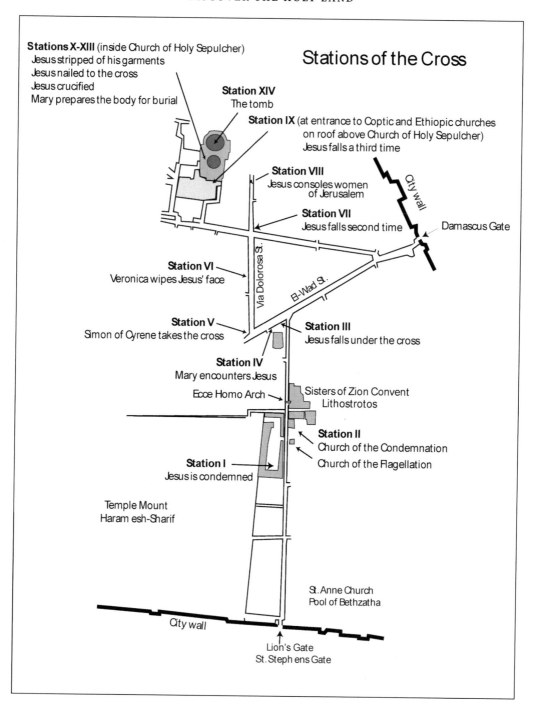

Stations X-XIII (inside Church of Holy Sepulcher)
Jesus stripped of his garments
Jesus nailed to the cross
Jesus crucified
Mary prepares the body for burial

Stations of the Cross

Station XIV
The tomb

Station IX (at entrance to Coptic and Ethiopic churches
on roof above Church of Holy Sepulcher)
Jesus falls a third time

Station VIII
Jesus consoles women
of Jerusalem

Station VII
Jesus falls second time

City wall

Damascus Gate

Station VI
Veronica wipes Jesus' face

Via Dolorosa St.

El-Wad St.

Station V
Simon of Cyrene takes the cross

Station III
Jesus falls under the cross

Station IV
Mary encounters Jesus

Ecce Homo Arch

Sisters of Zion Convent
Lithostrotos

Station II
Church of the Condemnation
Church of the Flagellation

Station I
Jesus is condemned

Temple Mount
Haram esh-Sharif

St. Anne Church
Pool of Bethzatha

City wall

Lion's Gate
St. Stephens Gate

Stations of the Cross

1st Station: In the al-Omariya School (not accessible). *Jesus is condemned in the Antonia Fortress.*

2nd Station: Franciscan Chapel of Flagellation and Chapel of Condemnation. *Jesus scourged and given the cross to bear.*

[**Ecce Homo Arch, between 2nd and 3rd stations:** Traditional spot where Jesus is presented in mock royalty (with a crown of thorns and in a purple robe) and Pilate says, "Behold the man." Nearby is the Church of the Sisters of Zion, and beneath that the Lithostrotos, earlier thought to be pavement from the time of Jesus. Actually, both the Ecce Homo Arch and the Lithostrotos date from a later phase of the city—Hadrian's Aelia Capitolina. The arch served as entrance to one of the city's marketplaces. Lines etched in the pavement apparently are from soldiers' games. Interesting also is the massive water cistern.]

3rd Station: Polish chapel immediately after turning the corner onto El-Wad Street. *Jesus falls under the cross.*

4th Station: Armenian Church of Our Lady of the Spasm. *The Virgin Mary encounters Jesus.*

5th Station: Franciscan Chapel at corner of El-Wad St. and the continuation (turn to the right) of Via Dolorosa. *Simon of Cyrene takes the cross.*

6th Station: Chapel of Saint Veronica, served by the Little Sisters, a Greek Catholic order: *Veronica wipes the blood and dirt from Jesus' face with her veil, leaving the imprint of his face on it.* The original cloth is kept in Saint Peter's Cathedral in Rome.

7th Station: Two chapels are connected. Note the column base near the entrance, which is a continuation of the Cardo. *Jesus falls a second time.* At this spot, it is believed, Jesus passed through the Gate of Judgment, leaving the city on his way to Golgotha.

8th Station: On the wall of the Greek monastery of Saint Charalambos, a stone with a Latin cross and inscription: "Jesus Christ is victorious." *Jesus consoles the crying women of Jerusalem.*

9th Station: A column built into the door of the Coptic church (on the roof of the Church of the Holy Sepulchre) *Jesus falls a third time, now within view of the place of crucifixion.*

[The remaining stations are inside the Church of the Holy Sepulchre, which encompasses both Golgotha and the tomb. When you enter the church, Golgotha is to your right, and stations 10, 11, and 12 are in chapels above Golgotha.]

10th Station: Chapel of the Divestiture. *Jesus is stripped of his garments.*

11th Station: Roman Catholic chapel above Golgotha, marked by beautiful mosaics. *Jesus is nailed to the cross.*

12th Station: Greek Orthodox altar and beneath it a silver disc marking the spot of the cross. *Jesus is crucified.*

[Near the Greek Orthodox altar is a Franciscan altar with a seventeenth-century wooden bust of Mary in sorrow ("Mater Dolorosa"). This statue was presented by the Queen of Portugal in 1778.]

13th Station: Stone of Unction (anointing). This is straight ahead as you enter the church. *Mary receives the body of Jesus after he is taken down from the cross and anoints it for burial.*

14th Station: The tomb.

Entrance to the Church of the Holy Sepulchre

The Church of the Holy Sepulchre

Soon after the Council of Nicaea in 325 CE, Constantine commissioned the building of a church over what early Christians believed to be the place of Jesus' crucifixion and tomb. According to Eusebius, bishop of Caesarea at the time, the place of the tomb had been covered with soil, paved, and desecrated with a temple to Venus.

> This sacred cave, then, certain impious and godless persons had thought to remove entirely from the eyes of men, supposing in their folly that thus they should be able effectually to obscure the truth. Accordingly, they brought a quantity of earth from a distance with much labor, and covered the entire spot; then, having raised this to a moderate height, they paved it with stone, concealing the holy cave beneath this massive mound. Then, as though their purpose had been effectually accomplished, they prepared on this foundation a truly dreadful sepulcher of souls, by building a gloomy shrine of lifeless idols to the impure spirit whom they call Venus, and offering detestable oblations therein on profane and accursed altars. (*Life of Constantine*, book 3, ch. 26)

Eusebius's account describes how at Constantine's command the pagan temple was demolished and even the polluted soil was transported to a far distance.

> This also was accomplished without delay. But as soon as the original surface of the ground, beneath the covering of earth, appeared, immediately, and contrary to all expectations, the venerable and hallowed monument of our Savior's resurrection was discovered... Immediately after the transaction I have recorded, the emperor sent forth injunctions which breathed a truly pious spirit, at the same time granting ample supplies of money, and commanding that a house of prayer worthy of worship of God should be erected near the Savior's tomb on a scale of rich royal greatness. (*Life of Constantine*, book 3, ch. 28)

Somewhat later there arose a tradition that Helena, Constantine's mother, had been involved in the discovery of the tomb, and that she had actually found the "true cross" in a cistern nearby.

According to Muslim tradition, Sophronius, patriarch of Jerusalem, was showing Caliph Omar around the Church of the Holy Sepulchre after the latter had taken Jerusalem in 637 CE, when they heard the Muslim call for prayer. Sophronius offered Omar a place in the church to pray and laid out a straw mat. But Omar declined, lest future Muslims claim possession of the church and convert it to a mosque. He exited the church, threw a stone, and prayed where the stone landed. On that same spot was built the Mosque of Omar.

The tomb of Jesus

This Church of the Holy Sepulchre has been damaged, restored, and modified time and again over the years. It was almost completely destroyed when the Fatimid caliph al-Hakim (996–1021) ordered the destruction of all churches throughout the Fatimid realm. What originally were two adjacent churches marking the traditional locations of Jesus' crucifixion (Golgotha) and burial (Joseph of Arimathea's tomb) were combined under one roof during the Crusader Period.

Minaret of the Mosque of Omar viewed from the entrance to the Church
of the Holy Sepulchre. It is only a "stone's throw" away.

The Garden Tomb

Edward Robinson, a leading nineteenth-century biblical scholar who has been called the father of biblical archaeology, contended that the Church of the Holy Sepulchre probably is not the correct location of Golgotha and the tomb. This was unlikely, in his opinion, because crucifixions and burials would have taken place outside the city walls during Roman times, and he believed that the site where the Church of the Nativity is built would have been inside the Roman Period walls. Toward the end of the nineteenth century, prompted by Robinson's argument, and popularized by the British Major-General Charles George Gordon, an alternative site was proposed for Golgotha and Jesus' tomb. Located north of the Damascus Gate and clearly outside the Roman Period city walls, this alternative site is known as the Garden Tomb or Gordon's tomb. It is a beautiful spot, especially popular among Protestants, and well worth a visit.

Neither the Church of the Holy Sepulchre nor the Garden Tomb can claim firm archaeological support. But the former does rest on Christian tradition going back to the fourth century whereas the latter is a relatively recent "traditional site" in the making. Other tombs have since been discovered at the Holy Sepulchre site, which seems to undercut Robinson's argument, but it may not be entirely certain that these tombs date from the Roman Period.

Museums in Jerusalem

In one sense Jerusalem itself is a vast museum. Simply to walk through the narrow streets of the Old City is a moving experience; the sights, sounds, and smells will be remembered and enjoyed for years to come. The Rockefeller Museum, just outside the northeast corner of the Old City walls, was the archaeological museum for Palestine during the British Mandate Period. Many artifacts from excavations conducted prior to the mid-1940s are displayed there. Some materials have been added since the 1940s, but most of the later artifacts are in either the Israel Museum near the Knesset building or the Jordan Museum in Amman.

The Israel Museum is nothing less than fabulous and includes on its grounds: the Bible Lands Museum, the Shrine of the Book, and a scale model of Second Temple Jerusalem. The Shrine of the Book displays Dead Sea Scrolls in a building specifically designed for that purpose. The Second Temple model is an excellent visual presentation of Jerusalem as it stood in the mid-first century CE, the time of Jesus' ministry and soon before the First Jewish Revolt. The Tower of David Museum, located in the medieval citadel next to the Jaffa Gate, focuses on the history of Jerusalem from earliest times to the present. And finally, there is the Holocaust museum, Yad V'Shem ("a hand and a name"). Allow at least two hours for this one.

A model of Roman Jerusalem

Bethlehem

Bethlehem is a short drive south of Jerusalem's Old City. But travel there requires passing through the security wall and checkpoint into the West Bank, Zone A, which is under Palestinian Authority administration. Bethlehem, Beit Jala, and Beit Sahur were once three neighboring villages, mostly Christian. Now they are three modest-size cities that run together, mostly Muslim. As you approach Bethlehem from Jerusalem, look in the distance to the southeast for a steep, isolated mountain. This is the Herodium, a fort built by Herod the Great at the edge of the Judean Wilderness. The Herodium had a double circular defensive wall strengthened by four towers. Josephus reports that Herod was buried there, and an underground chamber recently excavated among the ruins may have held his tomb. On the opposite (eastern) side of the Dead Sea is Machaerus, where Herod's son Herod Antipas imprisoned and executed John the Baptist. Near the checkpoint entry to Bethlehem is the traditional tomb of Rachel (see Gen 35:16–20). Before 1967 this was a Muslim shrine; now it is a heavily fortified Jewish shrine.

Bethlehem is an important Christian pilgrimage destination for three reasons. It was King David's ancestral home (see Ruth; 1 Sam 16; 2 Sam 23). According to Matthew and Luke, Jesus also was born there (Matt 2:1–16; Luke 2:4–15). And in 330 CE, Constantine founded the Church of the Nativity above the traditional spot of Jesus' birth. According to Jerome, who resided at Bethlehem from 388 until his death in 420 CE and translated the Vulgate (the Latin Bible) there, a grove sacred to Tammuz (Adonis) obscured the birth place during the two centuries between Hadrian's reign and the founding of the church.

In Bethlehem, behind the security wall

Grotto of the Nativity. Present-day pilgrims stand in reverence
before the shrine with a star that marks the place of Jesus' birth.

Once when David and his band of rebels were on the run from King Saul, roaming the dry and barren Judean Wilderness while a Philistine garrison held Bethlehem, he longed for a drink of water from the well in his hometown.

> David was then in the stronghold; and the garrison of the Philistines was then at Bethlehem. David said longingly, "O that someone would give me water to drink from the well of Bethlehem that is by the gate!" Then the three warriors broke through the camp of the Philistines, drew water from the well of Bethlehem that was by the gate, and brought it to David. But he would not drink of it; he poured it out to the LORD, for he said, "The LORD forbid that I should do this. Can I drink the blood of the men who went at the risk of their lives?" (2 Sam 23:14–17)

According to John 7:41–42 there were those who hesitated to accept Jesus as the Messiah because he was from Nazareth. This conflicted with the belief that the Messiah would be a descendant of David and come from Bethlehem: "Others said, 'This is the Messiah.' But some asked, 'Surely the Messiah does not come from Galilee, does he? Has not the scripture said that the Messiah is descended from David and comes from Bethlehem, the village where David lived?'" Matthew and Luke addressed this issue, explaining that while Jesus grew up in Nazareth he actually was born in Bethlehem. Yet their explanations as to how this happened differ somewhat.

Entrance to the Church of Nativity and detail of its shrine that marks the place of Jesus' birth

Matthew places Jesus' birth during the reign of Herod the Great and seems to imply that the holy family was originally from Bethlehem. They fled to Egypt, returned after Herod the Great's death (which occurred in 4 BCE), and decided to make their home in Nazareth in order to avoid living under Herod Archelaus.

> Then Joseph got up, took the child and his mother, and went to the land of Israel. But when he heard that Archelaus was ruling over Judea in place of his father Herod, he was afraid to go there. And after being warned in a dream, he went away to the district of Galilee. There he made his home in a town called Nazareth, so that what had been spoken through the prophets might be fulfilled, "He will be called a Nazorean." (Matt 2:21–23)

Luke, on the other hand, places Jesus' birth during the governorship of Quirinius (which began in 6 CE), and has the holy family making a journey from their home in Nazareth to Bethlehem in order for Joseph to register.

> In those days a decree went out from Emperor Augustus that all the world should be registered. This was the first registration and was taken while Quirinius was governor of Syria. All went to their own towns to be registered. Joseph also went from the town of Nazareth in Galilee to Judea, to the city of David called Bethlehem, because he was descended from the house and family of David. (Luke 2:1–4)

Historically the various branches of Christian clergy have not gotten along well in the Middle East. Nowhere has this been more evident than at the Church of the Holy Sepulchre in Jerusalem and the Church of the Nativity in Bethlehem. In Jerusalem, privileges are shared by the Eastern Orthodox, Roman Catholics (Franciscans), Armenians, Syrian (or Syriac) Orthodox, Copts, and Ethiopians. In Bethlehem, privileges are shared by the Eastern Orthodox, Roman Catholics, and Armenians. In 1757, Eastern Orthodox priests at the Church of the Nativity encroached on some of the rights previously held by the Franciscans. Then in 1847, almost a century later, Eastern Orthodox priests removed the star with its Latin inscription from the grotto of Jesus' birth. The Franciscans appealed to the French ambassador in Istanbul, who pressured the Ottoman Sultan Abdul Mecit I to restore to the Franciscans their pre-1757 privileges. But then in 1852, championing the Eastern Orthodox cause, Tzar Nicholas I of Russia forced Abdul Mecit to issue a *firman* (official decree), known as the *Status Quo*. It reinstated the post-1757 practices and granted still other Eastern Orthodox demands. This conflict and the *Status Quo* firman contributed to the outbreak of the Crimean War (1854–1856), and the *Status Quo* was reaffirmed by the treaty that concluded that war. It remains in effect still today, defining and regulating the privileges that the different clergy groups enjoy in both the Church of the Nativity and the Church of the Holy Sepulchre.

Historical Highlights of the Church of the Nativity

- 339 CE—Original Church of the Nativity was completed, having been commissioned by Constantine and his mother, Helena. A fragment of Mosaic floor preserved beneath the present floor probably belonged to this original church. This original church was largely destroyed during anti-Byzantine disturbances early in Justinian's reign.

- 557–565—Justinian repaired and expanded the church. The nave and Corinthian columns date from this building phase.

- 614—Most Christian churches in Palestine were destroyed by Persian invaders, but the Church of the Nativity was spared, probably because of mosaics on its interior walls that depicted the wise men, whom the Persian soldiers associated with their own priests.

- 1169—The Crusaders made restorations and enhanced the church with decorations. The recently restored wall mosaics were commissioned by the Crusader king Almaric I and Byzantine emperor Manuel Comnenus. The grey marble slab floor probably dates from the Crusader Period.

- Mamluk Period (mid-thirteenth century and following)—Entrance to the church was reduced in size to prevent entry on horseback.

- 1448–1480—Church of the Nativity was in poor condition, several European states provided resources for repair.

- 1847–1855—Conflict between Greek Orthodox priests and Franciscans contributed to the outbreak of the Crimean war (1854–1856). The treaty concluding the war reaffirmed the status quo firman that Ottoman sultan Merit had issued in 1852. This *Status Quo* arrangement remains in effect still today.

Christian pilgrims through the ages have associated the angelic appearance to shepherds on the night of Jesus' birth (Luke 2:8–20) with the slopes and fields east of Bethlehem, where the Central Hill Country begins to give way to the Judean Wilderness. John Wilkinson traces the following description preserved in a twelfth-century source to the fourth-century pilgrim Egeria.

> Not far from there [Bethlehem] is the church called At the Shepherds. A big garden is there now, protected by a neat wall all round, and also there is a very splendid cave with an altar. It is the place where the angels appeared to the shepherds as they kept watch, and brought them the news of Christ's birth. (Wilkinson, *Egeria's Travels*, p 90)

Present-day pilgrims usually visit either of two Shepherds' Fields, one Roman Catholic maintained by Franciscans and the other Greek Orthodox. Both sites exhibit church and monastery remains dating back to the Byzantine Period. Both have large caves that may have been used to shelter sheep during times past. And both sites are enhanced by modern churches that focus thematically on the angels' appearance. The Roman Catholic church was designed by Antonio Barluzzi to imitate a shepherd's tent.

From Jerusalem to Caesarea Maritima

The book of Acts continues Luke's Gospel with an account of the postresurrection circle of believers in Jerusalem and the beginnings of apostolic activities. Three places between Jerusalem and Caesarea Maritima figure prominently in the Acts account: Emmaus, Lydda, and Joppa. Caesarea Maritima itself emerges as the hub of the early apostolic movement.

Emmaus

Luke 24:13–35 tells how Jesus appeared to two men who were walking on their way toward Emmaus and talking about the recent events that had led to Jesus' crucifixion. Jesus joined them without revealing his identity and listened while they described how angels had appeared that morning to some women who visited the tomb and found it empty. Then Jesus began to interpret for them the meaning of the events: "Oh, how foolish you are, and how slow of heart to believe all that the prophets have declared!" (v. 25). As they reached Emmaus, the men invited Jesus to stay with them for the evening. Finally, at the evening meal when Jesus broke the bread, blessed it, and gave it to them: "Then their eyes were opened, and they recognized him; and he vanished from their sight" (v. 31) "They said to each other, 'Were not our hearts burning within us while he was talking to us on the road, while he was opening the scriptures to us?'" (v. 32).

The Emmaus mentioned in this passage has not been located with certainty for two reasons. First, Emmaus was a fairly common appellative name—the Greek and Latin form of Semitic *Hama* (variants include *Hamath* or *Hamat*), which referred to a warm spring or a bath. So more than one place will have gone by that name or some variation of it. Second, there is a discrepancy in the manuscript readings for Luke 24:13. Some manuscripts read: "a village called Emmaus, about *sixty stadia* from Jerusalem." Others read: "a village called Emmaus about *a hundred and sixty stadia* from Jerusalem." The manuscript traditions generally considered to be most trustworthy favor the shorter distance: sixty stadia or about seven miles. Three candidates come into play in this case: Abu Gosh and Qaloniyeh, both west of Jerusalem, and el-Qubeibeh, more to the northwest of Jerusalem.

For the longer distance—a hundred and sixty stadia, or about twenty miles—the obvious candidate is ancient Nicopolis, represented by ruins north of the Latrun Monastery and near the Canadian Park. These ruins date largely from the late Byzantine

Period (fifth century to seventh century), but are dominated by a Crusader-era rebuild on a smaller scale of a Byzantine church. Whether or not this is the Emmaus of Luke's Gospel, Nicopolis apparently did go by the name Emmaus during New Testament times, and it appears as such in 1 Macc. 3:40—4:15. The name was changed to Nicopolis ("city of victory") in the third century by the Roman emperor Elagabalus (reigned 218–222 CE). Arab villagers who occupied the site centuries later called it Amwas—i.e., an Arab pronunciation of Emmaus. Their descendants lost most of their land with the establishment of modern Israel. Arabs who remain in the vicinity find jobs either on Israeli farms or in construction work.

Emmaus: Abu Gosh

Authentic or not, Nicopolis/Amwas is the site that most Christian pilgrims from the fourth century forward took to be the New Testament Emmaus. And it is the one favored by both Eusebius and Jerome. Yet the possibility remains that Luke's Emmaus was one of the places by that name nearer to Jerusalem, but that for whatever reason pilgrims began to come to the Nicopolis site instead, and some of the early manuscripts of Luke's Gospel were corrected to fit.

Emmaus: Nicopolis

Lod/Lydda

Approximately five miles south-southeast of the Ben Gurion Airport is the site of ancient Lod (1 Chr 8:12). It appears in the New Testament with Greek pronunciation as Lydda. According to Acts 9:32–25, Peter visited the early believers in Lydda and healed Aeneas who had been paralyzed and bedridden for eight years. All the people of the village and surrounding area saw him and were converted.

Saint George, the soldier saint, was revered especially among eastern Christians before the Crusades. Details of his life and martyrdom are obscure, but he also is associated with Lydda. The most popular medieval story about Saint George, *The Golden Legend,* probably was compiled during the thirteenth century as the Crusades were winding down. It identifies him as a knight from Cappadocia who rescued a maiden princess from a dragon in Libya. This led to many converts in that region, according to *The Golden Legend,* and eventually to Saint George's own torture and beheading during Diocletian's persecutions. So how did a knight from Cappadocia come to be associated with both Libya and Lydda, and kill a dragon in the process? Possibly folk memory has entangled stories about more than one martyred Saint George, along with the Perseus and Andromeda myth (see below).

Approximately eight miles south of the Ben Gurion Airport is the site of Ramla. Founded by the Umayyad caliph Suleiman ca. 700 CE, Ramla served as an important administrative and commercial center along the coastal route (Via Maris) between Damascus and Fustat (predecessor to Cairo). Both Lod and Ramla were Arab towns before the establishment of modern Israel, at which time most of the Arab population from both towns was displaced.

Joppa (Jaffa, Tel Aviv)

Ancient Joppa, present-day Jaffa in Arabic, and Yafe in Hebrew, was situated on a high hill with a good overview of the sea. The ancient Semitic name meant "beautiful." A chain of rocks in the sea created a small natural harbor for ancient vessels, but one that had to be entered carefully from the open sea through a gap between sharp rocks.

Jaffa's harbor was protected by offshore rocks

This was the scene of one of Perseus's adventures in Greek mythology. Cepheus was the Ethiopian king of Joppa. His wife Cassiopeia boasted that she and her daughter Andromeda were more beautiful than the Nereids (sea nymphs). The Nereids complained to Poseidon, who sent a flood upon Joppa, and also a female sea monster that devastated all of the surrounding coastal region. Cepheus consulted an oracle and was told that, for relief from the monster, he must sacrifice Andromeda to the monster. So he had Andromeda bound to one of the rocks and left her for the monster to devour. Perseus, passing by on his way from Egypt, saw the naked maiden bound to the rock with Cepheus and Cassiopeia watching from the shore. He fell in love with the maiden on the spot, negotiated with her parents for marriage if he could save her, and killed the monster. As suggested above, this myth may have contributed the dragon episode to the folk memory of Saint George of Lydda, less than twenty miles away.

Another story associated with Joppa probably has more historical basis, although perhaps much enhanced in the retelling. Papyrus Harris 500 includes a portion of a tale about the taking of Joppa by an Egyptian general named Djehuti. According to the tale, Djehuti smuggled soldiers into the city by hiding them in big clay jars, supposedly filled with produce intended for the city market. Once inside the city, the soldiers climbed out of the jars and captured it. Most scholars think this story would have had its setting during the reign of Tuthmosis III (ca. 1457–1425 BCE), the same pharaoh who claimed victory at Megiddo and may have campaigned in the Transjordan.

Joppa appears several times in the Old Testament. Cedar was shipped from Lebanon to Joppa and from there to Jerusalem for Solomon's temple (2 Chr 2:16). Jonah fled to Joppa and boarded a ship to Tarshish rather than honor God's command to preach to the Assyrians (Jonah 1:3). In the New Testament, Peter's evangelizing moved from Lydda (Acts 9: 32–35) to Joppa (Acts 9:36—10:23) and from there to Caesarea Maritima (Acts 11). At Joppa, he revived Tabitha/Dorcas, resided with Simon the tanner, and had a dream that prepared him to receive Cornelius's messengers.

Jewish immigrants inspired by the Zionist dream founded a settlement on the outskirts of Jaffa in 1909 and named it Tel Aviv. Theodore Herzl, one of the chief founders of Zionism, had written a book titled *Altneuland* (*Old-New Land*). Among the Babylonian cities where Jews were resettled during the exile was one named Tel Abib (Ezek 3:15), which could be taken to suggest a combination of "old" and "new." A *tell* (Hebrew *tel*) is of course a mound containing the stratified remains of an ancient city; *Abib* or *Aviv* is a spring, which implies freshness, constant renewal. The name Tel Aviv was chosen for the new settlement, which grew into a city and in 1950 was merged with Jaffa. Now Jaffa is essentially an older section of metropolitan Tel Aviv.

Caesarea Maritima

Perhaps more than any other place, Caesarea Maritima illustrates and symbolizes the Roman Empire setting of the gospel narratives and Acts of the Apostles. The gospel narratives unfold in small Galilean villages and Jerusalem for the most part, so they make no actual mention of Caesarea Maritima. But this important city was the headquarters of Roman administration in Palestine and the commercial center of the region, thus very much in the background throughout Jesus's earthly ministry. Also, it was the main gateway port to the Roman world beyond Palestine, so when the first apostles set out to spread the Christian message to that broader Roman world, Caesarea Maritima served as the hub of their missionary activities.

Caesarea Maritima was named after Caesar Augustus and built by Herod the Great, both of whom had long reigns, significantly transformed their respective realms, and initiated dynasties that dominated political affairs in Palestine while the New Testament events unfolded. Herod the Great's successors, the Herodian Dynasty, ruled locally in Palestine, but subject to Augustus's successors, the Julio-Claudian Dynasty, that ruled from Rome. Caesarea Maritima is an ideal place to review connections between the Roman emperors, Herodian rulers, and New Testament events because Caesarea Maritima played a central role in that story and is crucial for understanding it.

Caesar Augustus, after whom both Caesarea Maritima
and Caesarea Philippi were named

Caesar Augustus and Herod the Great

Augustus's long and prosperous reign (27 BCE—14 CE), remembered as the Age of Augustus, was a threshold moment in Roman history. Under Augustus the Roman Republic gave way completely to Imperial Rome—an empire ruled by emperors with virtually unlimited power. In spite of some really bad emperors who followed Augustus, the empire remained generally stable and internally secure for more than two centuries ahead, a situation known as the Roman Peace (Pax Romana). According to Luke's

Gospel an even more wondrous event also occurred during the Age of Augustus that was a threshold moment for all of human history, the birth of Jesus (Luke 2:1).

Herod, who had been loyal to Mark Antony before the Battle of Actium and Mark Antony's suicide, affirmed his allegiance now to Augustus and continued to rule as a totally loyal client king to Rome. And having built a fortification in Jerusalem and named it the Antonia after Mark Antony, he began building this port city in 22 BCE to be named Caesarea after Caesar Augustus. Augustus expanded Herod's realm over the course of Herod's long reign (37–4 BCE) so that eventually Herod's kingdom included virtually all of Palestine west of the Jordan River and considerable territories in the Transjordan. Herod gained great wealth, undertook major building projects, and came to be known as Herod the Great. I have described already how he rebuilt and expanded the city of Samaria, added a temple dedicated to Augustus, and renamed that city Sebaste (the Greek equivalent of Augustus). Herod built the Augusteum at Paneas, which his son Philip later renamed Caesarea in honor of Augustus. Herod lavishly rebuilt the Second Temple in Jerusalem and surrounded it with the massive temple compound protected by the Antonia fort. He also funded building projects, festivals, and games in various other cities outside his kingdom (in Athens, Rhodes, Antioch, and Damascus, among other places).

Herod's Caesarea

Herod envisioned Caesarea Maritima as a port city and chose for its location a site on the sandy coast south of present-day Haifa. This segment of the Palestinian coast had been controlled by various rulers, most recently by Cleopatra. And a landmark structure known as Straton's Tower had stood at the site selected. But there was neither water for a city nor a natural seaport, so Herod's builders constructed a long aqueduct to bring water from the foothills of Mount Carmel, and a massive artificial harbor. Various other structures typical of Roman cities were added—a theater, hippodrome (horserace track), palace, and a temple dedicated to Caesar Augustus and Roma (Rome's city goddess), which looked out over the harbor toward Rome. Caesarea Maritima would serve as the chief commercial and administrative city of Palestine through the remainder of the Roman Period and the Byzantine Period. It would be expanded and modified over time, so some of the archaeological remains visible at the site today represent later Roman or Byzantine construction. But through the Byzantine Period the basic layout of the city remained much as Herod the Great had set it up.

Caesarea Maritima: Overview of the excavated area

Pontius Pilate at Caesarea.

At Herod's death, when his kingdom was divided among his three surviving sons (Herod Archelaus, Herod Antipas, and Herod Philip), Archelaus received the larger portion with the title ethnarch. His ethnarchy included Judah, Idumea, and Samaria. Archelaus proved to be a problematic and cruel ruler, however, so Augustus exiled him in 6 CE. After that, the territory of Archelaus's ethnarchy was administered by Roman governors who resided in Caesarea. Among these was Pontius Pilate, and an inscription pertaining to Pilate has been discovered at Caesarea. Jesus' ministry unfolded during the generation following Herod the Great. The Herods he knew were Herod Antipas and Herod Philip. Pontius Pilate had come from Caesarea to Jerusalem to be on hand at the time of the Passover, which explains why he was in Jerusalem for Jesus' trial and crucifixion.

Caesarea Maritima in the Book of Acts

Roman governors residing in Caesarea Maritima continued to administer Archelaus's former ethnarchy until Claudius added this territory to the kingdom of Herod Agrippa I in 41 CE. Meanwhile, Herod Philip had died in 34 CE, Herod Antipas had been exiled in 39 CE, and Claudius's predecessor Caligula had granted their territories to Agrippa. For a short time, therefore, until Agrippa's death in 44 CE, Herod the Great's former kingdom was reconstituted under the rule of his grandson Herod Agrippa I. After Agrippa's death, former Herodian Palestine reverted to direct Roman administration and was governed by Roman proconsuls residing in Caesarea Maritima, until the Jewish Revolt in 66 CE. There was one notable exception. Claudius transferred the area of Paneas/Caesarea Philippi to Agrippa's son Herod Agrippa II shortly before his own death in 54 CE.

[CAESARIEN] S [IBUS]   To the people of Caesarea
TIBERIEUM   Tiberium
PON]TIUS PILATUS   Pontius Pilate
PRAEF]ECTUSIUDA[EA]E   Prefect of Judea

Facsimile of the Pontius Pilate inscription discovered at Caesarea Maritima

It was against this political background that the events described in the book of Acts unfolded. The earliest apostles set out from Jerusalem but eventually found their way to Caesarea Maritima. Philip preached to the villagers in Samaria, turned next to Gaza, and preached his way from Azotus (Ashdod) to Caesarea (Acts 8:4–40). Peter followed Philip to Samaria, healed Aeneas in Lydda, and went from there to Joppa, whence he answered Cornelius's call to come to Caesarea (Acts 9:32—10:48). Herod Agrippa I probably resided in Caesarea Maritima most of the time, and he was the Agrippa who, according to Acts 12, executed James the brother of John, imprisoned Peter, and died a terrible death: "On the appointed day Herod, wearing his royal robes, sat on his throne and delivered a public address to the people. They shouted, 'This is the voice of a god, not of a man.' Immediately, because Herod did not give praise to God, an angel of the Lord struck him down, and he was eaten by worms and died" (Acts 12:21–23). Josephus provides an alternate account of Agrippa's horrible death (*Ant.*19:343–52).

Paul's Trial before Felix Festus and Agrippa II

Although the chronology of Paul's career remains somewhat uncertain, his conversion and time in Damascus, preaching and disputation with Hellenists in Jerusalem, and his return his home to Tarsus (Acts 9:1–30) must have occurred during the 30s and early 40s CE, probably before the death of Herod Agrippa I. His missionary journeys described in Acts 13–28 would have occurred during the late 40s and 50s CE, during the reigns of Claudius (41–54 CE) and Nero (54–68 CE), with most of Palestine again governed by Roman officials residing in Caesarea Maritima. Among these were Antonius Felix followed by Porcius Festus.

Having returned to Jerusalem after his third missionary journey, Paul was accused of bringing a Gentile into the temple. This roused an angry mob, and Roman soldiers arrested Paul for his own protection. But the tribune allowed him to address the crowd, which made matters only worse. About to be scourged, Paul made it known that he was a Roman citizen. Next came a hearing before the chief priests and council, followed by another eruption of religious anger, and word of a plot to kill Paul. At his wit's end, and aware that he was responsible for the safety of this Roman citizen, the tribune sent Paul by night and under heavy guard to Antonius Felix in Caesarea Maritima (Acts 21:29—23:35).

Ananias the high priest and other elders followed from Jerusalem to make their case against Paul before Felix. Paul made his defense. Felix apparently realized that Paul had done nothing deserving of punishment, but did not wish to offend the Jews, and at the same time hoping Paul would offer a bribe, delayed his decision for two years. Paul spent two years in Caesarea, therefore, during which time he probably was allowed some freedom of movement around the city rather than being confined in prison (Acts 24:1–27).

After two years, Porcius Festus arrived to replace Felix as governor. Agrippa II and his sister Bernice came to add their welcome to the new governor. At Agrippa's request, Paul was called in to make his defense before Felix, Festus, Agrippa II, Bernice, the military tribunes, and other prominent men of the city (Acts 25–26). Then he was sent by ship to Rome for trial before the emperor (Acts 27–28). This would have been approximately 60 CE, during Nero's reign. The book of Acts concludes with Paul in Rome, apparently having been there for about two years. According to early Christian tradition, both Paul and Peter were martyred in Rome.

Caesarea Maritima: Foundations of the palace

Whether the gospel applied to Gentiles as well as to Jews was a controversial issue for early Jewish Christians. Both Peter and Paul concluded that it did, but this would have been a much more radical and difficult decision for Peter than for Paul. Peter was an orthodox Jew from a small fishing village, who would have been taught from child-hood to follow specific food laws, avoid close contact with non-Jews, and certainly never to sit and eat with Gentiles. Breaking the food laws and preaching the gospel to a Roman soldier would not have come easy for him, and one wonders whether he was ever entirely comfortable with the idea. On the other hand, as a Roman citizen by birth, having grown up in Tarsus of Cilicia (one of the empire's important crossroads cities), well educated beyond his Jewish religious training, and at least bilingual, Paul likely found it the natural thing to do. Already before setting out on his missionary journeys Paul had preached the gospel to Hellenist Jews in Jerusalem (Acts 9:29). Preaching to "Godfearers"—Gentiles who turned to synagogues in search of religious truth (Acts 13:26)—would have been a natural next step.

The First Jewish Revolt

Caesarea Maritima had a mixed Jewish-Gentile population. They were constantly at odds with each other, with occasional riots on both sides. According to Josephus, it was one such incident that touched off the First Jewish Revolt in 66 CE.

> War broke out in the twelfth year of Nero's reign and the seventeenth of Agrip-
> pa's [Agrippa II], in the month of May. In comparison with the fearful disasters

to which it led, its pretext was insignificant. The Jews in Caesarea had a synagogue alongside a piece of ground belonging to a Greek citizen. This they had repeatedly tried to acquire, offering many times the real value. Scorning their requests, the Greeks further insulted them by beginning to build a factory right up to the dividing line, leaving them a narrow and utterly inadequate passage. The immediate result was that the more hot-headed of the young men jumped in and interfered with the builders. When this display of force was suppressed by Florus [Roman governor of Judea after Felix and Festus], the leading Jews, among them John the tax-collector, having no other way out, gave Florus a bribe of 8 silver talents to put a stop to the work. As nothing mattered to him but money, he promised full co-operation; but as soon as the money was his, he left Caesarea for Sebaste, allowing party strife to take its course as if he had sold the Jews permission to fight it out!

The next day was a sabbath, and when the Jews gathered in the synagogue, a Caesarean partisan had placed a large earthen vessel upside down at the entrance and was sacrificing birds on it. This infuriated the Jews, . . . [For the rest of the story, read Josephus, *The Jewish War* 2:284ff. (Penguin ed., 142ff.)]

This incident touched off a revolt that spread rapidly throughout Judea. Nero sent Vespasian to suppress the revolt, and he and his son Titus used Caesarea Maritima as their main military base while conducting the war. According to Josephus, twenty thousand Jews were slaughtered in Caesarea itself within an hour. Jerusalem fell to Titus and the temple was destroyed in 70 CE. Jewish rebels held out at Masada until 73.

Caesarea Maritima: The Mithraeum

Origen at Caesarea

Christianity spread across the Roman Empire with increasing momentum over the next century and half. Organization and structure followed quickly—the offices of bishop, presbyter, deacon, deaconess emerged. Caesarea Maritima and Jerusalem became the main Christian centers in Palestine. In 215 CE, the bishops of these two centers invited Origen, a rising Christian theologian in Alexandria, to visit and teach in Caesarea.

Christianity and Influential Theologians from the Jewish Revolt to Origen

Late 1st century—The Flavian Dynasty ruled in Rome (Vespasian, Titus, Domitian). Most of the New Testament books probably were written toward the end of this first century, while the Christian movement separated more distinctly from Judaism. The authentic letters of Paul would have been written earlier, and perhaps some of the New Testament books (2 Peter, 1–3 John) were written as late as the early second century.

Early 2nd century—Era of the good emperors (Trajan, Hadrian, Antoninus Pius, Marcus Aurelius). The Roman Empire was at its peak. Prominent Christian leaders included Clement of Rome, Ignatius of Syrian Antioch, Polycarp of Smyrna, Papias of Hierapolis (present-day Pamukkale, in Turkey), and Justin Martyr of Neapolis (present-day Nablus, in the West Bank). Their writings, some of which came to be known as the works of the Apostolic Fathers, were widely read and respected, but they were eventually excluded from the Christian canon. The Marcionite schism occurred ca. 144 CE when Marcion of Sinope distinguished between two gods—the Old Testament God of the Law and the New Testament God of Love—and held a Docetic view of Christ as God's emissary on earth.

Late 2nd—early 3rd centuries—Severan Dynasty (Septimius Severus, Caracalla, Elagabalus, Alexander Severus). Christian churches and leaders had become increasingly visible and public by the mid-second century in spite of sporadic persecutions. Church leaders of this period included Irenaeus (bishop of Lyon, writing in the 170s), Tatian (born somewhere in Syria, produced the *Diatessaron*, an early Gospel harmony, in 170s), Clement of Alexandria (wrote ca. 190s, died before 215), Tertullian of Carthage (died ca. 215/220), and Hippolytus of Rome (died ca. 235). Origen taught at Caesarea Maritima between ca. 215 and 254.

Origen was born to a Christian couple in Alexandria (ca. 185 CE) and emerged as an exceedingly devout and notable theologian among the Christians in that city. When his father was martyred during the reign of Septimius Severus, Origen wanted to join him in martyrdom but was prevented by his mother, who hid his clothes. Taking Matt 19:12 literally, he emasculated himself. He served many years as head of the Catechetical School in Alexandria, during which time his notoriety spread to other Christian centers. Thus in 215 (during Caracalla's persecutions), the bishops of Caesarea and Jerusalem invited Origen to visit and teach among the Christians under their charge.

This displeased Origen's own bishop, who apparently thought it inappropriate for Origen to be engaging in a preaching mission because he was still a layperson. The bishop recalled Origen to Alexandria where he spent the next decade and a half writing. In 230 CE, during the turbulent reign of Alexander Severus, we find Origen back in Palestine, having been ordained as priest now by the same two bishops of Caesarea and Jerusalem who had invited him to their cities earlier. Origen established a school in Caesarea Maritima where he continued to teach, preach, and write for the remainder of his life. Among his writings is *Hexapla*, a comparative study of the Old Testament text in six parallel columns—the Old Testament in Hebrew, in Greek transliteration, and in four versions of Greek translation (Aquila, Symmachus, Septuagint, and Theodotion).

Alexander Severus's assassination in 235 CE ended the Severan Dynasty and introduced a period of political instability that lasted the next half century. One emperor after another would emerge from the military and rule for a short time only to be assassinated and replaced. This endless imperial rivalry, along with breakaway movements in North Africa, Gaul, and Syria, meant almost constant civil wars. Among the short-term emperors of this period was Decius (reigned 249–251), who seems to have been a conscientious ruler, but he issued an imperial edict in 250 requiring all Roman citizens to offer sacrifice for the emperor's well-being. This edict may not have been directed specifically at Christians, but surely Christians accounted for a major portion of those caught up in the resulting persecution. And among those who were caught up in this net was Origen. He was put in chains, tortured (apparently his legs were pulled four paces apart), and survived, but died soon after (ca. 254).

Decius's edict was short-lived; efforts to enforce his edict seem to have died down already before his own death in 251. Aurelian (ruled 270–275) issued two edicts in 257 and 258—this time directed specifically at Christians. Perhaps he deserves the blame for conducting the first focused and systematic attempt to stamp out Christianity. But his program was suspended by his son Gallienus in 260.

Pamphilus and Eusebius

In an effort to restore order and reverse the empire's decline, Diocletian (reigned 284–305) divided the empire into two parts—west and east. Each part was to be ruled by a separate emperor bearing the title Augustus and by a coemperor with the title Caesar. Diocletian chose to rule the eastern part of the empire from Nicomedia (present-day Izmit), across the Bosporus from Byzantium, and Byzantium soon was renamed Constantinople). Diocletian's coemperor/Caesar, Galerius, resided in Thessaloniki. Diocletian and Galerius attempted one more time to stamp out Christianity, and many Christians were martyred, including Pamphilus, bishop of Caesarea (executed in 310). But their effort also failed for lack of local support. Among Christians in Caesarea who managed to survive this last persecution was a student of Pamphilius, Eusebius. He took the name Eusebius Pamphili and was elected bishop of Caesarea about 314.

Diocletian abdicated the throne in 305 with a plan in place for his succession. But the plan got off-track and civil war followed from which Constantine emerged as the new emperor. Christianity gained legal status in the process (Edict of Milan 313), and one of Constantine's first acts as emperor was to organize an international conference of Christian leaders from throughout the empire—the Council of Nicaea (325). Eusebius witnessed the radical shift in Christianity's legal status, therefore, from a systematically persecuted religion under Diocletian to the favored religion of the Roman Empire under Constantine.

As bishop of Caesarea, Eusebius found himself in a position of significant leadership. He played a central role in organizing the Council of Nicaea and led the large moderate party that submitted the first draft of what was to become the Nicene Creed. He also wrote important documents intended for the clergy. These include his *Historia Ecclesiastica,* which continues the story of the early Church from the Book of Acts to Constantine; *Vita Constantini* (*Life of Constantine*); and *Onomasticon,* a list of Old Testament place-names with notes about their locations and Greek names. One cannot overestimate the importance of these documents for us today as we attempt to understand the early church.

Herod's one-channel aqueduct was later retrofitted for a second channel

Byzantine, Arab, and Crusader Caesarea

Caesarea Maritima continued as an important commercial, administrative, and intellectual center throughout the Byzantine Period. It continued to expand in size as well, while its leaders participated actively in the various theological debates and church councils. Caesarea surrendered to the Arabs in 640 CE—the last Palestinian city to do so—and then declined under the Umayyad, Abbasid, and Fatimid Caliphates. Yet it remained a port of some consequence, surrounded by a substantial wall, until Crusaders arrived in 1099. Marine archaeologists discovered in the harbor a trove of two thousand gold coins from the Fatimid Period (eleventh century). This money may have been sent to Caesarea for payment of salaries to the Fatimid military garrison known to have been stationed there. Or possibly it belonged to a large merchant ship that sank in the harbor.

Crusader walls built by Louis IX during the Seventh Crusade

The first wave of Crusaders reached Palestine in 1099, Caesarea capitulated to them in 1101 after a two-week siege, and they erected fortifications near the ancient harbor. Saladin recaptured Caesarea in 1187, a follow-up to his victory at the Horns of Hattin. Crusaders recovered it in 1191, during the Third Crusade led by Philip of France and Richard of England, and Caesarea remained a Crusader stronghold for the next half century. In 1251–1252 Louis IX built the fortifications evident at Caesarea today. Caesarea fell to Baybars in 1265, who systematically destroyed the city and left it in ruins. These ruins would serve as a quarry for nearby villages throughout the subsequent Mamluk and Ottoman Periods.

Your Visit to Caesarea Maritima

Several archaeological teams have excavated at Caesarea over the past century, and work continues. Due to the city's size, however, especially in Byzantine times, archaeologists have barely scratched the surface. Review the site plan provided below before visiting Caesarea, keeping in mind that the area open to tourists represents only part of the once-expansive city, and that the visible archaeological remains represent essentially three different phases of history:

- *Roman Period*—Look for two dashed lines marked "Roman wall" on the site map provided below. One of the lines is in the upper-right quadrant of the site plan; the other is near the bottom margin. These two lines indicate the approximate northern and southern extent of Caesarea during the Roman Period.

- *Byzantine Period*—Look now for the dashed line in the upper right corner marked "Byzantine wall." This shows how far the city expanded during the Byzantine Period. The eastern and southern lines of the Byzantine wall would be off the site plan.

- *Crusader Period*—Look finally for the lines of the Crusader wall. The settlement had been reduced to approximately the area enclosed by this wall when the Crusaders first arrived.

The following notes correspond to the numbers on the site plan.

1. Your visit to Caesarea probably will begin or end with a stop outside the main archaeological site to view a surviving section of the aqueduct that brought water from springs at the base of Mount Carmel to the Roman and Byzantine city. It was built by Herod the Great, originally with one water channel, but it was later modified to support two additional channels. For a short distance along its nearly ten-mile route the water flowed through a tunnel underground. A dotted line on the map indicates the aqueduct's original route from the surviving segment into the city.

2. Your tour of the city itself probably will begin with the theater, also built by Herod the Great. It seated four thousand spectators and remained in use through most of the Byzantine Period. Almost certainly the centurion Cornelius would have attended performances here.

3. On a small peninsula or promontory that juts out into the sea are the remains of a palace from the Roman and Byzantine Periods. On display in its forecourt is a reproduction of the inscription discovered at Caesarea that mentions Pontius Pilate.

4. North of the promontory palace and stretching along the shore is a long U-shaped structure that the Jewish historian Josephus referred to as an amphitheater (*Ant.*

15:341), but it served also, if not primarily, as a race track. This also was built by Herod.

5. Apparently during the Byzantine Period and after the amphitheater/race track was no longer in use, a large public bath was built at its northern end. Public bath houses of the day served many purposes other than being places for baths. They were more like community centers, with gardens, libraries, and other amenities where people could spend leisure hours with friends.

6. In addition to the worship of traditional Greek and Roman deities, many eastern religions and cults flourished in cities throughout the Roman Empire. Caesarea would have been no different, as illustrated by the Mithraeum excavated among the ruins of the commercial district. Mithras was a Persian god whose cult was especially popular among Roman soldiers. Typically, its rituals were celebrated in an underground chamber known as a Mithraeum.

7. After the Mithraeum, pass through the opening in the Crusader wall and exit at the harbor. Note that Herod's harbor (indicated by dotted lines and dark grey) was much larger than the present-day harbor, which itself is more of a tourist area than a functioning port. Herod named his harbor Sebastos, which is Greek for "Augustus." Facing this harbor, and also facing Rome, Herod built an imposing temple dedicated to Roma and Caesar Augustus. The temple stood on a massive stone platform that elevated it above the city. Much of the platform remains, but the temple itself was replaced in time by an octagonal church, then by a mosque, and eventually by a Crusader cathedral.

8. Continue around the temple area to the Crusader wall and exit to the parking lot. Remember that this is not the original Crusader wall (which was destroyed by Saladin in 1187) but a later wall built by Louis IX in 1251–52. Also known as Louis the Pious, this French king organized two crusades and built this fortification during his first one (the Seventh Crusade).

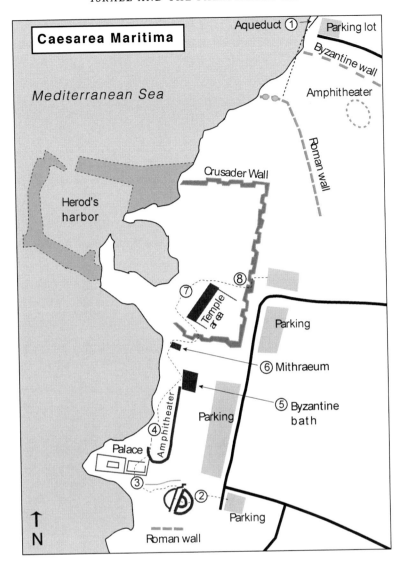

Judean Wilderness and the Dead Sea

Between Jerusalem and the Dead Sea is the Judean Wilderness (the Badlands of Palestine). This rugged, dry, thinly populated area was an ideal sanctuary for outlaws and rebels in ancient times. David and his soldiers roamed the Judean Wilderness while avoiding Saul. Jewish rebels retreated there when the First Jewish Revolt and later the Bar-Kochba Revolt were crushed.

Masada and Qumran focus our attention again on that First Jewish Revolt that broke out in Caesarea Maritima in 66 CE, resulted in the destruction of the Jerusalem temple four years later, and ended with the fall of Masada in 73 CE. The Dead Sea Scrolls discovered at Qumran shed light on a Jewish sect active while the first Christian apostles were beginning to spread the Christian gospel abroad, and the Qumran community itself seems to have ended as a result of the First Jewish Revolt. The destruction of the Jerusalem temple in 70 CE was to have a major impact on both Judaism and Christianity. The Gospel of Mark alludes to this moment in its so-called Little Apocalypse (Mark 13), which serves as a clue for dating the Gospel of Mark, which serves in turn as a benchmark for dating the other Gospels.

Qumran

Where the rugged terrain of the Judean Wilderness meets the northwestern shores of the Dead Sea are Wadi Qumran (a usually dry streambed) and Khirbet Qumran (archaeological ruins near the mouth of the streambed). Here the first of the Dead Sea Scrolls were discovered in 1947. Although their origins are debated, most scholars believe that these Qumran scrolls were left by a Jewish religious community, apparently the Essenes, who occupied Khirbet Qumran from some time in the second century BCE into the first century CE. Presumably the Essenes hid their library in nearby caves shortly before their community was destroyed by the Romans during the First Jewish Revolt. Qumran is maintained by the Israeli government as a national park. Many of the scrolls are on display at the Shrine of the Book of the Israel Museum.

Khirbet Qumran in the foreground. Dead Sea and the Transjordanian Highlands beyond

Qumran Cave 4

The Scrolls are of two sorts: manuscripts of the various books of the Hebrew Bible/ Old Testament; and other documents relevant to the Qumran community's organization and worship. They are useful to biblical scholars for two corresponding reasons. The manuscripts of the Old Testament books are the oldest surviving biblical manuscripts, while the nonbiblical documents provide valuable firsthand information about a sectarian Jewish community during New Testament times. By comparing the beliefs and practices of this Qumran community with those of the earliest Christians, we can better identify and understand essential features of early Christianity.

Chronology of Dead Sea Scrolls Discoveries

- 1947—Mohammad ed-Dib, a Bedouin shepherd, discovers the first scrolls

- 1948–1949—Archaeologists trace the scrolls to Qumran, discover and clear Cave I

- 1951—Bedouins make further discoveries at Murabbaat Caves

- 1952–1956—Ten more caves are discovered at Qumran, and excavations at Khirbet Qumran are conducted by Père Roland de Vaux

- 1953—Y. Aharoni conducts a brief survey of the Israeli sector of the Dead Sea area (from En Gedi to Masada).

- 1955—Mar Yeshue Samuel, Syrian Orthodox Patriarch, having brought the scrolls discovered by Mohammad ed-Dib to the US, sells them to Yigael Yadin for the State of Israel for $250,000.

- 1960–1961—More thorough exploration of Israeli sector occurs, and discoveries are made in Nahal Hever ("Cave of Horror" and "Cave of Letters")

- 1961–1964—Construction begins for the Shrine of the Book, to house and display the scrolls.

- 1967—Yigael Yadin acquires the so-called Temple Scroll.

Continuing south from Qumran along the western shore of the Dead Sea, one reaches the vicinity of En Gedi (Ain Gedi in Arabic). The name means "spring of the kid"; the spring is above the cliffs that overlook the Dead Sea, and it can be reached by a trail from a visitors' center. Archaeological investigations in the vicinity of the spring indicate settlements from the Chalcolithic Period, the time of the Judean monarchy, and the Hellenistic, Roman, and Byzantine Periods. According to 1 Sam 24:1, David once escaped from Saul to "the wilderness of En Gedi." In Song 1:14 the poet compares his "beloved" to a "cluster of henna in the vineyards of En Gedi." En Gedi is mentioned also in Josh 15:62; 2 Chr 20:2; and Ezek 47:10.

Emerging from the rugged and barren wilderness area between En Gedi and Masada are Wadi Murabbaat and Nahal Hever. Archaeologists recovered manuscript fragments from a cave in Wadi Murabbaat in 1951. The so-called Cave of Horror and Cave of Letters, discovered in Nahal Hever ten years later, produced more artifacts and manuscript fragments. Whereas the Qumran discoveries relate to the first century CE, those from the Wady Murabbaat and Nahal Hever date from the second century, especially from the time of the Bar Kochba Revolt.

Masada

This is the largest and most famous of Herod the Great's mountaintop fortifications. The mountain itself is an isolated plateau with steep sides. It had been fortified by the Hasmonean ruler Alexander Jannaeus and served later as a haven for Herod's family when the Parthians invaded Syria-Palestine in 40 CE. The Parthians placed Antigonus on the throne in Jerusalem, who then imprisoned Herod's brother Phasael and attempted to arrest Herod as well. But Herod, who had been serving as tetrarch of Galilee, was forewarned, managed to escape with his family and a military guard to Masada, and gain control of its fortress. Herod then left his family at Masada under the protection of eight hundred men and enough provisions to withstand a siege while he hurried first to King Malichus of Petra, then to Cleopatra in Egypt, and eventually to Rome in search of additional military support. On the advice of both Octavian and

Mark Antony, the Roman senate authorized Herod to replace Antigonus and sent him back with an army to recover the Hasmonean realm. Antigonus had laid siege to Masada meanwhile, so Herod's first military priority upon return was to lift the siege of Masada and rescue his family. The wintry battle for Sepphoris and Herod's capture of Jerusalem followed. (*War* 1.261–94; Penguin edition pp 55–61).

Masada, center of photo

Immediately after taking Jerusalem in 37 BCE, Herod set about to rebuild Masada on a much grander scale. He encircled the crest of the rock with a double wall, prepared cisterns and storehouses to ensure an almost inexhaustible water and food supply, engineered an impressive three-stage bath (frigidarium, tepidarium, caldarium), and constructed two elegant palaces. The western palace was more centrally located. Near the western defensive wall and approximately midway along its length, this palace probably served a more functional role—as a royal residence, as a place where administrative matters were handled and where ceremonies took place. The northern palace was more isolated and private. It was nearer to the bath, and offered a commanding view. It consisted of three levels resting against the northern end of the mountain.

Masada: North Palace

Masada received its real test as a military stronghold during the First Jewish Revolt, which erupted more than a half century after Herod's death. According to Josephus, who provides our chief and virtually only written source of information about Masada, Jewish zealots (Sicarii) seized the fort at the beginning of the revolt. More rebels fled to Masada when Jerusalem fell to Titus in 70 CE. Not until 72 CE, however, did the Roman military governor of Jerusalem, Flavius Silva, attack Masada. Using Jewish prisoners captured during the revolt, he constructed a massive earth and stone ramp up the west side of the mountain in order to gain access to the fort's western wall. After almost a year of siege the Romans were able to breach the wall and destroy any hopes the zealots had of defending their position.

At that point, according to Josephus, the zealot leader Eleazar conceded that God either had not supported or had abandoned their cause and called on his fellow rebels to commit mass suicide with their families rather than to submit to Roman torture and slavery:

> We ought perhaps to have read the mind of God and realized that his once beloved Jewish race had been sentenced to extinction. For if he had remained gracious and only slightly angry with us, he would not have shut his eyes to the destruction of so many thousands or allowed his holy city to be burned to the ground by our enemies . . . Not even the impregnability of our fortress has saved us. Although we have plenty of goods and weapons, and more than enough other supplies, God himself without a doubt has taken away all hopes of our survival. The fire which was directed toward the enemy lines did not

turn back of its own accord toward the wall we had built. These things are God's vengeance for the many wrongs which we in our madness have done to our countrymen. For those wrongs let us pay the penalty to God, by our own hands and not to the Romans. It will be easier to bear. Let our wives die un-abused, our children without knowledge of slavery. After that, let us do each other an ungrudging kindness, preserving our freedom as a glorious winding sheet. (*War*, 7:323–36; Penguin edition pp. 385–386)

The rebels heeded Eleazar's appeal, according to Josephus. Each of the men killed the members of his own family, then they committed suicide themselves. By Josephus's figures, 960 people died; only two women and five children survived by hiding in an underground cavern.

Josephus's dramatic account of the fall of Masada has been scrutinized in recent years and its accuracy challenged. While he may have had access to field reports from the Roman army, Josephus was not present himself during the siege, and clearly he tells us more about the episode than he actually knew. This would have been true especially of Eleazar's speech, which probably reflects Josephus's own sentiments more than those of the rebel leader. Josephus, it must be remembered, had been captured, defected to the Roman side, and served as informant and translator for Titus during the siege of Jerusalem. His account of the mass suicide also has been challenged on the grounds that this is a stock literary theme—mass suicide to avoid capture by the Romans—that turns up in other literary sources including Josephus's account of his own capture by the Romans. But stock literary theme or not, desperate resort to suicide to avoid death by torture would not have been an uncommon occurrence when Roman armies crushed resistance and may well have happened at Masada.

Masada was known to earlier travelers and archaeologists, but it took a hardy soul to climb the Snake Path to the ruins on top. The Snake Path was still the only way up when I visited Masada for my first time in 1966. Now there is a cable car, Masada is perhaps the most visited tourist destination in Israel, and is included on UNESCO's World Heritage list. Much of the credit belongs to Yigael Yadin, who directed excavations at the site between 1960 and 1965. Hundreds of volunteers came from all over the world to help. Yadin's abilities as an archaeologist were matched by his abilities to communicate his discoveries. Other archaeologists have continued to explore Masada, and some of Yadin's interpretations of the evidence have been challenged. But his name remains linked with that of Masada in much the same way that Heinrich Schliemann's name is associated with Troy, Arthur Evans's with Knossos, and Howard Carter's with Tutankamun.

5

Present-Day Jordan, Israel, and the Palestinian Areas

My focus throughout this travel guide has been on biblical times and places, and I emphasized at the outset that the Holy Land does not correspond to present-day political boundaries. Nevertheless, the actual destination of present-day Holy Land travelers is either one or both of two modern nations: Jordan and Israel. These are neighboring nations, each with its own national story, political complexities, and corresponding terminologies. Some of the highlights require review in order to understand current political terminology that one is likely to hear during a trip to the Holy Land; terms like "Hashemite," "Israeli Arab," "Palestinian areas," and so forth.

Hashemite Kingdom of Jordan

For approximately four centuries leading up to World War I, all of the Levant including historic Palestine was part of the Ottoman Empire. During the war, Hussein Ibn Ali, Sharif of Mecca, and his four sons (Ali, Abdullah, Faisal and Zaid) led an Arab uprising against the Ottoman government. They were urged to do so by the British, encouraged by the famous Lawrence of Arabia, and promised independence at the end of the war. When British and Arab forces secured control of Syria-Palestine toward the end of the war, Sharif Hussein's son Faisal set up a provisional government in Damascus.

After the war, European diplomats charged with dismantling the Ottoman Empire decided that the former Ottoman territories in the Middle East—historic Mesopotamia, Syria, and Palestine—should be governed by France and Britain as *mandates*. Essentially, they became colonies of France and Britain. The basics of this mandate arrangement were worked out at the San Remo Conference in July of 1920. France received Syria as its mandate and took possession soon after the conference, displacing Faisal. Britain received Mesopotamia and Palestine as its mandate, but Faisal's older brother Abdullah entered the Transjordan with a Bedouin army, presumably poised to challenge the French in Syria.

With Abdullah and his army still in the Transjordan, Winston Churchill organized a conference of Middle Eastern leaders and experts to work out how the British mandated areas should be administered. The conference was convened in Cairo during March 1921. Among the experts were T. E. Lawrence and Gertrude Bell. And it was decided that Britain's mandated territories would be divided into three separate political entities, all three under British oversight. Mesopotamia became Iraq, ruled by Faisal as king. Transjordan became Emirate of the Transjordan ruled by Abdullah as emir (prince). Palestine west of the Jordan remained under direct British administration and came to be known as the Mandate of Palestine. Its residents—Arab, Jew, Armenian, whoever—were known officially as Palestinians.

Abdullah chose Amman as his capital, little more than a village at the time. Britain granted limited independence to the Emirate of the Transjordan in 1923, but remained suzerain, and reserved the right to maintain military bases there. At the end of World War II, prompted by the loyalty of Abdullah's government through the war,

Britain recognized Transjordan as a fully independent emirate. Jordanians celebrate May 25, 1946, as Independence Day.

Britain withdrew from the Mandate of Palestine two years later (May, 1948), while Israel simultaneously proclaimed itself an independent nation in what had been the Mandate of Palestine. Armies from surrounding Arab nations, including Abdullah's Emirate of the Transjordan, attacked in an effort to prevent this from happening. Israel was able to defend its existence as a new nation, but at the end of the fighting was in possession of only part of the former Mandate of Palestine. Armistices were negotiated during 1949. The armistice between Israel and the Emirate of the Transjordan, signed on April 3, left Abdullah's troops in control of the West Bank—the core of the Central Hill country west of the Jordan River. Abdullah annexed the West Bank, including the walled Old City of Jerusalem, to his emirate soon after (1950), changed the name of the emirate to the Hashemite Kingdom of Jordan, and upgraded his title to king. While worshiping at the al-Aqsa Mosque in Jerusalem the following year, Abdullah was assassinated by one of his new West Bank/Palestinian subjects.

Abdullah was succeeded by his son Talal, who soon was removed from office, and the crown was transferred to Talal's son Hussein. Supposedly Talal had psychological problems, but his resistance to continued British oversight may have been a contributing factor to his being replaced. Talal's son Hussein, seventeen years old at the time, was recalled from school in England and proclaimed king on August 11, 1952. Hussein was to enjoy a long reign—forty-seven years—characterized by moderate, pro-Western policies.

Israel captured the West Bank including Jerusalem during the so-called Six Day War in 1967. But Palestinian militants under the leadership of Yassar Arafat continued to use northern Jordan east of the river as a base of operations against Israel, and by 1971 they posed a threat to the stability of the Kingdom of Jordan itself. Civil war erupted in September of that year (called Black September). Hussein's Jordanian army defeated Arafat's militants and expelled them from Jordan. Arafat shifted operations to southern Lebanon at that point, where he and his followers would figure prominently in events leading up to Lebanon's civil war (1975 and following).

Jordan relinquished all claims to the West Bank in 1988. And in 1994, following the Oslo Peace Accord, King Hussein signed a peace treaty with Israel. The Peace Accord specified that Jordan would retain guardianship of the Dome of the Rock, al-Aqsa Mosque, and enclosed area of the Temple Mount/Haram ash-Sharif. Along with other benefits, the accord rendered Jordan more available to tourism. King Hussein died in 1999 and was succeeded by his son Abdullah II.

The native population of Abdullah's Emirate of the Transjordan was primarily Bedouin. One of the consequences of the 1948–1949 hostilities—in addition to the establishment of modern Israel, the annexation of the West Bank to the Emirate of the Transjordan, and the change of the emirate's name to the Hashemite Kingdom of Jordan—was a wave of Palestinian refugees into the West Bank and Transjordan from what became Israeli territory at that point. The Six Day War in 1967, which ended with Israel in control of the West Bank, also prompted another wave of Palestinian refugees into the Transjordan. Then came an infusion of Iraqi refugees and immigrants following the US/coalition invasion of Iraq in 2003. Since 2010, Jordan has struggled to absorb thousands of Syrian refugees.

Israel

As I explained above, all of historic Syria-Palestine had been part of the Ottoman Empire for approximately four centuries leading up to World War I. Toward the end of the nineteenth century, pogroms in Russia and anti-Semitism in Europe gave rise to the Zionist movement and ever-increasing Jewish immigration to Palestine—to Ottoman-held Palestine at first, then to the British Mandate of Palestine after World War I. There had been hopes that the peace settlement following World War I would designate part or all of Palestine as a homeland for Jews. This did not happen; the British Mandate of Palestine was established instead. But the Balfour Declaration, issued in 1917, gave reason to believe that this might happen eventually. There remained strong support for a Jewish state in Palestine among some British diplomats, and Jewish immigration to Palestine increased significantly during the Nazi era (1930s and early 1940s). Serious conflicts between the rapidly increasing Jewish population and the native Arab inhabitants of Palestine had emerged by the 1930s and reached new levels of violence after World War II (the King David Hotel bombing occurred in July 1946; the Deir Yassn massacre in April 1948).

Great Britain, having granted independence to the Emirate of the Transjordan in 1946, announced that it would terminate its mandate over Palestine on May 14, 1948. Israel proclaimed itself a nation on that date and the United Nations, which had already passed a resolution favoring the establishment of a Jewish state in Palestine, recognized the new state. The United States also recognized Israel without hesitation, followed by a number of other nations during the months ahead.

But there was also opposition, especially from neighboring Arab countries, whose armies attacked the fledgling Jewish state from different directions. In addition to preventing the birth of this new Jewish state, the Arab rulers wished to expand their own boundaries into former Mandate of Palestine territory. When the dust settled from the fighting and armistice agreements were signed in 1949, the new state of Israel had managed to defend its sovereignty over a large part of the former Mandate of Palestine, but Syria held the Golan Heights, Egypt held the Gaza Strip, and the Emirate of the Transjordan held the West Bank including the walled Old City of Jerusalem. Israelis refer to this war as the War of Independence. Former Arab residents of the Mandate of Palestine and their descendants speak of it as al-Nakbah (the Disaster).

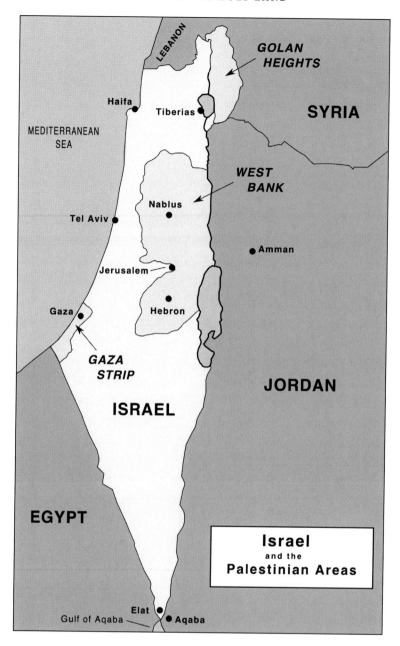

Israel
and the
Palestinian Areas

Arab residents of the former Mandate of Palestine who remained in what became the new state of Israel were granted Israeli citizenship and are known as Israeli Arabs. But most of the former Arab residents of what then became Israel had fled their homes during the hostilities to the areas that ended up in Syrian, Egyptian, and Jordanian hands: the Golan Heights, the Gaza Strip, the West Bank, and East Jerusalem. Over time, many of these refugees and their descendants emigrated to surrounding Arab countries and further abroad. Both those who remained in Palestine and those who have emigrated abroad regard themselves, and are known internationally, as Palestinians.

Israel has emerged since 1948/49 as an exceedingly successful and powerful nation. It is a major player on the international scene in virtually every category that comes to mind—economic strength, military clout, scientific and technological advancements, intellectual influence, and on and on. And for its citizens, Israel represents a rare democracy outside the Western world.

Palestinian Areas

The so-called Six Day War in June 1967 was a major turning point for both Israelis and Palestinians. Israel gained control of the Golan Heights, Gaza Strip, West Bank, and East Jerusalem. The Palestinians who lived in these territories, some of whom had fled there only two decades earlier when the state of Israel was established, were now under Israeli occupation but without citizenship. This Palestinian population has increased in number since the 1967 war and continues to do so. Israel's continued occupation of these territories with their ever increasing, non-citizen, Palestinian population presents demographic, legal, and ethical problems yet to be resolved. Your Holy Land tour almost certainly will include visits to places in one or more of the following Palestinian areas.

The West Bank

The 1949 armistice between Israel and the Emirate of the Transjordan left a large enclave west of the Jordan River and Dead Sea in the hands of the emirate. Emir Abdullah annexed this West Bank to the Emirate of the Transjordan in 1950, and it remained under Jordanian rule until the 1967 war when it fell into Israeli hands. Israelis generally refer to this West Bank territory as Judaea and Samaria, and since the 1970s, beginning with a Likud administration, has encouraged and subsidized Jewish settlements in the West Bank/Judaea and Samaria. Palestinian resistance, the First Intifada, erupted between 1987 and 1993, during which time Jordan renounced its claim to the West Bank (1988). This turbulent period led to the Oslo Accord (1993) and the peace treaty between Israel and Jordan (1994) that remains in place.

The Oslo Accord called for a "peace process" that began with dividing the West bank into three zones. Zone A, representing approximately 18 percent of the West Bank, was to be administered by a newly established Palestinian Authority; Zone B, approximately 60 percent, was reserved for potential expansion of Palestinian administration; and Zone C, approximately 60 percent, was designated for Israeli settlements and security. This peace process has not been successful, but the zones remain in place. A Second Intifada, more violent than the first, followed the collapse of the Second Camp David conference, in 2000 involving President Clinton, Prime Minister Barak, and Palestinian leader Arafat.

Israeli settlements continue to expand in the West Bank. These settlements are connected now by limited access "security roads" that tend to separate the Palestinian areas into isolated segments. Israeli construction is well underway on a security wall that surrounds and intrudes on some of the West Bank.

East Jerusalem

The minority-Jewish inhabitants of Jerusalem's walled Old City fled their homes during the 1948–1949 War of Independence/Nakbah. But their Jewish comrades in arms managed to secure a corridor from the coastal plain to the western side of the Old City. Over the next two decades—between 1948–1949 and the 1967 war—a modern Israeli city emerged in the corridor. Meanwhile, the Old City itself remained in Jordanian hands, and Arab suburbs continued to expand beyond its walls and outside the Israeli corridor to the north, east, and southeast. There emerged essentially two cities of Jerusalem, in other words, one Jewish and the other Arab, until Israel gained military control over both in 1967. Israel unilaterally annexed the Old City with its Arab suburbs, calling the annexed parts East Jerusalem. Israel has also expanded the official limits of East Jerusalem so that it now stretches deep into the West Bank.

The Golan Heights

After the 1949 armistice between Israel and Syria, the Jordan Valley north of the Sea of Galilee remained in dispute. Syria contended that the armistice agreement designated this valley as no-man's-land. Israel contended that it belonged to itself and began establishing farm settlements in the valley. This prompted Syria to shoot down on the Israeli farmers from the Transjordanian highlands that overlook the valley from the east—more specifically, from the Golan Heights. At great expense in human life on both sides, Israel conquered the Golan Heights during the 1967 Six Day War. Control of the Golan Heights became a key issue in subsequent peace negotiations between Israel and Syria, and the Golan frontier with Syria remains troublesome. Most of the current Arab inhabitants of Israeli-controlled Golan are Druze with close family connections across the Syrian border.

The Gaza Strip

The 1949 armistice between Israel and Egypt left Egypt in control of Sinai and a narrow strip of territory surrounding the city of Gaza. This Gaza Strip has an especially dense Arab population because so many Palestinian refugees fled there during the hostilities. Israel overran the Gaza Strip and the Sinai in 1956 (in the Port Said Conflict), in 1967 (during the Six Day War), and in 1973 (during the Yom Kippur War). Sinai was returned to Egypt after the first Camp David conference in 1978, involving President Carter,

President Sadat, and Prime Minister Begin, leaving the Gaza Strip in Israeli hands. The political status of the Gaza Strip paralleled that of the West Bank after that, except that Palestinians in the Gaza Strip were more isolated, their living space more cramped by settlements, and security measures more restricting. Not surprisingly, Gaza became a political "basket case" with militant factions, primarily Hamas, dominating the local scene. Israel unilaterally withdrew from the Gaza Strip in 2005, but with Egypt's support Israel controls virtually all access between the strip and the outside world. Palestinian elections in 2006 resulted in a split between the two main parties, Fatah and Hamas. Fatah continues to administer Zone A segments of the West Bank under Israeli oversight, while Hamas governs the Gaza Strip internally.

This brings us to the end of our journey through the Holy Land. We have explored it from east to west—from Amman and Petra on the fringes of the Syrian-Arabian Desert, and Mount Nebo that overlooks the Jordan River Basin, through Galilee and the Central Hill Country, to Jaffa and Caesarea Maritima on the Mediterranean coast. While focusing on places mentioned in the Gospel narratives and Acts of the Apostles, we have been attentive as well to the long sweep of history that has unfolded in this ancient land. We have seen Bronze Age tells and biblical sites from Old Testament times, walked among the remains of Hellenistic-Roman cities, explored churches from the Byzantine Period, Crusader castles, and Arab-Islamic monuments. All of these are the heritage of present-day Jordan, Israel, and the Palestinian areas.